DURING:

A Couple's Intimate Experience with Breast Cancer Treatment

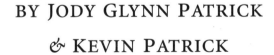

BY JODY GLYNN PATRICK

& KEVIN PATRICK

VCC *VEDA COMMUNICATIONS CO.*

FRESNO, CALIFORNIA

Copyright © 2004 by Jody Glynn Patrick & Kevin Patrick
ISBN 0-9749562-1-X

Publisher: Veda Communications Co.
                4709 N. El Capitan, Suite 103
                Fresno, CA 93722
                www.vedacc.com, 559-276-8495

More information about the author and this title is available at *www.DuringBreastCancer.com*

R-05-04

DEDICATION

Family is a central theme in *During*. It was written for our family – for Summer, PJ, Brook, Paddy, and Patrick – and the book is dedicated to them with great love.

However, **During** was *published* for the cancer community, and so we are contributing a percentage of profits to both the Ronald McDonald House and Gilda's Club. Jody is former manager of the Chicago Ronald McDonald House, and we hope to be a contributing influence in bringing a *red door* — Gilda's Club Madison, Wisconsin!

Finally, we'd like to share this opening sentiment with anyone who has been diagnosed with cancer, and with all who may be in the future:

When you come to the edge of all the light you've known,
and are about to step off into the darkness of the unknown,
faith is knowing one of two things will happen.
There will be something solid to stand on...or you will be taught to fly.
—From ***The Edge*** by Patrick Overton

During*: The Lesson is *FLIGHT.

Jody Glynn Patrick
Kevin Patrick

3

DURING

CONTENTS

CONTENTS

Jody Kissing Kevin

ACKNOWLEDGEMENTS

We would like to publicly praise Dean Medical Systems oncologist Michael Frontiera, and Dean Medical surgeon Carl Sunby. Quite succinctly, they saved and extended Jody's life and gave us profound encouragement and support. We are also grateful to the skilled oncology nurses and technicians at Dean Medical, St. Marys Hospital (*especially* Dr. Michael Foley), and the University of Wisconsin Hospital's Comprehensive Cancer Care Center in Madison, Wisconsin.

Just as important to Jody's recovery were the many friends and co-workers who helped prop up our family. Special thanks to Donna and David Gray, and to *every one of our friends* for embracing this project with such whole-hearted support.

Of course, we are most grateful to our family. Summer, Brook and PJ have been graceful about our telling of their most difficult times. We are mindful that this book is also part of son-in-law Paddy Cassidy's history, and grandson Patrick's legacy. *During* also received a "Yes!" from Jody's brothers, Robert Hawley and Kurt Shryack, which meant a great deal to us because we love them very much. We also thank our special family angels – Daniel, Joyce, Lucille, Betty, Hugh, and Michael. They are gone from our world but remain very much alive in our hearts.

And finally, we would like to thank our publisher, Mike Neer, President of VEDA Communications, who provided the most astonishing editing! However, we are most impressed with the passion he brought to this project on behalf of cancer patients everywhere. His enthusiasm was infectious and, frankly, he made it fun along the way.

DURING

INTRODUCTION

**Life's defining moments -- *Before* & *After* ● The
decision to journal ● Kevin's promise to record
what is often unsaid**

JODY:

Though undeniably a *defining event* in my life, the diagnosis of late-stage inflammatory cancer — the rarest, most deadly and aggressive form of all breast cancers — was not the worst thing that ever happened to me. Certainly the two subsequent mastectomies flattened me like a steamroller, but years before, I had been leveled by bigger cosmic machinery... by a trauma that arguably could have been the trigger that set the cancer cells in motion.

August 27, 1991 was like many Wisconsin late summer days. It was hot outside, the sky clear, with no ominous weather — no sudden hail storm or tornado warning, not even a light rain — to foreshadow or cause the single-car accident that would claim my son's life that afternoon. Daniel-Paul was driving home from the orthodontist's office, the braces finally removed from his teeth, and most likely he raised his eyes from the country highway to check out his new smile in the rearview mirror. At the self-conscious age of 16, he wouldn't have given his reflection more than a cursory glance at the dental clinic, but while driving home alone, the impulse to look in a mirror must have been irresistible. That's the way I imagine it happening, anyway.

I immediately understood that someone had died when I received the telephone call, but back then, dead bodies were routinely reported to me. I was the crisis intervention counselor who performed face-to-face death notifications for all shifts for our suburban-Milwaukee police department, and we had a clearly established protocol. My pager was supposed to go off; I wasn't supposed to get a call at home because home telephone numbers were regarded as sacred. I said to him, "Wait a minute ... back up...."

"There's no mistake, ma'am. I'm sorry to say it outright like this, but your son Daniel died today in a car accident. He was dead when police

9

arrived at the scene."

Suddenly I had a glimmer of understanding that this man wasn't calling for my help.... then I couldn't respond in any way... couldn't speak, couldn't make my legs work. I had been standing when the phone rang, but my knees buckled and I crumpled on the floor. Summer, 14, was first into the kitchen; at the sight of my tears, she grabbed Brook's hand, stopping the 11-year old in her tracks, too. Nothing seemed real, and I stared at the girls, wondering how much they had already heard. It was as if I was watching someone else's family, and I needed a clue from them how to proceed. Five-year old PJ crawled into my lap, crying. I held my youngest son close to me, though I no longer seemed to be in my own body. From some far-away place, I asked for the details.

The car's right front tire apparently meandered onto a loose-gravel shoulder and the car went nose-first into a steep ditch. It flipped end-over-end, propelling Daniel nearly 100 yards into a thick cornfield. He was dead before a witness and police could locate his body in the field.

Any bereaved parent will understand that the most difficult moment occurred at the gravesite. I wanted to kiss my first-born child one more time regardless of his injuries; and so the coffin was opened again. The funeral director and I reached the intersection of cross purposes when I wouldn't allow him to seal it a last time and proceed with the burial. I couldn't do what was being asked of me... couldn't be a willing participant in a ceremony that would conclude with putting a child of mine into a gaping hold in the ground. But I only managed to stall the inevitable.

On the day of their births, I had promised each of my children a million kisses. Had I given Daniel enough kisses to send him on this journey? Surely Daniel extracted a million tears from our family in only days. It was unthinkable that the world continued on without him and I found it incomprehensible that the "real me" was not already buried alongside my child.

Two weeks after Daniel's death, the chief of police ordered me to a civilian psychologist to be certified as fit to return to service following a traumatic incident.

"What do I say to a grief counselor about grief?" the psychologist asked. "I won't pretend that I know how you feel, because I don't. But I do understand that your life will never be the same as it was before."

I was jolted back to a memory of death notifications — those I gave and those I've since received — upon hearing the diagnosis of cancer. That pronunciation cut like a knife, cleaving yet another easily definable *before* and *after* marker in my own timeline. Before breast cancer. After breast cancer. My life would never be the same as it was Before. Unlike tragedy, however, I soon discovered that cancer treatment has three parts: *Before* and *After*, but also *During*. I kept a journal *During*. More important, I compiled my contributions to the book *After* because an honest telling of what it is to be a cancer patient is most genuinely written in hindsight. Active patients often do not want to worry their familial and physician caretakers with full accounts of the dark places to which their minds and bodies are sent as they are methodically poisoned. We don't want to add to the burden that we have already become. Even survivors willing to review the horror may have an almost superstitious fear of revisiting the trauma. Why tempt whatever fates blew us to Cancer Hell in the first place? It feels almost sacrilegious to question the treatment that still offers the best hope for life.

However, when survivors do talk, our stories offer similar accounts of a search for dignity in treatment. Also, many report that a life review was part of the necessary work during their journey to remission. But each tale is as unique as the teller. For example, I personally found it a struggle to advocate for the most proper treatment. At times, I had to wrestle not only with the doctors caring for my body, but also with myself in order to maintain a faith base that was additionally tested by my mother's concurrent cancer diagnosis.

And yet, there were so many precious moments that my new husband and I managed to pull from the experience.

Our family has indeed changed, and the experience has returned to me a part of myself that I (*Before*) believed to have died with Daniel. From this up-close-and-personal, near-death experience came a renewed thankfulness for life.

KEVIN:

After Jody's diagnosis, family and friends were naturally anxious for word of how she was doing and how they could help. When the demands of individual correspondence overwhelmed her stamina, my wife emailed a single *Friday Update* message to the group as a whole. This frank review became so popular that the weekly recipient list swelled to over 150 people and just as quickly to a hundred more. Many of the journal entries in this book are exact excerpts from those reports.

In the middle of umpteen reasons to cry with Jody, you will also find ample opportunity to chuckle. It sounds weird, but it's true that Jody's life is sometimes so darn sad that it's just downright funny and she's usually the first to laugh.

DURING

For my contribution, I'd like to clearly state the purpose for the book, which is this: to record what other people normally leave unsaid. To my astonishment, writing everything proved to be a heart-wrenching cathartic experience and I'm the better for having done it, though it meant putting numerous relationships under a magnifying glass and sharing the most intimate moments and thoughts. My wife asked that I describe what it was like to stepparent a teenager when I was already an exhausted husband, employee, housemaid and caregiver. Jody asked that I put into words the inexplicable: what ran through my mind when I first saw her chest after surgery. She asked me to admit to you the dread that surfaced after her concept of money took a 180-degree turnabout. Forced celibacy was no picnic, and then there was the constant threat of losing my best friend.

On the other hand, survival is the story of meeting adversity head on. It's the art of finding faith in fear and solidarity in pain. Or maybe it's really just the luck of the draw and, finally, we get the card we hoped for. Regardless of how or why, we're just very glad to report that survival is the other half of our story.

This moment, Jody is in full remission and we both are thanking God. As a couple, we triumphed over the first year of treatment. Admittedly, we still lack the confidence to make plans very far beyond the day after tomorrow, but regardless what the near future holds, Jody's spirit will forever prevail ... and it is strong enough to carry yours with it.

CHAPTER 1: May
Discovery of lump • The harried doctor • Bruised doubts

Wednesday, May 10
<u>KEVIN:</u>

A wristwatch with a morning alarm function set for 5 a.m. beeps, the sound muffled. I've tucked the watch beneath my pillow because my bride of less than one year is sensitive to sounds. Although faint, the beeping is persistent enough to wake me, though when it does, I am reluctant to climb out of bed and take a shower. Instead, I set aside my normal workday routine to gently nuzzle closer to Jody, who has turned away from me in her sleep, leaving me with a profound sense of skin-hunger.

I kiss the back of her shoulders and reach for her, only to remember in the second before my fingers would light on her skin that I'm not to touch her *there*. I pull back my hand, mindful that a lump is growing in her left breast despite a doctor's insistence that a negative ultrasound six weeks ago means she's fine. She was told *probable cyst* and *menstrual cycle fluke* and *don't worry* when she called for another appointment so soon after the ultrasound. But I've not approached her in a sexually provocative manner since we discovered the lump two weeks ago. She has a morning appointment for a recheck and we've agreed that if the doctor dismisses the lump after examining it today, we will relax.

I just pray that is the case. I've seen a lot as a surgical and clinical technician during a more than twenty-year tenure in the Navy, but even when I initially felt the small mass, something about the nodule made me immediately queasy. I couldn't get past it and mentioned it mid-fondle.

"What's this, right here? Have you felt this little hard spot? This wasn't here when you had the ultrasound, was it?"

Jody brushed away my advances with the pushing away of the hand on her chest. She muttered, "I didn't get into bed for an impromptu breast exam," and turned to her other side, making it clear that there would be no bedroom fireworks. I knew in that instant that she had already noticed the

13

lump and had come to a conscious decision to ignore it. She wasn't prepared for me to discover it so soon and force the issue.

Generally I pick my battles carefully, but especially with Jody because she has a compulsive need to control everything in her world. Usually when we have a difference of opinion or preference, I acquiesce because I recognize that being in control is her Achilles heel. But the lump was not going to go ignored. I persisted and eventually extracted a promise that she would risk feeling like a hypersensitive hysteric by calling the doctor back, which is exactly how she said she felt when she did. But today both of our small humiliations will be worth it when we get some answers.

I already know without touching the breast that the lump is still there. It has become large enough to see and I continue to harbor a lurking dread about it.

She shifts positions to her back and sighs, draping one long leg over mine. She was late getting into bed last night, brooding about the doctor's appointment. Even later, I suspect, getting to sleep. Her eyes flutter but remain closed. I count off two minutes and then carefully slip my leg out from under hers. Half an hour later, I whisper, "Have good news," and kiss her softly good-bye.

A firm believer that the best way to handle adversity is to expect it, I do some worst-case scenario planning during my 50-minute drive to work. When dealt a load of lemons, why just settle for lemonade? Explore options, taste the peel. Nonetheless, as I'm sorting through what we might do with our own bushel basket of uncertain outcomes, I say a silent prayer, begging God for a reprieve from a cancer diagnosis.

I arrive at work early, Navy training a hard habit to break though I'm now the human resources director for a large manufacturing company. Lori is already at her desk and that makes my load a little lighter because if my wife does have cancer, this colleague will be a lifeline. There are few with whom I can speak openly because of my function at the company, but Lori has become a friend; she laughs at my jokes and tolerates my abstract ramblings during departmental meetings.

Lori must know something is wrong when I linger in the doorway of her office, but it isn't her nature to be intrusive. I give her the opening she needs: "I may have to take off early today. Jody is having a follow-up breast exam and I know it's probably nothing. But if it is, I'm planning to leave to be with her."

Concern flashes across Lori's face, though she states flatly that she's sure it's nothing. She then points to a co-worker currently undergoing chemotherapy following a double mastectomy. Lori self-censors how painful it has been to watch the woman endure treatment, nor does she remind that it was our joint decision to pursue short-term disability status for the employee.

Instead, she focuses on the positive: "We have every reason to believe that she's going to make it, Kev, and that wasn't even detected until it was pretty far along. Medical advancements in this area are incredible and they're saving women who would have died if diagnosed only a couple years ago. I know Jody will be fine. Most likely, it's just a harmless cyst."

"It probably is just a cyst," I agree wistfully.

"And probably 99% of all cysts turn out to be benign."

That's almost a word-for-word replay of what I said to Jody recently, though my wife argued that her research indicated that as many as 186,000 women are expected to be diagnosed with breast cancer this year alone. Damn her need to know every fact, thinking it will help her cope! It doesn't help anybody's immune system to delve into depressing statistics. I certainly don't repeat the prediction to Lori because I came to her for reassurance. Although... I only realize at this moment that it isn't something Lori can really give me, nor can I give it to myself. There will be no relief until I get the "all clear" from Jody.

I linger for another couple of minutes of forced conversation but leave as soon I can politely extricate myself. I sit down at my desk and shuffle papers and stare at the computer screen, hoping no one has any problems today because I'm not sure if I could maintain my usual objective demeanor.

JODY:

A round protuberance about the size of a robin's egg is lodged just under the skin over the top of my left breast. A clear mammogram six months ago makes me think it can't really be cancer, and a more recent ultrasound showed no serious abnormality. But the lump is beginning to feel vaguely creepy, as if it is taking on a malevolent personality of its own. Even though logically I know nothing is wrong, I am struggling with a superstitious feeling that things have been almost too good this past year since marrying Kevin — and perhaps, in only a few moments, the other shoe will drop.

I brought company financial records to review while waiting for the doctor, but the spreadsheets are no more than page after page of meaningless numbers. I traded a counseling career for the less dramatic and demanding field of publishing, and I should be immersed in plans to open a second magazine, a project in which I will be managing publisher and partner. But I can't get my mind off the lump. Will I have exceptionally horrid luck or get exceptionally good news today? I've been a peak-or-valley girl for 47 years with little middle ground, so it could easily go either way.

Finally it is my turn to be seen by the doctor. I slip in to a paper smock and awkwardly position myself as modestly as possible on the padded stainless steel bed. I am no sooner appropriately arranged than my primary care physician charges into the tiny examination room, shadowed by a male medical student. My doc is a tall, slender fellow in his early 60s who looks much younger because he works out religiously. He's been my doctor for two years, but it's a big clinic with a lot of patients. Usually he's very mild mannered, but even before the doctor glances at my chest, I can see that he is agitated about something.

"Sorry for the wait, but I'm leaving for China tomorrow," he says, "so the appointment desk double-booked every slot today. Point to the place you feel the lump, okay? Right there, I see... You know, even on a normal day, I'm expected to see patients ten minutes apart. It's ridiculous, the way the HMO runs this clinic. Twelve patients per hour is utterly unacceptable and I'm hopelessly behind. Is the lump painful in any way? Sort of painful? Okay. Were you waiting long? This assembly-line approach to patient care leaves the doctors overworked...."

I stop listening altogether. Doesn't he know that I am entertaining the possibility of having cancer? Although I have been seeing him on a fairly regular basis, he doesn't recognize me in any meaningful way and, without my chart at his fingertips, probably couldn't recall that he's recently seen me for a similar concern — a thickening he dismissed as *fibrous breasts*.

I don't really know him, either. Certainly not well enough to care about his damn vacation or the tile work he's having done in his condo. But maybe his prattle should be comforting, a sign he's seen breast lumps like mine many times and he is not worried. He even says this to me, as he continues to poke and prod: "It's a cyst, I'm pretty sure. I'll just aspirate it with a needle. We'll get fluid and it'll be gone. It's when you can't get clear fluid, or when you get blood, that you should worry."

The male student hovers, the doctor probes. The needle is big, the topical anesthetic worthless because I don't respond to most numbing drugs. But the real problem seems to be that he can't draw off any fluid. He stabs and stabs just beneath the skin and then deeper. Eventually he gets fluid, but it's not at all clear. He says, "This doesn't mean anything," referring to the blood. He says he just can't get to the actual lump because I have that darn thick shelf of breast tissue.

"But I'm sure it isn't cancer," he says again. "Cancer doesn't grow this fast." He tells me to go home and wait for one or preferably two menstrual cycles; if the cyst doesn't go away and if I'm still worried, he'll

16

make a referral then for a surgeon to drain the fluid using ultrasound. I falter, uncertain.

"I'm sure it's nothing," he repeats more forcefully.

I choose to believe him and so I go home and check the date of Brook's July graduation from the Air Force police academy in San Antonio, Texas. I circle the first workday after our expected return to Wisconsin, when I will have the lump checked again. I take an aspirin for a deeply bruised breast that already is very sore and multi-colored from the assault.

KEVIN:

Hours pass. The phone rings again and again, but it's not her. I keep myself busy. Finally, my wife calls.

"The doctor says I'm fine, honey. I'm just a little sore, where he tried to aspirate the cyst." She tells me what he did and what he was unable to do. "He was in a hurry today because he's leaving for vacation tomorrow," she adds, as if that would be an appropriate reason for not properly attending to it today.

Having worked with some excellent military doctors during my early years, I don't find this attitude to be acceptable medical care. I point out to Jody that this same doctor was harried and hurried when he gave me a routine exam a couple months ago, and his excuse that day was also that he was soon going on vacation. A few minutes after meeting him, I left unimpressed with his *thorough* physical exam and vowed never to see him again.

"Could you please just take the good news at face value and leave well enough alone?" Jody pleads. So be it. I don't *want* her to be sick, after all. I *want* her to be well.

I share the results with Lori, and the grin on my face is soon reflected on hers. I'm glad not to have to burden her with the role of being an emotional rock.

When I get home, Jody shows me the site, which has become a deep red-purple. It's also warm, as if the area is actually infected now that he stirred it up with a needle. I'm even less impressed with her physician, but I "leave well enough alone" as requested.

CHAPTER 2: July

More tests • Diagnosis • Sitting on the steps • When Kevin met Jody • Family and friends react • Biopsy • Mom's Diagnosis • Two not-so-happy birthdays • Haircut • The golf outing • Mastectomy • Kevin seeks perspective • The Slashing Beast

Tuesday, July 25

KEVIN:

The lump has grown. If touching it didn't cause Jody to wince with pain, I could feel it without having to do more than lightly graze the skin. It actually looks angry, this red and hot-to-the-touch nodule.

It hasn't been but two months since the doctor pronounced my wife to be worried about nothing, but he now would prefer to defer a third assessment to a surgeon, who is expected to do a proper needle aspiration this time around. Good, I said. If my bride has to go through that again, it should be by someone who has the experience and the TIME to do it right. I am reminded that 50% of all doctors finish in the *bottom half* of their class. I wonder where *her* doctor finished.

Jody insists this is no big deal and sends me off to work. I want to believe her, so I go. I don't believe her, though. I know it could be a very big deal indeed.

Once again, I find myself outside Lori's door. I'm matter-of-fact now: "Jody has another appointment today. The lump has grown. You know the drill." I can't meet her eyes, but I hear Lori's words: she's sure it's nothing, and if I need to go, I should leave.

I nod and move on.

JODY:

Yesterday I reached my doctor's nurse by phone and described what was continuing to grow in my breast. She abruptly put me on hold, then announced that the doctor wanted me to make an appointment with the first available surgeon to have the cyst aspirated. Her sense of urgency was a little disconcerting and sparked my own, but soon the worry, tentative touching, and wondering would be put to rest once and for all! The

18

mass has become so predominant that my nipple is actually inverted due to the swelling around it, so the cyst should be easy to spear. Kevin offered to go with me, but I laughed off the offer. Why act scared, when he already is frightened? I went to my own office as though nothing was amiss, where I told Tracy, the sales manager, that I had a routine doctor's appointment at 11:00 but would be back in time for an afternoon meeting.

Once I'm properly papered, I again wait atop a cold examination table. I look around the room thinking, Remember this, because these could be the last few minutes that everything in your life is the way it should be. For the magnitude of the moment, the tiny room is disappointingly sterile. One pastel watercolor poster well branded with the logo of a medical supply company is thumb-tacked to the wall. For such a dramatic possibility, it would be nice to at least have an original piece of art to remember.

Finally the surgeon comes into the room, introduces himself, and shakes my hand. He is an attractive, dark haired man in his late forties with a serious, no-nonsense approach. He is very purposeful: "What have we got here? I don't believe we need an ultrasound to do this, do you? Pretty straight forward, I'd say, from the size of the protuberance. You don't need a local anesthetic, do you, because you're going to feel at least one poke either way. Good. Let's just do it and get you on your way."

His direct attitude is very heartening, which makes me brave. I nod permission. He expertly inserts the needle once, twice. Moves the needle around. Goes in another spot. And another. Damn, that hurts! The look on his face changes.

"I'll be right back, Ms. Patrick. I just want to check that last ultrasound again before we continue."

I forget to breathe, realize I'm not breathing, and take a deep, shaky breath. I count my exhales. One.. two... fifty... eighty... two hundred sixty... three hundred seventeen.

The surgeon re-enters and crosses his arms over his chest. "I've made arrangements for you to have another mammogram right now, to be followed by an ultrasound. I assure you, it's no big deal for me to have these tests repeated, just to be safe. It's fairly routine and the good news is that you won't have the typical wait; I'm made arrangements for the lab to do back-to-back procedures right now. I want to see what I'm trying to get at, because that cyst must be moving under the skin. I can feel it but I can't seem to get at it so I want to see it first. Then you'll come back here and we'll discuss whether I have to do the aspiration with aid of another ultrasound or not."

At first, the mammogram technician's handling is routine, almost brusque. Then she checks the films and discovers a reason to take a couple more views. Now the woman is very kind, very gentle, and she calls me "honey" in the tone of voice that a mother would use with an injured child. I am afraid to move any further forward into this day, and I stay in my seat, looking to her for... I don't know what, exactly. Help of some sort. She gives me a slight nod of her head. "Good luck, sweetie," the woman adds, and I get up and move deeper into the medical complex, more deeply into the web. I am trapped now and I know that the word "cancer" will surely be said before I can escape. I think of walking out now, before it can be named and take on a life of its own in my conscious world. I want to run away, but people seem to expect me to act civilized and to move on. There is protocol to be followed. You can't walk out on your own destiny... can you?

The ultrasound tech also is very thorough. She moves the probe over my skin, over my nipple, and over the right breast, too, so that there can be a comparison. I am very close to screaming because I do not like to be touched by strangers. I am feeling a little claustrophobic and want to be anywhere else but lying on the table, bare-breasted, exposed. The phone rings, the interruption created by a specialist looking at my images on a monitor in another room. Is it the radiologist? Is it the surgeon? I don't know. Now the woman moves according to the stranger's directions. Back over the lump, a little harder. Back and forth, back and forth. I clench my hands together to feel my fingernails in my palms so that I do not scream. I will myself to be calm. Be calm.

I am returned to the surgical treatment room. Now I am feeling resentful that there is not something special to look at, to grab hold of, if only with my eyes.... something special to take with me into the future.

Within ten minutes, the surgeon strides into the room. "You have a small cyst," he begins. [My relief is actually palpable. My thoughts race: How silly I've been! How relieved Kevin will be! How lucky I am! How thankful that I don't have to tell the children that I—] "The cyst is like a little ball," he adds, meeting my eyes. "But over that, there is a very large tumor, and I believe that it sits on the smaller cyst like a ball glove resting on a ping pong ball. It appears to be a very aggressive cancer. I'm not going to lie to you; I believe it's very fast growing and I believe it is likely a malignant tumor. I'd guess it's a very serious cancer."

I look at him, dumbfounded.

He continues: "I'd like to schedule a biopsy for tomorrow at St. Marys Surgical Center. And then, on Friday, we'll talk about my treatment plan, which might take place as early as next Monday, because we need to act quickly."

I continue to stare, speechless. He waits.

"Okay." I finally manage to get that single word around the lump in my throat. Then: "You mean I'll need a mastectomy?"

He nods. "There's no easy or gentle way to say this, Mrs. Patrick, and I'm sorry for that, but a mastectomy is exactly what I expect is needed, and as quickly as it can be arranged. I'll give you a few minutes for this to sink in and to get hold of your emotions."

I don't understand what he means about composing myself. I am not crying or screaming. I tell him I am fine. He waits, expectantly, and I don't know what to say, but it's obvious he thinks it is still my turn so I whisper, "Thank you."

He seems to take this as a sign that I can handle more. He says, "After you get dressed, you'll need to call the hospital and give them your pre-admission insurance information. They'll give you their instructions, too, because there are some things you can't do before surgery and other things you should do to get ready. My nurse will get them on the phone. Just go into the office across the hall and sit down at the desk. Nod your head if you understand what I'm saying to you. Very good. Okay. After you call the hospital, you need to go down the hall to see your primary care physician, who'll do your pre-op. Then you'll have a chest x-ray so that you'll be admitted for surgery tomorrow. I've already talked to your doctor; he's expecting you."

Wow. Everything is arranged. He stares and I realize it is my turn again. He needs a sign that I'm still with the program. "Okay," I croak.

"You can stay in here a couple extra minutes if you need, though. Take as long as you want."

I do not take a couple extra minutes. I don't have time to waste on hysteria; I have to get this ball-glove tumor off my chest. I dress quickly, sit at the assigned desk, and almost immediately am connected to the hospital. I read aloud my insurance card number but have to ask twice when I'm supposed to stop eating because I can't mentally process everything being said to me.

I have to get to my doctor's office down the hall. He has a student with him, of course, though I suspect the young man is being used as a witness this time in the event that I might be in an agitated state and/or confrontational. As directed, I climb onto the examination table and open my blouse, trembling. He asks quite nicely, "Would you mind if the student feels the tumor, too?"

Would I mind?! I want to scream at him, "I hate you, you incompetent fuck! You wait-and-see hack! I hate your little protégé, too! I hate him this minute just for being here in this room! I hate everyone standing in line to touch my tumor!" This is what I would say if I could talk, but I can't get the words out. My mouth isn't cooperating and... I'm tired, so tired... and... I may need this doctor in the future and suddenly I fear alienating him. I nod permission for the student to touch what may be his first real, live cancer tumor. Whoopee.

The physical exam takes less than two minutes. Then my doctor asks if I wear a seatbelt when I drive. I am caught off guard and look to his eyes for clarification. All I can discern is that he is serious. I nod. "Good," he says, and glances down. Where did that clipboard come from? His eyes remain on the checklist in his hands. "And do you have a carbon monoxide detector in your home?"

Are you worried about saving me from flying through a windshield or succumbing to toxic fumes? I wonder. The sheer idiocy of his ideological concern is insulting. Are you implying there may be pending disasters for which my own irresponsibility will put me at risk? Or are you deflecting attention from the obvious and immediate situation? I study him like a bug under glass and decide that he's not smart enough to pull off such a diabolical ruse. The questions must be part of the latest HMO survey or a new protocol for physicians. I remain mute and eventually he gives up and sets the survey aside. "Very well," he sighs. "You have more pressing concerns, I suppose."

It takes all of my strength and self-control to dress, get out the door, and find my way to the x-ray department.

This latest lab technician wants to know when my surgery is. "Tomorrow," I tell her. This is the only word I will say because the mass in my throat feels as real as the one in my chest. I will cry if they make me talk anymore and I can't cry because there isn't time. I have to hurry and get the tumor off my chest.

I sit and wait while she checks to see if the films are acceptable. It is now 1:30 in the afternoon and I haven't called anyone yet. Not the office, not my husband. I realize I cannot go back to work as expected, yet I can't call them or Kevin right now because I can't speak without crying and I don't want to cry in front of strangers who might think that touching me might make me feel better. I will scream and scream and never stop, I know I will, if one more person puts one more hand anywhere on my body.

I get dressed. Before hooking my bra, I inspect the traitor breast. It feels hot, sick. There is no longer any sentimental attachment to the flesh.

I want it gone. I want the cancer gone. I realize that soon I won't have a nipple on that side of my chest, but I've breastfed my last baby anyway. Good riddance.

I make it to the parking lot before I break down. Then, sitting in a hot parked car, I allow myself a good hard cry. I put my head on the steering wheel and sob for maybe five minutes. I look up to discover my doctor and the medical student who has touched my breast, both stopped in their tracks gaping at me, obviously startled to see a crazy woman crying in her car. Did they come out for a quick stroll? A cigarette, perhaps? My doctor recognizes me and looks away. Funny that he would be embarrassed for me now, when he wasn't at the time I was most exposed and vulnerable in Exam Room #4.

I long to be home with Kevin. I drive oblivious of the route or even the experience, startled back to reality as I coast into the garage. I have had no thoughts, not a single one. I made my head stay empty so that I might just get home and not kill some innocent bystander in a freak accident along the way.

I walk into the kitchen and call my husband. He is not in his office so the call is forwarded to voicemail. My sudden wailing startles the dog. In a long rambling message, I beg Kevin to come home because… things are not okay, just please come home. Then I go outside and sit on the steps to wait for him.

I sit on the front steps of my home, just as I did so many years ago after learning Daniel was dead. I didn't know what else to do then either, when shock and disbelief rendered me useless. That night back then, I could only think to call my best friend and my pastor and then I put myself on the steps and waited for help. Just as I am doing now. I thought I was prepared for the worst today, but…. I would prefer to sit on the curb, even in the gutter… that seems right… to be in the gutter… but it is too far to walk. So I will stay here until Kevin comes and does whatever he is supposed to do with me.

I put myself on the steps. I will stay here until Kevin comes and does whatever he is supposed to do with me. This is as far ahead as I can think or plan.

I put myself on the steps….

KEVIN:

The morning drags by. I check my watch at 11:00, at noon. I wait until 1:00 to grab a chicken sandwich, certain Jody must have gotten an *all-clear* and returned to work. To tell the truth, I'm a little miffed that she didn't call and tell me. She should have known I'd worry.

There's a meeting scheduled for 1:30 and I go into it prepared to have my mind 100% on work issues again. When I return to my desk, there is a voice mail waiting. It's Jody and she's crying, repeating, "Just come home."

I immediately dial home. No answer. I am at Lori's office in seconds and interrupt a conversation between her and a colleague to state bluntly that I've got to leave. I can tell by the look on Lori's face that my own must be colorless. "Be careful," she cautions. "And give Jody my best."

A quick nod and I race to the parking lot. Despite my need to be home with my wife at this very second (THIS VERY SECOND!), I am rational enough to realize that a car accident would not ease our situation. I intend to speed home, but speed prudently.

Driving, I just naturally review our too-short relationship in my head. She is my every thought right now, my wife, this beautiful woman whom I first met through a mutual friend who arranged a telephone conversation between us on Mothers Day, 1999. After a 99-minute phone call, we agreed to take it a step further and talk face-to-face. Not one to waste time, Jody invited me to meet her for dinner the next evening.

In truth, she didn't invite me so much as she challenged me to have dinner with her. I surmised that she wanted to get the date out of the way to pacify her matchmaker friend and possibly also to teach her ex-boyfriend a good lesson, a legislator with whom she'd only called it quits the previous Friday. Then she likely would go back to him. I expected no more than that. However, I wanted to meet the woman who had fascinated me for an hour and a half on the phone.

On the evening of our dinner, I arrived early at the agreed upon restaurant so that I might see her before she saw me. Even approaching the door of the restaurant, Jody had presence. She moved with a combination of grace, elegance and confidence. She was also drop-dead gorgeous.

If this is not Jody, I thought, *I'm going to have a hard time concentrating on whoever my real date turns out to be, with this woman in the same restaurant.* I was enthralled.

"You must be Kevin," she said, extending her hand.

"If not, I should return his suit to him," I replied, hoping she shared an affinity with other women who said they most valued a sense of humor in a blind date. I wanted to score points with this lady, and fast.

Once seated at our table, the conversation flowed as if we had known each other for years. When asked for our drink order, I requested tea. Jody was obviously pleased by the choice. "I don't drink and drive," I explained. "And I almost always drive."

An hour later, I was so captivated that most of my food was yet untouched. The waitress interrupted a third time to inquire if the entree was to my liking. "It's fine," I admitted, "But we are kind of busy falling in love right now, so could you please stop asking?" Then, because doing impressions is a passion of mine, I slipped into a George Bush voice: "Interrupting again wouldn't be prudent at this juncture."

Jody chuckled and I knew in that instant that my heart was completely and forever hers for the taking. After dinner, she noted that we both would pass by her office on our respective paths home. "Would you like to see where I work?" she asked. It was in that very office that very night that I proposed on bended knee. And that very same night she said yes.

Memorial Day, I was on my knees again as I slipped an engagement ring on her finger. We were married July 5. A month later, we moved into a new home, the first house we looked at. Within five days, we were completely unpacked and Jody had redecorated the house, including new wallpaper and paint.

Yeah, things happen fast with her.

I pull into the driveway and Jody is on the front steps. As I drive into the garage, she slips inside the house. I find her on the stairs leading up to our bedroom. Her face is blotchy red, and it is apparent that she has been crying for some time. I take her in my arms and the tears begin to flow again. I try to kiss them away but there are too many, so I just hold her. I fight back my own tears as she explains, through sobs, that the doctor thinks she has an angry form of cancer. A very aggressive form.

To say that I am unhappy with her primary physician would be a severe understatement. But I have no time for anger now. I have only time for Jody.

JODY:

My husband takes me into his arms, and I cry and cry. He touches my face, cradles me. His touch is good.

PJ walks in half an hour later and goes right to the refrigerator for a Pepsi, oblivious that Kevin and I are cuddling on the couch. Kevin calls out that dinner is going to be a little late and PJ responds that he doesn't care because he ate a pizza at a friend's house. He's fifteen, that awkward age when so much goes unspoken, his emotions and thoughts impossible to articulate to people as dense as parents. Thursday nights are reserved for *family night*, not Tuesdays, and so he feels no obligation to talk to us now. He's visibly annoyed when we stop him from going directly to his room.

"What?" he challenges. "I want to get on the internet."

I look at my son, who is quickly growing into a handsome young man. He's already as tall as I, at five-foot-six, though the pictures taken at the wedding showed him to be inches shorter. He's shot up in the last 13 months! His hair is still blonde… I figured it would be brown by now, like his father's, but all of the children apparently inherited my hair color. He has piercing green eyes and I can see the faint blonde hairs on his face, the beginnings of a mustache and a few coarse whisker hairs on his chin. When did that happen?

Kevin gives PJ the news because I truly can't. The delivery is delicate because Kevin thoughtfully neuters the words: "Your mother has a medical problem, but we found it in time to be able to get treatment which will include surgery tomorrow and maybe again soon, and then she'll have to take some medication that will make her pretty sick for quite a while."

"Do you have cancer?" PJ asks me bluntly. His tone sounds accusing.

"Yes, I do, honey. But it's treatable."

"That sucks." Then PJ shrugs, uncertain what we want from him. We don't know, either, so no one speaks for an awkward moment. "Well… okay," he finally says, and he goes to his room. He surfaces half an hour later to ask if he can spend the night at another friend's house. We say okay, knowing he is not okay, nor are we, nor is anything.

The diagnosis will affect friends as well as family. There is a question about what to do next because we expect that soon Joe will come through the door. A few months ago, I hired him to be the editor of our Madison magazine and, because Joe lives 90 miles away in Milwaukee, he sleeps at our house on Tuesday nights to knock out one commute a week. We call the office to see if there is somewhere else he might go this night, while the shock of the diagnosis is so fresh and close to the surface. No answer.

Joe gives a couple quick knocks on the door and then opens it, right on schedule. He sees Kevin standing in the kitchen, but he doesn't see me, where I have retreated back to a makeshift bed on the couch in the family room. Joe walks into the kitchen and tells Kevin, "Tracy told me Jody went to the doctor. She must be pretty sick, not to call to let us know she wouldn't make the staff meeting." Kevin shrugs. Joe then catches sight of me and gives a quick wave. "I see you're alive after all," he teases.

Joe and I have been friends for more than a decade and worked at two newspapers together before coming together again in Madison. He takes off his suit jacket and loosens his tie, a tall man in his early 40s who is as comfortable in our house as his own. He makes his way up the stairs to put his suitcase in the guest bedroom, and I know he'll then wash his hands for dinner, expecting that we'll eat in the family room while watching Friends on television. We have a routine. He found my disappearance worrisome because we are predictable to each other, as close as brother and sister. In fact, I've known him since before he lost his hair. Likewise, I marvel, soon Joe will be able to say that he knew me long before I lost my breast.

When he comes back downstairs, Joe sits on a couch adjacent to mine and he asks me directly if I feel okay. I shake my head. Kevin makes a lot of noise moving pots and pans in the kitchen. Joe takes my hand. "What's up, Jo-Jo?" he says softly.

I begin to cry. "I have breast cancer and… it seems to be pretty far along, Joey."

The color drains out of his face and Joe soon leaves the room, overcome with emotion. My husband holds out his arms and pulls our friend into an embrace. I watch but say nothing because that damn lump is back in my throat. I realize that this will be a new role for Kevin with all of our friends, even while he must be struggling to come to grips with his own grief. They will come to offer comfort to him, but that is not how it will be. He naturally takes care of people and they can't help but respond to him.

Summer, my daughter, telephones soon after dinner and Joe discretely leaves the room, knowing I haven't told her yet. Now 22 years old, Summer is enrolled in pre-med studies in Chicago, where she lives and works part-time, though presently she's in Denver. The whole purpose of the westward winding bus and train trip was to introduce Paddy, her Irish immigrant fiancé, to our far away family members. It was an adventure that was inaugurated with homemade sour mash made by my free-spirited brother Kurt in Missouri, and now is winding down with my equally unpredictable mother and conservative brother Bob, who lives with her in Denver. It's Summer's first trip to Grandma Joyce's house since Grandpa Wayne died of cancer last year, and I'm thankful that this trip is spurred by a joyous occasion rather than a tragedy. I'd like to see to it that the return trip is just as pleasant for her.

"Hey, Mom, Grandma's in the hospital," Summer says without preamble. "Uncle Bobby took her there this afternoon. You know that pain she keeps having that her doctor said was from a bad back? Well, it got really bad today, and now they think it's from pneumonia! They said she'll probably be there for a few days at least, so Paddy and I are going to take a quick trip up into the mountains. I thought I'd better call and let you know in case you call and nobody's here."

I exchange a few pleasantries with Paddy, struggling to understand his thick brogue and odd pronunciations, then Summer is back on the line.

I broach the fact that I will be having a minor procedure and she immediately peppers me with questions. I tell her as little as possible, limiting the scope of the expected surgery to a minor biopsy.

"Do you want us to come there now?"

I do not. "Summer, your grandmother and I have danced our dances and had our share of romantic mountain getaways. Now it's your turn. Give us both something positive to think about. Go to the mountains."

After we say goodbye, Kevin hugs me tight. Tears spring to the surface again. I don't know what I would do without him. I know he will *be there* for the children – for PJ and Summer and Brook. Even while my world is falling apart, I feel him putting it back together minute by minute, encouragement by encouragement.

Wednesday, July 26
KEVIN:

Things are moving very fast, though if I could, I would wish this day already gone altogether. But I keep my demeanor light as we check into St. Marys Hospital as directed at the front information desk.

After the paperwork is finished, I have my first opportunity to meet the surgeon who made the initial diagnosis. He's a tall man with a ruddy complexion and dark goatee and mustache. Although very matter-of-fact about what he expects to find, he will not discuss a plan of action until the lab analyzes the biopsy. A by-the-numbers guy. I respect that.

He launches into a brief but practiced pre-operative chat with Jody, spelling out what she should expect during the biopsy surgery, and then he sends me to the waiting room with a promise to speak to me as soon as the operation is finished. Jody is responding well to the pre-op shot in her butt; she smiles, already relaxed.

That makes one of us.

I wait an hour, alternately turning the pages of a magazine in which I haven't the slightest interest, and staring at the clock. It's 8:30 a.m. Will this day never end?

Suddenly the surgeon steps off a nearby elevator. His eyes flit from person to person and I realize that he doesn't recognize me. My initial amusement quickly turns to concern: my wife believes that her survival chances will be enhanced if her doctors develop a personal relationship with her/us. His apparent failure to pick me out of a group of only eight indicates that even a tenuous bond has not yet been established. I will need to cultivate a relationship.

I nod when his eyes come my way again and he motions to me. "Come in here, where we can talk," he says, pointing to a conference room. Apparently it doubles as a nurses' training room, as it's now occupied. Somewhat annoyed, the doctor scouts for another spot. I follow him from place to place as he becomes visibly more agitated. I can't stand the suspense a moment longer and tell him to please just tell me right here in the waiting room. Expecting the worse, I silently steel myself to absorb every syllable the man might utter.

"Your wife came through the operation just fine, as expected, but my original diagnosis is correct. The frozen section revealed that the lump is malignant cancer."

While intellectually I had prepared myself for this inevitability, I had still held out some hope that this was just a horrible mistake. The surgeon, into whose hands I will place Jody's life at least one more time, tells me to wait in the recovery room for her. I thank him, marveling that he has forever and profoundly changed my life with only two sentences, and marveling also at what he has not said.

A nurse wheels the love of my life back into the recovery room and I manage a weak smile. "The surgeon wants to see us on Friday," I say. Jody nods, still groggy from the anesthesia.

As soon as we are home, I put her to bed. I explain to P.J. that nothing is certain at this point; we'll know more on Friday. My stepson seems to accept this statement, but with him it is hard to know. He's a private lad and I'm sorry at this moment that this is the case because I could use someone to talk to, and I expect that he could, too. Still, he retreats to his room and to his video games, to his comfort zone.

Jody sleeps all day. I vegetate before the television, checking on her during every commercial break. She rouses toward early evening, but only to be helped to the bathroom and back to bed. I wonder how it will be after she has the more serious operation, and how long she will be down. I suspect not as long as predicted but this is new ground for us. I haven't a clue.

There is just so much that I don't know anymore....

Thursday, July 27
JODY:

Happy birthday, Brook! Even though you'll spend it on patrol at Patrick Air Force Base in Florida, and there is no way that I can celebrate with my beautiful 20-year old today, you are my first clear thought upon waking at 7 a.m. I miss you so much!

Rising causes me to hurt in places I never imagined, but I will not be a patient again today. I gingerly push off the bed and reach for my robe. Bad enough that I lost yesterday to cancer, falling asleep as soon as we returned from the hospital. An entire day of my life – Poof! Gone! Kevin helps tidy the house because Beverly, my dearest girlfriend, is expected to arrive in Madison around 10 a.m. She lives in California and makes annual pilgrimages to Milwaukee to visit her mother, when we typically steal a couple of days together. I can't wait to see her!

The bandages over the incision itch like crazy, but I hold off taking a pain pill so that I won't appear dim or drugged. The irritation increases as I putter around the house until I go half berserk with an aching desire to scratch. Finally I relent and pop a pill, rationalizing that the narcotic will lessen the itching sensation and ease the throbbing.

The doorbell rings. I had talked with Bev on the phone earlier about my condition, but I was unprepared for what came through the door. While Beverly's normal personality is effusive, she lunges into the house and scoops me into an enthusiastic hug, nearly manic in her desire to literally and figuratively hold me up. Moments later she is mournful, sobbing, openly grieving. I can't resist teasing that my disease has apparently triggered a bi-polar episode for her. She acts as if she does not hear me, as if she is absorbed with spreading out the cloth over which she will serve me Holy Communion. Bev is a recovering Catholic earning a Ph.D. in ministry and is intensely reverent about anything she perceives to be spiritual, which is everything. More than a decade ago we recognized the connection of both being peak-and-valley wild women and we forged a bond based largely on a similar skewed perception of the world. High-high-high to low-low-low.

She holds my hand and earnestly prays aloud for my eternal soul. Then: "You can't die and leave me," she wails. "I love you too much! I would just hate you if you died on me!"

"You just offered up my body and soul to Christ yourself," I remind.

"Screw you," she says, but she laughs at her own extreme reactions and whenever she laughs, I can't help but laugh with her. That's part of what makes her special, I guess. She hands me a miniature It's-Good-to-be-Queen keepsake.

"Queen of what?"

"Queen of yourself, Queen of this house, Queen of your treatment." Bev acts as if my domain and power is self evident. "You know, QUEEN," she prompts.

I put the little plastic power icon on a bathroom shelf above the toilet, the closest thing to a throne in our house.

Joe and Tracy appear at the door bearing flowers from the collective magazine staff. I introduce Tracy to Beverly and the two strangers hug and cry together. Joe is an awkward non-participant, unsure if he is expected to jump in or stand stoically by to comfort the women when they separate. He looks to me, but the Queen is fresh out of commands. I take another pain pill to further distance myself from all of them. I want to be in the audience for the play unfolding in my living room, despite having been cast in the center-stage role of *tragic heroine*. I never asked to play that part. The phone rings and Joe dashes off shouting, "I'll get it, I'll get it," to three women who are making no move to answer it or to stop him from doing so. (Shhh... actors are the most comical when they are unwittingly funny.)

Joe hands me the receiver. Nancy, the boss' wife, is calling to relay their shock and support. She openly appeals to my fighting spirit and offers the names of more oncologists, reminding me that she works at a lab and has the inside track. After we disconnect, I fight a strong sense of déjà vu, as if Nancy and I have already had this conversation in a dream. Or perhaps I was in a fog just now. It's too confusing, so I put it out of my mind altogether. I may have taken the second pain pill too close to the first.

Joe and Tracy leave, but Bev stays until 3:30. She cries and cries now that it is time to say goodbye for another uncertain year, and I comfort her as best I can. I've played the piano for her and not wavered in my bravery; I am proud of myself. PJ calls to say he's going to stay at the mall and he'd like to be excused from family night because he and his friends have plans to see a movie. I am feeling very disjointed. I suspect we all need family night, but I'm equally relieved to skip it. "Go, go. Have fun," I tell him.

After Bev leaves, I collapse into the folds of the red leather couch in the living room. Foley has been slipping me dog kisses about every five minutes for the past few hours; bumping his way between our thighs to deliver his little missiles of love and concern. Now the German shepherd settles into a fitful sleep by my feet. Although he appears to be unconscious, my faithful companion is easily startled, perhaps sensing something is very wrong because I very seldom sit still this long.

The surgeon's office calls to push back the consultation appointment tomorrow. Roused from my stupor, I call my boss and ask him to come by Saturday to talk about what we're going to do now about our new business venture. Friends check in who just got word and they all want details. Joe calls, though he only left an hour ago. As the conversation continues, he asks more and more pointed questions, apparently now the go-to guy for concerned employees who lack the confidence to ask such personal questions themselves. Like me, he's been assigned a reluctant starring role in this little drama. The phone rings and rings and the calls run together … until Brook telephones.

Our birthday girl! Brook thanks us for the present we sent and asks if I'd also consider co-signing a loan for her car, since she needs private transportation at this new Air Force base. It's wonderful to discuss something so normal! I wonder, Why not just give her the money she needs? What are we saving for? I announce that we'll put the money in her account to purchase the car outright! I quickly override her half-hearted protest. "It's done," I tell her. "The car is yours, no strings or payment books attached. Happy birthday." While she's still got her head in the clouds, I offhandedly mention what's going on, though, of course, Summer has already given her sister every detail known to her. It doesn't really matter because Brook and I are most comfortable talking about the car and we easily steer back to that discussion.

Almost all of our family birthdays fall within a two-month window and I've set a heck of a precedent for gifts this year…without even conferring with Kevin, whose own birthday is tomorrow. His was to be an extravagant gift already, a country club membership so that he might play more golf this season. I haven't signed the paperwork, but I'll take care of that small detail after the surgery, when my head is clearer. In the meantime, I could give him a symbolic gift tomorrow of a picture of golf clubs. Tomorrow… after we meet with the surgeon to discuss the biopsy and pending mastectomy. What a peak-and-valley week we're having, but that's *par for the course*. Ha ha.

Friday, July 28
KEVIN:

It's my birthday. It's also a Friday. Normally both days would hold some significance for me, but right now the only thing on my mind is the visit with the surgeon when Jody and I will find out about the rest of our life together.

We both claim a work vacation day, certain we will need some time to ourselves after the appointment. The drive to the clinic is tense, our conversation sparse. I drive. This in itself is unusual, since we are in Jody's car and she is subject to motion sickness when she doesn't drive. However, she has taken a Lorazapam to calm her nerves and I suspect she's taken a pain pill too, so when I insist on driving, she doesn't argue. In our own way, I think we are both beginning to realize that our life is about to spin off in a direction beyond our influence.

We are led into the examination room after a short wait. The doctor is delayed in surgery; we wait longer. She holds my hand even after he enters the room.

After a quick check of Jody's incision, the surgeon pulls a stool next to her and begins to sketch on a pad of paper, drawing what he has found and what the lab has confirmed.

"You have invasive lobular carcinoma," he begins slowly and precisely, unsure of our educational levels or familiarity with medical terminology. I interrupt him to explain that Jody has had extensive interaction with cancer patients when she employed as manager of the Chicago Ronald McDonald House. I also assure that I had some medical and surgical experience in the Navy, and so he should feel comfortable with technical explanations. (If I can't change the news, at least I can make sure that bad news is not drawn out and repeated several different ways to make sure I understand it.)

Hearing this, the surgeon's demeanor changes, softening, and he mentions that he served as a Navy doctor earlier in his career. *This could be the bond we need with this doctor,* I dare to hope. He picks up the pace, explaining this particular form of breast cancer and the treatment options available. Jody and I have already decided that if the surgeon thought a mastectomy was her best option, we weren't going to worry about more cosmetic surgeries just yet.

A mastectomy is the *only* option, he says. To be certain that the subsequent chemotherapy and radiation therapy follow the correct protocols, he suggests that lymph nodes be removed from under Jody's left arm and inspected to see if there are any cancer cells present beyond the tumor. Because of the rapid growth and the size of the tumor (classified as *large*), her cancer is determined to be at Stage 3A. If lymph nodes are involved, it will be downgraded to 3B. If found in the lungs, brain, bones, or any other organs to which this type of cancer is known to spread, it will become Stage 4 – the last number on the scale. The higher the number, the lower the odds of survival.

JODY:

The verdict is almost anticlimactic. It is what I expect. The mastectomy is scheduled for Monday, and overall chances of survival are estimated right now at less than half for best scenario – if it is still Stage 3A and the lymph nodes are clear. The tumor, we're told, is over 6 cm. large and likely is doubling at the rate of about every 100 days. I count back to May, estimating what my chances might have been had it been diagnosed then, but this serves no constructive end. The surgeon is saying that following surgery I will be sent to an oncologist to begin what is expected to be an aggressive chemotherapy and radiation program.

I ask the surgeon to recommend an oncologist. "They're all good," he hedges.

Kevin cuts in: "If it was your wife — and let's hypothesize that you

33

love your wife because that's important in this equation — then who would you recommend? Really. We're not leaving this room without a name."

Finally he relents. "Mike Frontiera with Dean Medical Center would probably be the most aggressive. And he has a very direct manner. You two seem up to that."

I jot down the name, knowing it's a moot point because I'm going to the competition for treatment, to the University of Wisconsin's Comprehensive Cancer Care Center. I already have an appointment with a university oncologist, though I don't mention it because it would just be dumb to alienate a surgeon before surgery. Today I am simply covering all bets and the name he supplied will be reserved as a backup oncologist.

KEVIN:

During the drive home, we talk about what needs to be done prior to surgery, what to tell the kids, and how much to tell Jody's mom. There is no need to inform anyone on my side of the family; both of my parents died of cancer several years ago. Two sisters and two brothers live in other states and don't know that I live in Wisconsin. They've never even heard Jody's name. Years ago I decided that contact with them was not in my best interest, after being called one too many times to save a sibling from the repercussions of their own *free spirit* lifestyle.

As we enter our home, Jody apologizes again for not having baked a cake. She wants to give me a present, though, and says that she has purchased a local country club player's membership.

"I won't be playing much golf this year," I remind, taking her into my arms. "But I do appreciate the thought." What I don't say is that despite having good medical insurance, our income soon will be diminished by co-pays. If your insurance company is about to billed in excess of $500,000, you're going to feel their hand in your pocket. "Given the situation, could we just pretend that today is not my birthday? I really don't need to be getting any older anyway."

"Ok, if that's the way you want it, but P.J. wants to take you golfing today. That's his present to you."

JODY:

I am almost frenetic in my research. Web page after web page, article after article on breast cancer. I can't learn fast enough, I can't find enough resource books! I can't understand how my own DNA turned on itself, or why a dormant cancer cell would suddenly activate. What does that mean?

34

What is going to happen to me next? And then, what's going to happen after that?

Patient-oriented cancer guides suggest women get their hair cut before beginning chemo to feel they have some control over making the change from hair to bald — as if that interim step will cushion the blow. In case there is the slightest emotional help to be found in sabotaging my own self image, I decided to have my hair cut very, very short while Kevin and PJ play golf today.

Then I called my mother, only to find out that she was diagnosed to have Non-Hodgkin's lymphoma. She found out that the *pneumonia* was actually cancer, learned it the very same day my cancer was discovered, but she kept it from us until she felt strong enough to say the words aloud. We spoke just before I left the house.

Weird. I mean, this can't really be happening. Not to my mother, too.

The woman who cuts my hair is nice. I tell her very dispassionately that I am about to have a mastectomy and begin chemotherapy, and I direct her to cut it shorter than a guy's typical hairstyle. She does. It makes me feel like I am in control of having little hair. It feels good. I know I won't be able to wash it by myself for awhile because they're going to take lymph nodes, too, and I won't be able to lift my left arm over my head, but Kevin has already volunteered to do it.

I go into JC Penney's and buy some nice lightweight cotton pajamas. Front buttoning. And slippers. My mother has cancer, too…. Why would we both be diagnosed on the same day? I can't believe this is true. There must be some mistake. I wanted to buy Kevin something special. I wanted to bake him a cake, but we don't even have a mix in the cupboard. What kind of a kitchen do I keep? What kind of a wife am I? He's very clear that he no longer wants the country club membership and so he doesn't even have a present. I don't know what to give him because what he really wants, I can't give to him. He wants this to be over. He wants me to be me again.

I'm taking Valium and pain pills. I don't want to wake up until after the mastectomy because this is scary as hell, and I can't let the fear race to my belly yet — not if I'm to be brave for the kids. I have no right to drive a car, but if I didn't, I'd be too dependent too quickly. That will come soon enough. This is how I rationalize what I know to be irresponsible behavior.

I stop at a big grocery store intending to buy a cake mix. It is unfamiliar territory and I can't find the right aisle. Eventually, wandering through the maze, I forget why I am here. I buy Foley a bone rather than walk out empty-handed, because the last thing I need right now is someone thinking I might be a shoplifter. In an emotional rush of gratitude for the dog, I buy three bones to reward him for his loyalty. Just as I get into the car, it hits me that I forgot the cake mix. I am a lousy wife. I open the car door to go back into the store to fix everything, but then another voice argues that if I do buy Kevin a cake, he'll lose his composure. He's like me. He normally doesn't like to cry in front of people. We're kind of pretending that this isn't really his birthday so that it won't forever be tainted by the news. And so he won't have to cry… yet.

Driving home, I remind myself that I don't need two breasts to play the piano. It isn't like the surgeon wants to take my hand, though I'm but an amateur pianist anyway. I only play Moonlight Sonata, Hill Street Blues, and If I Fell, but I'm too sentimental to sell the piano because sometimes Summer accompanies me on the duets that I taught her when she was a little girl. I always thought that someday she'd ask for the piano. Or maybe I'd take more lessons – enough to be able to play Canon in D. Today I very deeply regret that I cannot play that beautiful music for myself.

KEVIN:

P.J. hates golf but likes to drive the golf cart, so we select a course where they don't pay too much attention to the age of the person steering. During the round of 18, we mostly speak of my inability to hit the ball straight and of his inability to drive the cart any straighter. In less than a year, I am going to be teaching him to drive a car … a sobering thought.

Toward the end of the round he gives up any pretense that he came to golf. He came to drive a golf cart and he's bored having to play alongside me. It's a mutual decision that he is now relegated to chauffeur. Finally the subject of the surgery comes up. We talk about what will happen and what is to follow. I tell him that I'm going to be relying on him to help out more around the house because his mother may be pretty incapacitated by her medication. I also point out that we have to make more of an effort to get along.

P.J. listens quietly, offering only an occasional mumbled okay. I don't know whether he is agreeing with me or is just acknowledging that he has heard and understood what I said. I don't press for clarification.

As soon as I slide into the car, P.J. puts one of his most obnoxious rap CDs into the car's player, looking for a reaction from me. I say nothing, letting the raucous tunes play. In fact, neither of us has much to say as I drive the 35 minutes to home. Certainly I am more preoccupied with my own thoughts than concerned about his limited taste in music.

As we make our way, I remember past birthdays and holidays also punctuated by disaster and gloom. My older brother was a young man when he died on Father's Day. My uncle, aunt, grandfather, great grandmother, and mother had all died on either a holiday or family birthday. We used to joke that it was a family curse... but I'm not laughing now. In fact, my own birthday was rarely fun in my youth and so by adulthood, I had come to regard it as more *significant* than *celebratory*. At best I've remained suspicious of obligatory celebrations, never able to enjoy even the best of them because I was always waiting for Disaster to rear its ugly head.

We come home to Jody's note, folded over and addressed to me. She has gone shopping but wants me to know that she has already re-written her will, spoken with one daughter, left a message for the other, and broken the news to her brother and her mother, whom (her message continues) was also declared to have cancer *today*.

Happy freaking birthday!

JODY:

As I pull into the driveway, I realize that I'm free of fear at the moment. This is nearly exhilarating, and, I know, a brief reprieve. I enter the house as if it is any other day. I wave offhandedly at my husband and son, not stopping to show off my haircut, pausing only to give the dog a pat and a bone. I march upstairs to my office to email reassurances to staff. I email cancellations to any pending meetings. I am extricating myself from my life, memo by memo, while still in this good space that doesn't have fear in it. I sense I can't stay here forever, and so there is an almost frenzied push to do what I can in the moments immediately before me.

Happy birthday, Kevin. I'm sorry there is no cake. I'm sorry there is no wife. There is only me and I'm not here because you are letting me be where I need to be. Wherever that is.... I WON'T believe my mother has cancer. No one can make me believe it. NOT EVEN HER!

Monday, July 31
JODY:

It is early in the morning and we have reported, as scheduled, to St. Marys Hospital. I will likely only stay one night and to tell the truth, I'm honestly not afraid of the surgery. I think it's odd that the biopsy hurts so much, but they'll cut off the hurt and it'll get swallowed up in a bigger hurt; except that it won't be there anymore at all, will it? It'll be a phantom pain in the truest sense.

I have read enough to know that I am at the slash stage of the slash-poison-burn treatment regime. I look down as Kevin helps me into the hospital gown. Good-bye breast. When I wake up, you'll be gone, old friend. Good riddance, Cancer.

The hospital wants my signed Living Will before surgery. I put in writing that Kevin can pull the plug. It's comforting to know that death might be so antiseptic and legal. I get a shot to calm me although I'm not upset. A young man comes to get me, wheels me down the hall, helps me onto a different bed, straps down my arm. I say hello to the surgeon, who is becoming a familiar face. Hello again to the anesthesiologist, met a couple hours ago; hello to the nurses, hello to… ["When you wake up, you won't remember anything."]. Goodbye to….

<u>KEVIN:</u>

Sitting alone in her hospital room awaiting her safe return from surgery, I reflect on the weekend. Jody, with her once long and unruly curly hair now shorn closer than my own, had posed on the stairs for a few *before* shots. Wearing a low-cut top, she smiled into the camera lens and bent over to show off her lovely cleavage. While my wife certainly doesn't define herself merely by her looks, her appearance and her perfectly-shaped bosom are admittedly a source of self-confidence. She and I both consider this surgery to be a necessary maiming. But regardless how necessary, the physical and psychological aspects could easily be devastating to both of us.

I am alone for but a short while before Jan comes by to lend her support. I've only met this friend of Jody's once, though she enters the room as if we are old buddies and quickly offers a hug of reassurance. Red eyes belie her smile and it is obvious that she is fighting back yet more tears.

Despite the situation we are facing, I find it a kind of comic irony that Jody's friends seem to be taking the news harder than we are. Hugs intended to console Jody or me often become long hangings-on until the well-wisher is able to let go.

Jan has brought a get-well gift and waits with me for Jody's return. Then Jody's boss and good friend joins us. Soon after meeting Jody, I had been introduced to Bill, whose approval was important to her. Fortunately, I guess I made a good impression, and in turn, I like both him and his wife Nancy. As we shake hands, Jody is wheeled into the room. Still asleep, she looks so fragile now. Bill turns away, head bowed, shoulders shaking, choking back tears. I don't know if the emotion is sparked by his fear at seeing her so ill, or if the tears are in relief that she made it through surgery. I put my hand on his shoulder and whisper assurances that she'll be okay. He replies that of course she will. "Tell her that the whole staff is pulling for her," he adds and excuses himself from the room.

Jan and I wait in silence. Suddenly Salli, another of Jody's friends, startles us both with quick staccato raps on the door. She peeks in, wearing her best 'I-know-you-two-can-beat-this-thing' grin.

"Hi, honey," my wife whispers, hoarse. I kiss her lips and offer water. As she sips, she notices that Jan and Salli are in the room. A smile lights her face as handclasps and well wishes are exchanged. Jan says she must leave, but offers to help in any way needed. I thank her, insisting I'll let her know, but for now we are fine.

Of course we are not *fine*, but I'm thinking that control of whether or not we are to ever be fine again lay in my hands and in the soul and determination of my lover and wife. Salli rouses me from this thought by ordering that I get something to eat. She will stay with Jody until I return. I am becoming amazed at the depth of feeling others have for Jody and, now by extension, for me. While I'm happy for Jody, I am not sure how to respond because this sentimentality is alien to me.

I was raised in Louisville, Kentucky, the older middle child of six. My parents were exceptionally bright people who worked hard and did their best to feed, clothe and instill a sense of morality and responsibility in their children. However, their lack of formal education kept my father in a blue-collar trade and the number of offspring kept my mother at home. The unexpected loss of my older brother in a car accident seemed to take the wind out of their sails and they soon distanced themselves from their living children.

At age 12, I became the eldest son and took on the responsibility of family peacemaker and example-setter. Often I would take that to the extreme and too quickly accept blame or make a sacrifice just to avoid confrontation or arguments. This led to my being labeled by my siblings as a "martyr" and created somewhat of a rift between us, even then. Meanwhile, my parents were preoccupied with their grief, and the closeness we once shared became a memory.

I didn't fare much better in school. Small and rail-thin, I was untrained in athletics and often a target of larger students. In high school, I drifted along until finally I forged a small circle of only two friends; in them I found a place for my trust, as I had a secret. My parents, who had always had alcohol as part of their lives, were now relying on it heavily. I was embarrassed and ashamed. I trusted only Dale and Steve with that information or to come to my house to visit. Eventually the circle was tightened to only include Dale and this pattern of having only one friend at a time continued when I joined the Navy. It was easiest to only have one good friend at each duty station served. It simplified things and made me feel safer.

When I met Jody, she became my closest friend. Her friends became my acquaintances, but she was the only friend I needed or wanted. She's planned all of our social activities and with her, I reach out to a larger community. However, a work-related golf league has been the sum total of my explorations without her.

Now my best friend is lying on a hospital bed with tubes sticking out of her and one of her closest friends is trying to look out for my best interests. My life — our life — has begun unraveling. I realize that I can't mend it alone but I don't know how to ask for help and I'm not sure who to ask anyway, or even to trust.

I buy a sandwich, eat it, and go back to Jody's room with a barking toy puppy purchased in the hospital gift shop. Jody is asleep. Salli leaves amid reassurances and offers of help and prayers. I put the toy by Jody's head so that she will see it when she next wakes up. *It's not as good as Foley,* I think. But they wouldn't let him in the room anyway. I smile when I think about how our devoted canine has missed his *Mom* and how he will probably be returning the kisses that Jody has previously bestowed upon him. Jody plays the *million kisses game* with her children, too. It's amazing, really, her capacity for love and her ability to express it.

I sit quietly next to her bed, stroking her face just the way she likes me to. When she surfaces again, I tell her a story in the voice of Obadiah, a character I invented who tells her bedtime stories when we travel and she has trouble sleeping in a strange bed. She manages a smile and falls back to sleep... as I know she will do over and over today.

Alone with my best friend asleep beside me, I cry.

JODY:

I wake. I don't remember the recovery room and, true to the promise, I don't remember the surgery. I only remember being told that I won't remember. I try to smile for Kevin. "People were here before, right?"

"Yes."

"Salli? Jan? Tracy? And Bill...was Bill here?"

"Yes."

"Good. I thought I dreamed that part."

I'm not dreaming now. I have two tubes sticking out of the bandages. There is bloody yellow fluid accumulating in them. It's gross. A nurse asks me if I'd like to order a special mastectomy bra. She says the insurance company will pay for it, as if this should be a deciding factor. Sure, what the hell. Under the bandage is a dull ache the size of Texas, but no sharp pain. "The surgeon had to cut through quite a few nerve endings," the nurse explains. "Your chest may be numb for a long time. Maybe forever."

Good, I think. Otherwise, this would hurt like hell.

Is it over, then? I sleep. I wake. I sleep. There are flowers, so many flowers. While I sleep, somebody smuggles in helium balloons. I wake to take pain medication. I try and eat from a dinner tray and I call PJ to reassure him everything is fine and I think I do pretty well; I'm not sure what I eat but PJ says he's just happy I'm okay. Kevin has given me a little doggie toy with a little scarf around its neck. He has to leave now. He kisses me goodnight. I sleep fitfully, never comfortable on my back, but unable to pick a side because of the IV needle and the bandages.

Suddenly some huge animal slashes my chest with a swift, clawed paw. I run into a mouse hole. My chest burns! My mother is calling to me, but I can't help her. Her voice is far away. "I'll come get you," she calls. "No!" I shout. "Don't come here. Do NOT come here, Mama!" You can't help me escape this if you're inside here, too. Stay outside of this!

I wake drenched in sweat and request a stronger painkiller. A hospital should give its patients better drugs. One shouldn't have to dream after surgery! How can anybody get any rest this way? A nurse responds and sleeping pills are added to the growing list of drugs that I've decided to demand as "support medications."

What nonsense is all this? My mother cannot have cancer, too.

Of course I know she is hospitalized and already receiving chemotherapy. I called the Denver hospital just last night and Mama cried when she tried to be brave and strong about my surgery. I didn't cry for either one of us. Whatever will be, will be. I look down at the bandage. Que sera, sera…. Maybe if I didn't swear so much… I could be a better person that way, right? I recognize a classic stage of grief; barter. I am trying to barter back a missing breast, or at least talk God into a pardon from imminent death. Better to fight with some big phantom dream cat or whatever the hell was chasing me than to waste time trying to barter with an equally mean-spirited god. Irony is not lost on me; when I wanted to die after Daniel's death, God spared me. Now that I have reason to live….

I'm going back to sleep. Perchance to Dream. Hopefully not.

41

CHAPTER 3: August

Post-surgery routines • Jody and son are tested • First oncology visit • What's *inflammatory?* • Daughter's pregnancy announced! • Spending (like there's no tomorrow) • Recharging emotional battery • Port surgery fiasco • Chemo: Meet *The Red Devil* • Emergency transfusion • Kevin reacts to scars

Tuesday, August 1
KEVIN:

After a none-too-restful night, I need to prepare for Jody's return from the hospital. P.J. is still asleep; I call the dog up from my stepson's basement suite so that Foley might do his business outside of the house rather than in P.J.'s room. No need to start the boy's day off with that kind of surprise. I let Foley off his leash when we get back inside and he bolts up the stairs to look for his mom. I hear him leap onto our bed.

"She's not home, boy," I call after him. Whimpering, he descends the stairs, his tail hanging limp. I call down to P.J. to let him know I'm sending Foley back down and that I'm leaving to pick up his mom.

The drive to St. Marys is my fourth in less than a year, three of which trips have revolved around the cancer. I'm glad the hospital is relatively close to our home. St. Marys reminds me of a small Wisconsin community hospital where I was once employed between Navy stints. Although a larger facility, it has the same small-town convenience and the staff is showing great compassion and care for my wife, a silver lining in this dark cloud. She feels safe in the spiritually-based hospital, a sentiment I can respect.

Jody is awake, eating breakfast. She smiles and we kiss each other lightly on the lips. Even a slight adjustment of her head to do this causes some discomfort. She is sore from the surgery and the *good drugs* are starting to wear off. I encourage her to keep eating; between bites, she tells me of her previous night, of the intermittent pain and numbness at the surgery site. She mentions how kind the nurses have been to her when, as if on cue, a nurse appears to take her blood pressure, careful to approach from the right side.

42

A sign above Jody's head warns, "LEFT ARM: NO BP, NO IV, NO INJECTIONS, NO NOTHING, NO KIDDING" because of the node removal; injury to that unprotected arm now could cause lymphodema, a painful and possibly permanent swelling condition. The nurse checks Jody's temperature while informing us that the discharge order has been written. I am amazed that modern medicine has advanced so far that a patient can go home the day after major surgery. She will help Jody dress while I fill some prescriptions in the hospital pharmacy for pain and infection. She instructs me where to park to meet them downstairs and I realize I have been efficiently dismissed. I go and do as I've been told.

The ride home is quiet. As I gingerly help Jody maneuver out of our car, I am reminded of the two flights of stairs in our quad-level home and the pain I saw on Jody's face from just this morning's brief kiss. However, our bedroom is on the top floor and that is where she needs to be. We walk up the stairs slowly. The stairway handrail is on the left side, rendering it useless to her. Resting her weight on me, we finally reach the top step. After carefully tucking her into bed, I lie down next to her and watch until she falls asleep. I kiss her on her cheek. Then I shut the door securely behind me, lest Foley streak past me in search of his missing parent and cause her pain with an enthusiastic doggy hello.

P.J. is still sleeping; I call the dog from his room and close his door. Lately P.J.'s been spending more time in bed than usual and I suspect it may be tied to a mild depression over his mother's condition. When he is awake, he prefers the solitude of his room, to which he has just recently added yet another television attached to every video game player available. He still ventures out to join his friends in some activity, or to check on his mother, but meals with us are less frequent. Occasionally he will slip out the back door to jump on his trampoline, but more and more time is being spent in a dark room racing pretend cars or killing phantom invaders. He doesn't want to discuss his reclusive nature of late; he's made that much very clear. And, honestly, I don't have the time or the energy right now to explore teenage issues. I'm not proud of this; I'm just sapped.

Besides, there is the house to clean. With a dog and two cats, it quickly gets dirty and hairy. I suspect that soon Jody will have visitors and I don't want the house to be an issue for her. Even though I know that people will come to see her (not our home), she will never look at it that way.

Cleaning keeps me occupied for most of the day. Jody awakens around two o'clock and I authorize one supervised visit with Foley. The two are ecstatic to see one another. The big dog is amazingly gentle, as if he realizes his mistress has been injured. He actually wails when he sees her and kisses her face over and over. Jody kisses his ears and head and gently hugs him. This is more affection than I've scored so far today and so I sneak in a kiss to Jody and a pat on Foley's head. I play nurse; give Jody her pain pills and fluff her pillow. I promise a light lunch of scrambled eggs and toast.

By the time I return with a lunch tray, Foley has arranged himself at the bottom of the bed. He won't easily be persuaded to move. I sit with my darling while she eats and I tell her about the phone calls and the well wishes and offers of support we've already received. P.J. makes a sudden appearance at our doorway. He tenderly hugs and kisses his mother. She pats the bed and he sits next to her.

"I'm really feeling better," she says, bringing a wide smile of relief to his face. They talk about the upcoming school year and he mentions the need to get him registered next week. They both look at me expectantly. Suddenly, I'm seeing my parental role expanding exponentially and my personal time rapidly diminishing. Selfishly, I allow for some internalized whining, though nothing I would admit aloud.

"When is it?" I ask. P.J. rattles off the date and time and I log it on my mental calendar. He offers to take Foley for a walk and I leave, too, to allow Jody more rest.

I finish my cleaning, make dinner for all of us and watch some television. P.J. will babysit his mother tomorrow morning so I will be returning to work. As I gingerly slip into bed, she stirs. I cuddle next to her, give her one last kiss and tell her I love her for the umpteenth time today. She murmurs a slurred "I love you."

The whisper of her even breathing eventually lulls me to sleep.

Thursday, August 3
KEVIN:

Life has settled into a new routine. I get up earlier these days to bank a few extra minutes lying awake next to my precious wife. I can't help myself; I watch intently for signs. I know she had a restless night and I certainly don't want to miss something not quite right. So I listen and watch. When reassured that everything is status quo, I dress for work, feed the animals and walk the dog. When did P.J.'s assigned tasks become mine? Seems as if my stepson is doing less and less lately. Didn't we have a discussion early on about my need for his help? I finish our chores and kiss my bride goodbye.

She murmurs, "love you," followed by, "drive carefully." I am not sure if she is awake or asleep but am certain she won't remember my leaving. I begin the sojourn to work wondering how this could happen to me.

A little over a year ago, I was a reasonably contented divorced bachelor just settled into a new condo, after relocating from Detroit for the Watertown, Wisconsin job. Looking back now, my lifestyle demanded very little responsibility for anyone other than myself. Two previous marriages had ended amicably and had not produced any children. There were no pets. Then, in less than five months in Wisconsin, I met my soul mate, and in less than seven, had made her my bride. Now, a little over one year from our wedding date (three stepkids, two cats and a dog later) the "in sickness and health, till death do us part" portion of our wedding vows is insinuating its way into our everyday lives.

Even so, loving Jody is still easy. Love is a verb, an important concept that I don't overlook. Even though it flows naturally with respect to Jody, I work at it. In fact, I truly enjoy doing things for her. She is my queen. In return, she appreciates everything I do and she also loves me; of that, I'm sure, even though I sometimes joke that I come fifth in a procession line consisting of her three children and Foley. (Of course, P.J. will then pipe up that Little Cat and Charlie Cat were also around before me, so I'm really *seventh*.)

Loving the kids takes a more concerted effort, though I have emotionally adopted them into my idea of family. I am still getting acquainted with the girls on many levels, and they don't really need another parent, so I don't pretend to be one. Not only are they young adults already, but they openly adore their father, which is great. However, I do think that they appreciate the fact that I make their mom happy and we can all agree that is my role. So I pretty much stay in the background unless they ask for advice or need another ear.

P.J., the child of Jody's other marriage, is a different story entirely. His relationship with his biological father is tenuous at best. He has seen the man on only a few brief occasions since I've been around. It would be natural to assume that Jody poisoned P.J. toward his father so that he'd better connect with the new stepfather and make her life easier, but this just isn't the case. Having tried to provide the man with every opportunity to see his son, and having watched the father pretty much turn his back, Jody has all but given up on being a catalyst for any meaningful interaction between the two. For whatever reasons, their relationship is simply not happening. Nonetheless, it is pretty obvious that P.J. wants and needs a father, and so she would now like me to be a surrogate.

Despite the fact that I've grown to love him, and I sincerely believe (in spite of all signs to the contrary) that he loves me, too, neither P.J. nor I think that I'm necessarily a great choice for that role. Never having been a parent myself, I have no life experience on which to draw. With P.J., it is baptism by fire; in a condensed period of time, I've learned that the role of stepparent is an almost completely impotent one. I have no real control over him or his

45

behavior, although I now have financial responsibilities on his behalf. And I'm really not happy with his *normal adolescent* disrespectful demonstrations toward me.

I find myself more and more often drawn into petty arguments with him and it demands a conscious willfulness not to get over-the-top angry. Sometimes I think that it would be so much easier to just have it out and be done with it, as maybe I would, if his mother wasn't sick. It takes a lot to get me mad, because control and restraint are virtues and I admire personal discipline — an area in which P.J. could use a male role model. But I have my breaking point too, and once angry, I stay mad for a long time. I try not to go there. I try to just peacefully coexist with him and remind myself that I'm the new guy. I'm the adult. I'm the interloper in his life. And I'm supposed to be the one to give and give in. And... his mother has named me in her will to be his guardian should she die, a request I have agreed to. As I pull into the parking lot at work, I find myself wishing that his father would be a real father. Or at least call the boy once in awhile.

I try to leave such thoughts behind in the car as I lock the door. I have enough problems of my own without worrying about Phil's missed opportunities with his son. P.J. also is my stepson, my responsibility now. And I will make sure he gets the support he needs.

Folks up and down the assembly lines who know about Jody's operation call out their best wishes as I make my way to my office. I thank them all, wave to acknowledge specific ones, and then go about my day as if nothing is wrong. Lori is looking for a sign that I might need a shoulder to cry on, but I've already moved beyond that stage. I'm into the *execution to resolve the worst-case scenario* phase. No more time for personal pity parties. However, I am secretly beginning to grieve, albeit in very tiny private moments. Should Jody's treatments not work, I will not have time to grieve, only time to console all of the others.

I have a stack of business to attend to, and attack it vigorously, thankful for the diversion. As the day progresses, I call home again and again to confirm that Jody is resting, as she's been told to do, because I know it is not in her nature. She initially admits that she is tired. Then she upgrades herself to okay. She gets up, begins moving around the house. She makes herself lunch and gets dressed. Next call, she is feeling better. I phone again and she scolds lightly, saying she is fine; in fact, she has called her office to set a few things in motion.

I leave work earlier than usual; she may be *fine* but I need to see her. Maybe then I could believe her.

My first thought on arriving home is that a neighbor must be having a garage sale; too many cars are parked in front of our house. I soon learn why:

many of Jody's employees are gathered around our dining room table, working on the next issue of the magazine. I shake my head in wonderment at my wife's energy. Apparently I am married to my own personal Xena, Warrior Princess. Nothing can keep her down! I allow myself the hope that she can keep this cancer at bay for a very long time.

As guests prepare to leave, offers are made to bring more food into our home so that I won't have to cook every meal. In fact, there is already a casserole in the oven for dinner. Jody seems pleased by the willingness of others to help, but I have a moment of uneasiness. The food triggers an old memory association, though I'm not certain just what. It is too vague a discomfort to label and so I quickly close that mental door. Instead, I smile and say repeatedly, "That would be nice," even while I have a lingering pang that it would not be nice at all. Jody seems to be feeding off of their energy; she is alert and talkative and smiling. I see this as a positive sign and my thank-you to the group is sincere, even though the impromptu get-together has thrown off our fragile routine.

Everyone leaves and the immediate change in Jody's demeanor is frightening. She obviously is completely drained, and now that she feels safe letting her guard down, she does. She is sweating from the exertion of just walking across the room. Has she been sitting all this time because she couldn't walk? I help her journey down to the family room, insisting that she stop working and just watch television. Then I go about picking up the glasses in the kitchen, mindful of her staff's teasing that this kind of meeting could become a daily event. While I'm at it, I extend some effort in the living room, too, where P.J. finds me. He asks what is planned for dinner.

"There's a casserole in the oven that somebody from your mom's work brought over. That's what we're eating, as soon as I finish with this, but you're welcome to have some now if you don't want to wait for us."

"That's garbage. I'm not eating that."

"Then why don't you make a pizza? There are plenty of other choices available that you can make."

"Why don't you make dinner yourself?" he counters. "You said you'd do the cooking now. So cook."

I am tired. Too tired. And so I take the bait and our conversation takes on greater volume and intensity. Screw my good intentions, I think. This kid could piss off a saint.

Jody yells up from the family room that P.J. should stop arguing and just eat the damned casserole. She's not sounding much like a saint herself at this moment.

He does, electing to eat downstairs in his room by himself.

We eat quietly because Jody now is immersed in a television program on breast cancer. Tomorrow night, she tells me, she wants to make sure to watch a special program on dying. Where were these shows before this happened to us? As I sit on our couch, with her feet resting on my lap, I long for the nights we used to watch mindless comedies and complain about the writing, and I wonder how much more our life will change.

"Stage-four cancer is still a death sentence, given the present constraints of Western medicine," I hear. I am utterly aghast, not just at what the program narrator says, but also at how she says it. She has delivered this proclamation with the kind of light conversational tone that one might expect if she were commenting on the weather. I'm grateful to clear our dishes just to have a reason to leave the room, though my first impulse was to throw a glass through our wide-screen television set. I say nothing to Jody at all, but I am seething at the irresponsibility of someone casually announcing in my living room that my wife's prognosis could so easily turn hopeless. In the few moments that it takes me to load the dishwasher, Jody falls asleep on the couch. I gaze at her, wondering what she thinks when she watches these programs. What is it like to be her right now? To be told that you are dying? Will she believe it and give up?

Will I?

I wake her so that I can get her settled into bed. We make the climb up the two flights of stairs and I tuck her in, then I lie down next to her and try to fall asleep. The brief walk upstairs has evidently cleared her head; she talks about her day and shares her plans for tomorrow. I'm glad I've cleaned the house because it sounds like we'll be having more company for certain.

As much as I'd like to go to sleep, I will myself to stay awake and listen to her, because I don't know how many more nights I'll have like this, with her head on my shoulder, murmuring to me.

Tuesday, August 8
KEVIN:

I've just discovered an up-side, albeit a small one, to our ongoing saga – I'm driving much more often than usual when accompanying my wife. We've set a course to her first appointment with an oncologist at the University of Wisconsin, and half hour after leaving home, we pull up to the parking garage. *This is first-class care*, I think, taking advantage of valet parking. Entering the hospital complex, I am overwhelmed by the actual size of the facility but this could be a good thing; surely the Comprehensive Cancer Care Center housed inside this massive building will have the resources to provide a cure!

The walls feature horizontal stripes of colored tape; the woman at the information booth tells us what stripe to follow. Very efficient. As we follow the curving designated path to the oncology department, I make a mental note to watch for landmarks because, marker or no marker, I could easily get lost. We check in at a processing area and Jody is given a permanent brown ID card with a magnetic strip. It will serve as her passkey to hospital services. We then are led to an examination room that reminds me of past days... which reminds me that we have yet to report our marriage to the Navy. If we do, Jody will be entitled to additional medical coverage. We need to get to a military base to get her Navy Dependent I.D. Why have we not done this already?

We wait over half an hour for the specialist, but when he arrives, he apologizes for the delay. He's a precise-appearing man with a neatly trimmed beard, and he greets us both in a professional manner. The gentleman appears to be empathetic about the diagnosis, which I very much appreciate. It is going to be challenging for him and for us, he says, but he believes he can *cure* Jody.

My heart skips a beat. Cure is not a word that has been used before. We've been hearing terms like *aggressive, angry, lobular,* and *potential remission* — terms that hardly instill hope. However, the oncologist just said it! He said the *cure* word and I have already taken it to the bank and cashed it. I believe him!

I look to Jody, but she's forging ahead with treatment questions. She asks what clinical trial she might benefit from, stating that the opportunity to be in a research facility is one of the reasons we chose the U.W. system over the Dean Medical system. The doctor answers that she will not, in fact, be eligible for any clinical trials because of her type of cancer. He throws in a new term: *inflammatory.* Jody physically shudders; I sense she is aghast at whatever this means. I'm right, because she immediately challenges the diagnosis.

I have no idea what is happening, but certainly *something* is. The University of Wisconsin doctor pulls out the Dean Medical post-operative laboratory report, on which is printed the diagnostic results of the exam. Jody points to the words *lobular invasive* and the oncologist counters with a discussion about a *pathological versus clinical* diagnosis. I sense they meet in the middle when he agrees to have his own U.W. pathologists inspect the tissue sample. Still, he holds to the bottom line that there will be no clinical trial.

Disbelief is written all over Jody's face but again, I don't know why. Although I thought I knew most medical jargon, they share a secret cancer language that I'm not privy to. I let it go; there will be time later to ask what the importance of this word *inflammatory* really is.

The specialist moves on to describe a protocol of drugs. The names Doxorubicin and Cyclo-phosphamide appear to be quite familiar to my wife. She hangs her head, says, "Oh, so we are starting with The Devil." He asks when she would like to begin, and she meets his eyes again and counters with a question about the advisability of a port, since she has only one arm in which any intravenous tube can be placed. She says she knows chemotherapy drugs can cause problems in the veins.

I can't help but wonder how she has gotten so learned so quickly. The oncologist agrees that a port is recommended and says he can set up the simple operation within a day or so. He notices me again and tells me that it will take no more than 30 minutes to implant the small round device in her chest and snake a tube into a vein. His casual manner gives me even more confidence in him. Apparently this is routine stuff. I'm glad we have chosen him.

He asks Jody if there is any other test or procedure she would like prior to beginning treatment. Sorry, but this strikes me as an odd question. How could she know what she needs? However, Jody surprises me again by suggesting a C.A.T scan and a bone scan. "I'd like a baseline for later comparisons," she says.

The oncologist agrees to the bone scan, and suggests that, depending on the results, he may also opt for an M.R.I. He'll check with her after the bone scan.

"Thank you," Jody replies.

We are sent back to the department clerk, who schedules the port surgery for later in the week and also makes our appointments for the scans and chemotherapy.

As Jody directs me along a different route home, I ask about her surprise when she found out about her ineligibility for clinical trials. "Maybe you don't need them," I offer optimistically.

"Kevin, he said I have *inflammatory cancer*," she answers. "I've done the research. It's the most fatal and most aggressive form of breast cancers. He won't let me participate in a clinical trial because my outcome could make his remission results seem less spectacular."

"Less spectacular? How?"

"If I'm an inflammatory, I'm statistically more likely to die than his average lobular. And much more likely to die than to survive."

My heart again skips a beat. And another.

Sunday, August 13
JODY:

Happy birthday, Summer! Twenty-three years old today!

I spend the morning catching up on all the financial records and filed papers that I've been meaning to get to. I keep our finances on computer with a hard copy of the checking activity in a notebook. When everything is entered, I show Kevin how it is done and where everything is.

"Do you want me to take over paying bills?"

"No."

He scowls. "Then don't show me this until you do. I know why you're doing this, and it's just morbid. Stop it."

Fine. I have other things to do. I work on memory book pages, penciling on the back of each scrapbook page which person I hope to get that particular page after I'm dead. I sort through picture after picture until tears drip off my chin; while I don't cry in public, I'm making up for it during private moments like these. I am going to miss these people so very much. There's Summer when she was two, and again at 10. In Denver and in Philadelphia and in Chicago and Milwaukee, but have I done enough with her? Here she is in Ireland, standing inside a castle wall. I can't bear to part with this picture.

I can't bear to part with her.

This is no way to celebrate the anniversary of my child's birth! I literally run to Kevin and beg him to accompany me to Chicago for a spur-of-the-moment dinner to celebrate with Summer and Paddy. We call and she is quite surprised that I feel up to the trip, but they'd love to go with us! I feel strong enough to take the wheel for the three-hour drive into the city, but I'll let Kevin drive us back to Madison. PJ has no desire to be in a car with his parents longer than half an hour, so he's taking a rain check. He'd rather take a bus to see his sister later, he says.

"Fine," I tell him, too pleased with the decision to visit to allow him to sully it with a pointless argument.

"Fine," Kevin agrees more convincingly.

"Fine," PJ counters. "Then you should give me money for pizza because you won't be here for dinner and there's only crap in this house to eat."

"Fine," Kevin and I agree in unison.

We cruise down Interstate 90 East. "She'll really love her present," I say.

"Yes, she will," Kevin agrees. "I hope at least half as much as you love giving it to her."

Yesterday we went shopping for Summer's gift together. While I historically spend about $100 per child per birthday, this year Kevin and I walked right into a music store and bought her an exquisite violin made in the Ukraine, with horsehair strings on the bow and a beautiful velvet-lined case. We also bought her the chin-shoulder extension rest and a huge book full of Irish tunes for the violin. And an electronic tuner, bar of bees

51

wax and a music stand. She's been taking violin lessons and struggling to make beautiful music on a cheap college rental but now she'll have her own wonderful instrument.

My thinking is rather transparent: I have lived responsibly and paid bills promptly all of my adult life. If I die soon, Kevin will have all the life insurance money needed to cover credit card charges and any other bills that I'm responsible for. Meanwhile, I'll have the joy of seeing Summer open the music case. If I live, then who cares about money? I'll pay it back! *Do other cancer patients go financially berserk, too,* I wonder? *Spend money as if there is no tomorrow?* I didn't see anything about fiscal responsibility in the fact sheets handed out at the cancer clinic.

We pick up *the kids* and hug Summer and Paddy tight. We will take them anywhere in the city they want to eat. The sky's the limit! While Summer considers theatre district restaurants, Paddy announces that he's always wanted to eat at the Red Lobster, but first he'd like to buy us all a pint of Guinness at The Six Penny, his favorite Irish pub. I've been advised not to drink alcohol. Kevin doesn't typically, but he says he might have "a taste o' the ale tonight." What the heck, maybe I'll have a sip myself! Let's celebrate!

Summer climbs into the backseat, where the violin case is adorned with a big bow. "Oh, my gosh!" she gushes. "Mother, what have you done now?"

"Exactly what I wanted to do, as is my habit these days."

Monday, August 14
JODY:

No one expected me back in the office for four weeks following surgery. It has been two. Three days after coming home from the hospital, I began hosting morning manager's meetings at my kitchen table. Afternoons were reserved for reviewing magazine proofs at the same location. Bill calmed my reservations about our pending partnership and the likelihood of opening a Rockford, Illinois business magazine while undergoing treatment: "You at half-capacity is worth anyone else at full," he insisted. "We can do this because you're going to survive. I won't let you doubt it for a second."

I will love him forever.

And so, confidence renewed, I delved into writing copy from home. The art director, staff writer and sales manager have rotated daily visits this past week. Faithful Joe has been invited to continue his weekly stay-overs with us and so I see him more often. Still, even with all the visits and help, if we're to stay on our publication schedule, I need to be at the office. It is eerie, however, to step back into Magna Publications, the corner office with all the windows that I love so much. It is exactly how I left it on that morning that I skipped out for a doctor's appointment. If I turn on the CD player, I know what will play. How can it be that here everything is the same, when.... The pictures on the credenza of my family smile back at me, all of them snapped before I knew I was in the process of actively dying. But I am actively living, my soul argues. Likely this will be a mind-soul struggle for months to come.

I send an email to all company staff: "Yes, I am back ahead of schedule. But please do not ask me how I am because I can't spend my energy on personal conversations. I have very limited energy reserves, and I need to put all my efforts into accomplishing a few specific things every day. Please help me do that. Thank you." I feel more like a battery with a set charge than a person. Everything I do drains energy from that battery, drains me ... until I have nothing left to give. When my battery discharges completely, I don't even have the energy required to fall asleep. There is no way to explain that feeling of total exhaustion that has nothing to do with time of day, everything to do with mental and physical activity. I now consciously choose every expenditure, knowing there is no longer a "second wind" or energy bank to draw from.

I have 108 emails waiting to be answered, many of a personal nature. I decide to write weekly updates to the entire lot. I know my status and so I personally gain nothing by answering health inquiries, yet I don't want them to stop because they are lifelines to the world that I once belonged in, and already feel I'm beginning to slip out of.

Tracy nearly tiptoes into my office as if hoping not to disturb me, then shuts the door and holds out her arms. She cries as she embraces me. "Welcome back," she whispers.

Denise closes the door behind her when she steps in, too. The art director holds a beautiful silk scarf open before her bearing an art deco painting. "I thought maybe you might want to wear this over your head when..." she falters. I take her in my arms and she cries.

Next is Abby, my precious Abby, once my assistant and now an editor. I am so very proud of her and am personally mentoring her for a managing editor's position. Does she know how much she means to me and to this company? I tell her when I hug her.

True to my request, no one asks me how I am. But the door keeps opening and closing, opening and closing. I am so lucky! So blessed! Did I know that a month ago? Did I fully appreciate it?

Nanette, our always-giggly receptionist, musters a broad grin as she taps on the doorframe to get my attention. She clears her throat, holds up a computer graphic with the words Jody's meeting. "Everybody knows that if they see that posted on the conference room door, it means that you are resting on the couch in there," she says, somewhat sheepishly. "We thought that you might not feel so good some days, and, well...."

I come from around my desk and hug her, too. "It's okay. It's a very thoughtful gift. Thank everyone for me, and I'm sure I'll use it."

Bill comes to my office. "I'm so glad to see you back," he says, holding open his arms.

I vow that this is where I will be every workday that I can physically get dressed in the morning. This is my second home and it is where I belong. It is a door to the life that is so very precious to me now. These people do not drain my battery; they recharge it.

Tuesday, August 15
KEVIN:

Things are going well on this, my second trip to the UW medical facility. Traffic is steady and I'm making good time. I actually know where I am going and again have a little hope that this might become routine soon. No big deal.

Jody preceded me to the hospital today. In light of the explanation of the simple port implant, we decided it wasn't necessary for me to miss any more work. Salli dropped her off at the hospital, and I was expected to pick her up. She pooh-poohed the idea of anyone *babysitting*. Twice I've called the hospital and twice been told she wasn't yet ready. Now I must admit I'm getting a little anxious, though I'm sure things are fine. I suppose surgery was delayed for some reason and so they must be a little behind schedule.

Finding my way to the oncology department is also much easier the second time around and I am directed without much comment to the recovery room. I scan the sitting area but do not see my wife. I stop a nurse; he recognizes her name at once. "Follow me," he says, and leads me to where she lay on a gurney in a tiny room behind a drape. I expect to see a smile on my bride's face; instead, she is a visage of sheer terror. Although shrouded in blankets, she is shaking uncontrollably.

"Kevin, it was awful!" she cries through chattering teeth. "You know how Novocain doesn't work with me? Or lidocaine or any of those drugs?"

"Yes...."

"That's what they gave me, a local anesthetic, and I said it didn't work. They did it again and it still didn't work, but even though they couldn't numb the area, they wouldn't put me under."

"They did surgery using a skin-surface anesthetic?"

"I was strapped down and the surgeon kept telling me that I couldn't *really* be feeling it, I couldn't *really* be feeling it, but they had a drape over my head and I told him when he cut me because I could feel *everything*. He kept telling me to lie still, lie still, he's cutting a pocket in my tissue, and he started yelling at the nurses to numb me, but they couldn't. It wouldn't work."

"Why wouldn't they put you under?"

"I had to be awake when they put it in because they were going to push a catheter into my jugular vein and the surgeon needed my help to do it."

This is news to me. "Why didn't the doctor mention that? We could have told him you wouldn't respond to topicals!"

"I don't know! The surgeon said he was going to make sure I didn't feel anything but I didn't know he meant with just a local and I.V. Valium. And when I realized what was happening, it was too late. But it got so bad that a nurse came under the drape with me and held my hand and kept apologizing to me and meanwhile the doctor is telling me, 'Hum, hum,' and I say 'What?' and he says, 'Don't say 'what', just hum!'"

"He wanted you to *hum?*"

"So I hum and the nurse says its because he needs my jugular vein to open wider because he's threading in a tube and he has to stitch it in place – and I know that because I can feel every push and prick and it hurt so much that I start crying and the nurse almost cries too and she just keeps saying, 'I'm so sorry we can't help you better than this.'"

I look from my traumatized wife to the male nurse standing at her other side. "This really happened?"

He nods. "I heard it was pretty rough. She's still a little shocky."

I turn back to my wife. *Pretty rough?* She has been such a trooper throughout this whole ordeal and now…. Suddenly it dawns on me that there was no delay; she has been like this for some time, waiting for me to come. The initial confusion is giving way to anger.

She continues between sobs, really upset now that she is reliving it: "The doctor yells at the nurse for talking to me and says there had better be only one voice in this operating room and it better be his because he is instructing the patient and he's in her jugular vein and does anybody have anything else to say to break his concentration? And he tells me that he's already given me liquid Valium and that should be enough to get us through this, but it isn't working and he has somebody else stitch me up. A student doctor, I think. He tells her not to use a continuous stitch, but to do each one separately, and for what seems like about 20 minutes I can feel each stitch, inside and out and I had to lie still with the drape over my face and I was strapped down and it was, it was, I can't even describe it, it was so horrible."

DURING

There is no way this could have happened at this hospital! I have faith in this hospital and these doctors and nurses. They are supposed to be the best in the business! I believe her and yet am still wondering how this happened. The male nurse wraps yet another heated blanket on my wife's quivering shoulders.

She has been here six hours. This is unbelievable.

I hold both of her hands in mine for comfort and warmth. If the oncologist had told us any of this, we could have informed him of her well-documented immunity to Novocaine, which forces alternative anesthesia during trips to the dentist. The entire family of "caine" drugs has been tried on her with no good result.

She complains that the tube extended into her jugular hurts her, which I can clearly see as a protruding bulge in her neck. I try to reassure Jody that the pain is likely temporary. When that obviously fails, I try to cajole her into a lighter mood: "It beats having your right arm turned into a pincushion by chemotherapy techs, doesn't it?"

The trembling slows and whether she agrees with me or not, she leans forward and whispers conspiratorially, "He wrote a prescription for Tylenol 3, but I still have Percocet left over from the mastectomy." She says this as if it is a coup d'état, as if she is now battling her caregivers and has won some small secret battle. Tylenol 3, huh? Comprehensive cancer centers pride themselves on a "zero tolerance" for pain. They supposedly have the techniques and the medicines to make an intolerable situation at least bearable. We have counted on the notion that Jody would be spared whatever pain possible. Sitting with my wife, I can't help but wonder if we have made the right choice coming to the U.W. It is so big and Jody is only one patient of so many. The doctor was so flippant about the surgery, and my wife so vulnerable.

I certainly am no longer the naïve 18-year-old recruit thrown into the world of surgery who once put both doctors and nurses on high pedestals. As a novice medical corpsman, I was programmed by the Navy to respect all doctors, regardless of merit. Perhaps I automatically carried this programming over into my civilian life. The U.W. facility had inspired a déjà vu expectation of institutional professionalism and, by extension, an expectation of competency. Now I am not so sure.

A basic life tenet was drilled into me by a commanding officer: "You get what you inspect, not what you expect." As I hold my *shocky* wife, I vow that I will not let her travel into this or any other hospital or facility without me again. Until she is strong enough to be her own advocate, I will protect her from her healers.

The blinders are off.

Wednesday, August 16
<u>JODY:</u>

My neck and the incision site are still raw from yesterday's port surgery, but the bone scan is accomplished without incident. Still, it's freaky to be back at the hospital so soon. I was quite claustrophobic during the test but it's important to take one day at a time, one procedure at a time. I've got a long road of challenges ahead and I can't start falling apart because of yesterday's bad experience.

We leave the UW, pick up PJ, and then go to St. Marys, where PJ will be evaluated for Attention Deficit Disorder on the recommendation of his school's psychological team. We've waited three months to get him before a prominent child psychologist, who told us to expect four hours of testing. Medical Test Anxiety: PJ and I now have this in common.

The psychologist spends about 10 minutes talking to Kevin and me. He should realize things aren't up to par in the emotional support department for my son, because I share my concern that stress from his grandmother's health and mine may be feeding his already-apathetic attitude toward school. PJ is then subjected to myriad computer tests, but the doctor only spends a few minutes talking with him. He motions for Kevin and me to enter his private office, where he shares his opinion that PJ seems "a little depressed but not overly." And PJ might have ADD "but not overly." He has an attention deficit proclivity "but… not overly." He might really benefit from medication, or it might not really make any difference at all. We could start with mild medication if we want. A judgment call, apparently ours to make.

He calls PJ into the room. "You aren't the kind of rubberhead that I usually see," he announces. "You're not one of those. We can get you into some counseling if you think it would be a good idea, but not the kind where they talk about touchy-feely stuff. I'm talking about the kind of counseling where you could just tell them why you think school is dumb; talk about stuff like that. No heavy stuff. That's not what you need, buddy."

In the next five minutes, he repeatedly uses the expression *rubberhead* in reference to children suffering from ADD who come to him for help. Kevin and I both quietly fume. This is the specialist we've waited so long to talk to? The man I had hoped might help my son through this very difficult period? I'm embarrassed that the insurance company will pay his bill, and resentful of the co-pay we'll be expected to kick in.

Thursday, August 17
<u>JODY:</u>

It is almost time for my first chemotherapy session and as I wait to be called for the quick pre-chemo consultation with the UW oncologist, I can't stop trembling. Then, to make matters worse, my mind flits to my Dean Medical Center surgeon and I'm further unnerved by the memory of angering a trusted physician ally. God knows they are hard enough to come by.

I have an independent insurance carrier and so can choose either of Madison's two fiercely competitive medical providers. My research showed that, while both had great reputations, UW seemed to be recognized more widely than Dean. I told my Dean surgeon, just after he removed the surgical drainage tubes sewn into my chest, that I was choosing to be treated by the other side. He was righteously and loudly offended, but I was undeterred in the decision. The situation is dire, since lymph nodes are involved after all. If there is any further progression, the language of *cure* is over and we begin talking *maintenance*. I need any edge I can find.

The visit with the oncologist today is simply precursory. He asks to see the sub-skin chemo port.

"That looks good," he decides. "We can use that today."

I don't tell him that his surgeon was an ass or that the mastectomy was less excruciating than the simple port surgery. I don't tell him that the night of the latest surgery, I woke at midnight suffering with a yeast infection, courtesy of too many antibiotics in too short a time. I don't tell him that I don't trust him quite so much anymore.

"The scans came back fine," he continues. "It shows some marked deterioration in your knees, but that seems to be a pre-existing condition. So a nurse will call your name and you'll be taken into a cubicle and we'll get you started on your chemo cocktail."

"Are you aware of any side effects other than those discussed in the literature?"

"The nurses will give you an information packet and go over all of that with you, okay? I'll see you again in a few weeks."

Soon Kevin and I are hustled into a little cubicle divided from the others in the huge chemo room by hanging drapes. I'm encouraged to eat a ham sandwich and a cookie because chemo is easier to tolerate on a full stomach. A pre-chemo drug is started via an IV line to deliver medicines and fluids that help cushion the impact of the medication known as The Red Devil, nicknamed for its color and its vicious impact on the body.

While this drug (also known as Adriamycin or Doxorubicin) kills cancer cells, it will also wipe out my body hair, including eyebrows and eyelashes. It will cause sensitivity to sweets that will leave me nauseous for months to come, and it will cause a very bloody metal taste impossible to rinse away. My skin soon will reek of it when I sweat.

Adriamycin is also hard on blood cells and the heart. My mother is receiving it and already has needed five blood transfusions. A friend of mine died of a heart attack while on an Adriamycin protocol. I have good reason to tremble.

After the pre-medications are given, a nurse appears wearing protective gloves. I'm given ice chips to suck to minimize the likelihood of mouth sores. She fingers the tubing that goes directly into the dragonfly needle anchored in the port next to my collarbone. "I'm going to push this medication into your veins very slowly," she says, brandishing a huge syringe full of red liquid that reminds me of the red sugar water we used to mix to attract humming birds to my mother's feeder. The nurse continues: "I'm going to do it over a period of almost an hour, to minimize your reaction to this first dose, though next time it might take only 20 minutes. This is potent stuff, but it has to be, and when we finish with this, you'll get Cytoxin as a bag drip."

And so we get down to business.

I am woozy. The pre-medications include antihistamines that make me drowsy, anti-nausea medicine, and steroids to protect my veins. I doze off and on, amazed that I no longer feel any stress, but certain that the indescribable smell of the room will always be with me. I've been told that eventually merely crossing the threshold to a chemo room will nauseate me, because my mind will connect what comes before with what comes after. But today, I'm an innocent. Today the room smells funny in a clean kind of weird way, my tongue is starting to taste funny, and I'm sleepy. Kevin talks to other folks in other cubicles and eats a sandwich he scored from a cafeteria vending machine while I dozed off. This will be our routine. I'll snooze, he'll schmooze, and we'll get through this. We can do this.

Between naps, I entertain myself with one of a long series of mental wrestling matches with God. Yeah, sure, God's will be done. Except… I don't feel it is my time to die yet. As if I have a choice! I hate it when people hold cancer patients accountable for their own mortality, as if just thinking good thoughts hard enough can change the outcome of their treatment. Why would cancer patients, whose very DNA has gone awry, be expected to be more in control of their own destiny than a heart-attack patient? It's absurd. This is a disease process and the chemo either will work with my blood chemistry and tolerances, or it will not. God doesn't have a whole hell of a lot to do with this just yet. Nor do I. We're both off the hook for the moment.

I rouse with a sudden realization that the infusion is finished. The nurse hands me a little folder with the results of my blood tests. It means nothing to me until she gives me a sheet of paper that explains what the ranges should be and what to watch out for. The little folder also has the date of my next chemo infusion, but nothing else.

"When am I supposed to have blood draws?" At least two blood checks between treatments is standard — one at about the ninth or tenth day because that's when chemo goes after red blood cells, and then again before treatment. Adriamycin and Cytoxin can be brutal on both reds and platelets, and white blood cells can drop so low that a patient becomes very susceptible to infections.

She takes back the folder. "You're right," she says, frowning. "That's odd. Let me go back and get those dates added."

She soon returns. "He doesn't think you'll need it. You must have really impressed him with your stamina."

This makes no sense. "I have a clear medical history of anemia. I was turned down by the Red Cross as a blood donor in the past year and received treatment for it. Tell him it's all in the chart that he has from Dean Medical. I don't think he wants to skip blood tests with me."

The nurse looks away, considering, but then shakes her head, apparently unwilling to second-guess him twice in five minutes. "He apparently thinks you won't need it," she repeats. "But I'll tell you what... don't hesitate to call any of the phone numbers on that little card we gave you earlier if you think you're anemic. Feel free to call right away."

Kevin and I follow maze markers out of KK or JJ or wherever we are; we circle back to the main lobby. To the uninitiated and barely conscious, UW Hospital is just too much of a good thing. Kevin steers.

"That wasn't so bad," my eternally supportive husband says, smiling. "One down. To celebrate, I'll make dinner tonight."

Oh boy. And I mean that. Really.

Friday, August 25
KEVIN:

The Red Devil has taken hold of my wife. Day by day she has grown more nauseous, become weaker and more tired. I call home from work several times to check on her. Thank goodness P.J. is still on summer vacation from school so that he can keep an eye on her between trips to the mall with his friends.

Jody is strong willed, which is part of what initially attracted me to her, but now her strong will has set events in motion that might not be in her best interests. While still recovering from three surgeries and now chemotherapy as well, she has conspired with Bill to put in a cable modem in her home computer so that she can work out of the house. She simply refuses to rest.

Today I come home to a stack of empty computer boxes. She has bought a scanner and new software and a printer; obviously, she's spent some serious money. A computer techie is working fervently to finish hooking up a cable modem to get her *connected*. Jody sits on her office floor, watching. They are locked in a conversation concerning his wife, apparently a cancer survivor.

I bend over and kiss her forehead. Lately I've been avoiding any prolonged kiss on the lips. The chemo has left Jody with very sour breath on which even the special alcohol-free mouthwash has little effect. I wonder, has she noticed that I now prefer kissing her forehead and cheeks? When I do kiss her on the mouth, I remind myself not to breathe in too deeply. This is hard, as I still desire intimacy, but.... Today marks the one-month *anniversary* of the discovery of the C-word. She is still talking but I kiss her on the mouth anyway.

"I'm tired," she whispers.

"Perhaps you should have napped rather than shopped."

The techie finishes her umbilical cord to the office, which obviously pleases her. He also leaves with words of encouragement about her condition, instruction from a caregiver who has been there and won. I walk him to his truck and privately thank him for his compassion.

"It can be done," he says of beating the disease.

Jody remains in her upstairs office, happy to be able to finally catch up on her email. "I don't know how I'm going to have time to answer all of these," she calls down to me. "There must be a hundred!"

I begin preparations for dinner: chili for P.J. and me, egg noodles for Jody, one of the few foods she tolerates. As the noodle water begins to boil, I notice that she has made her way partway to the kitchen. She sits on the stairs, her breathing quite labored. "I can't seem to get enough air in my lungs," she gasps. "I nearly fainted at the top of the stairs just now. I think my red cells crashed. I think I may even need a transfusion."

She is ghostly pale. I check the kitchen clock: 6:30 p.m. *Okay, stay calm and call the after-hours number on the emergency medical card.* I explain the situation first to a nurse, then to the oncologist on call. I am told to bring her into the U.W. Hospital's Emergency Room right away. I turn off the burner and shout to P.J. that he is on his own and that I'll call him from the hospital when I know something.

We're lucky to find parking close by. As soon as we give her name, Jody's blood oxygen is measured by a small device placed directly on her finger. "Your oxygen level is okay," the nurse comments, puzzled.

"It's great for each cell," Jody counters breathlessly. "There just aren't enough cells, so it isn't enough to keep my body going, even at 100% oxygenation. Have someone check red cell volume."

I settle in for a long night.

JODY:

What I likely will always remember about tonight is a doe-eyed male nurse telling a story about a little bunny rabbit patient. This may seem like a dumb thing to dwell on, but I can't get enough oxygen to think real clearly. At least this is my diagnosis, not that anybody is listening.

But let me back up, because I'm getting ahead of my story.

I was marked *urgent* by the triage nurse and then parked. Kevin and I waited in a jam-packed waiting room for almost two hours, calling home every half hour to reassure PJ. I groused to anyone who would listen that a hospital should be run like a grocery store; there should be an express line for people who know what they need.

Finally I was moved, although not to the expected oncology workup room. No, I was put in a cardiac emergency bed. Kevin and I exchanged confused glances, which became even more puzzled when I was given a hurried EKG, EEG and chest scan. A resident polled me for a cardiac patient research survey, and another inquired if my oncologist had mentioned that one of the chemo drugs is known for causing heart damage.

We spent an anxious but very boring four hours in the cardiac unit before the ER nurse broke out the rabbit story. As he fished with a needle to take a blood sample, he remembered aloud a different night in the ER. On that atypically slow night, a bunny rabbit had been rushed in from the parking lot where it had been discovered with a cut on its leg. The rabbit quickly was surrounded by residents, nurses, indeed anyone in the unit who could make their way to the treatment cot where the animal was being comforted in preparation of suturing his leg.

"So everyone is standing around the rabbit, see?" Nurse Bob continued.

I could *see* it in my head. Kevin nodded that he could *see* it, too.

"But what the docs here didn't know — that probably any vet in town could have told them — is that when you give a rabbit lidocaine, it instantly goes into a terrible grand mal seizure and drops dead."

What?! I laughed at the absurdity of it all, likening it in my mind to my own good doctor's attempts to help me by prescribing rat poison blood thinners and heart-attacking chemo medications.

The nurse smiled, obviously pleased to have finally made me laugh instead of wince.

"That's a hare-raising story," Kevin muttered.

Nurse Bob's grin widened. "Hope I don't have to do this to you again," he said, toasting us both with a vial of my blood as he backed out of the cubicle.

Within an hour, the cardiac unit doctor ordered two more blood samples to rule out systemic infection. I whined that it was a waste of time, to which Kevin responded that the doctor had the medical license and I had the health insurance. "Know your role," he advised sternly.

While the verdict is still out on the root cause of my distress, I have not once believed that I'm having a heart episode. The tightness around my chest is probably just a side effect of not being able to breathe well. Knowing that someone thinks my problems are of a more serious nature ironically makes me feel guilty for being here, as if I were a fraud given valuable bed space under false pretenses. Many times this long night I've imagined doctors yelling at me for being so stupid and panicky over a typical chemo reaction. They haven't, of course, because they still think I'm having a heart attack. But I suspect they could turn ugly if it turns out that I'm not dying.

And so the story has caught up with us.

If Kevin and I weren't so exhausted, we'd really be getting restless. The glass cubicle houses two cardiac beds and we can clearly hear anything happening on the other side of the curtain, where a woman is having stomach distress that she attributes to gas. Nonetheless, she apparently has other signs of cardiac stress and so they continue to take her blood, too. Poke, moan, fart, poke, moan, fart. It becomes routine. As does her friend's never-ending saga about not getting child support for 13 years from the bastard that gave her five kids.

I see my roommate for the first time when she lumbers out of the hallway bathroom where I happen to be next in line. "You're in the bed next to me, ain'tcha?" she accuses. I nod and step into the bathroom. And back out.

"They can discharge her now," I whisper to Kevin. "She's taken care of the gas." Still, I have to pee because we've been here forever, so I hold what precious little breath I have and quickly tend to my own business.

Back in the cardiac unit, she is soon dismissed, replaced by a woman having a serious heart attack. I hate to admit it, but it helps pass the time, listening to the doctors explain why they prefer doing an angioplasty instead of using clot-buster medication. It is educational if nothing else.

To my good fortune, the rabbit-nurse comes to tell me that (surprise, surprise) my heart is fine but I'm a couple units low of red blood cells and anemic. An oncology fellow orders me admitted onto the oncology floor for the actual blood transfusions.

Halleluiah and Amen.

KEVIN:

Around midnight, an on-call oncologist tells us that Jody needs a transfusion. She tells me to go home, but I'm reminded that you get what you inspect, not what you expect, so I'm staying until I see her in her room and the transfusion begun. Three hours later, they arrive to wheel her gurney chariot upstairs and I give in and kiss her goodnight.

Foley barks from his bed in P.J.'s room as I come through the door. I climb into my now very lonely bed and think how lucky P.J. is to have the dog's companionship. I am still awake when I see the hall light come on. Foley jumps on the bed. The big mutt licks my face and cries when he doesn't find Jody with me.

"Is Mom going to be alright?" P.J. asks from the doorway.

"It looks that way. She needs a quart or so of blood, though."

He seems satisfied with this and calls Foley to go with him back to his room.

I will myself to sleep but have nightmares and wake up frequently. During one waking, I suddenly know that Jody is soon going to want a second opinion. Too much has gone wrong in only a couple weeks, shaking her faith in her doctor. Next week, we have a scheduled visit with her surgeon to remove the mastectomy stitches. We might have to eat some crow, but I could learn to cook bird — certainly I will have to negotiate a referral for a second opinion between two very strong-willed people.

Oh boy. Are we having fun yet?

JODY:

The first bag of blood shows up at 5 a.m., as does the Valium requested because the woman in the next room is having a really rough night and her moans echo throughout the unit. ("God, please don't let this be visions of admissions to come," I pray selfishly.) An aid bearing warm blankets and extra pillows is a sweet woman but she has a most annoying habit of whistling as she walks up and down the hall doing good deeds. *Buffalo gal, won't you come out tonight, come out tonight, come out*

64

tonight.... She only whistles, but in my head, Kevin is doing his Ethel Merman imitation, singing the words. I feel like her whistling will make me truly crazy in a matter of minutes. I just want to hide under a warm blanket, and Valium is my blanket of choice.

I dream that a nurse sprays Lysol in my face as she cleans the room while I lie sleeping in the bed. She is accompanied by a little toy poodle that she tosses on my chest for me to play with. "Hey," I cry, "I'm only a couple weeks out of surgery and that hurts!" It hurts enough that I feel myself crying in my sleep, and in the dream, I call the unit station to complain to the charge nurse.

It is later in the morning, and though not dreaming, I'm not yet quite awake either. However, I confer with a group of oncologists making rounds who warn that I might become "transfusion dependent" because of the amount of blood I needed after only one treatment. That might indicate that I will need to rely on blood transfusions to maintain the level of chemo I am getting. They speak of iron panels and more tests. I listen politely as one tells me that all of my hair will likely fall out by next Thursday. He says he can tell things like that. "Hmm," I say, trying to act interested, but secretly deciding that I will shave my head and fuck up his prediction. Can he also predict with such certainty when I will die? I'm glad he isn't my doctor because he's a little too precise. They say a bunch of other stuff, too. I answer their direct questions and nod appropriately, but the minute they leave, I go right back to sleep.

I dream that nurses are tiptoeing into my room, a lot of them, whispering about who should hold my hands and who gets my legs to do this next procedure because I had been getting argumentative and they aren't going to get hurt doing it. I know I am dreaming, and try to wake up but I cannot. To save myself, I change the scene and imagine that my friend Salli is singing a commercial on television celebrating some event with an 80-year-old man. Although Salli has a pleasant speaking voice, I have no idea why I'm imagining her singing professionally. Then I dream that a stranger asks me where my mother and brother are living these days and I say, "Up in the mountains." But now I remember that they live in Macomb, my Illinois hometown. In a shack. I correct my story, except that they really both live in a nice home in Denver. Funny I don't know that. Except, of course, I do.

I wake to Kevin stroking my face. "You can leave whenever you want, but eat your lunch first," he says gently, kissing my face. He hands me a little monkey with Velcro arms to put around my neck, with a baby monkey attached to the mother monkey. "This reminded me of you and PJ," he says.

The monkey is so cute and cuddly and I love having it around my neck. Mostly, however, I am relieved it isn't a bunny. They kill bunnies at UWH... with lidocaine. I'm sure the murder was a fluke, but still... I feel that receiving even a fake bunny would be a bad omen.

If I have port surgery again, I'd like Kevin to sit next to me and talk me through it. I wouldn't want him to sing like Ethel Merman, but he does a really good Obadiah, an old black man who makes me feel quite safe and loved. Or he could just be himself, my real anesthetic in the midst of all these jabs.

Monday, August 29
KEVIN:

As we prepare for the Dean Medical Center surgeon to remove the mastectomy stitches, I watch Jody slip out of her blouse and struggle into a hospital gown, closures in the front. This is not my first glimpse of the scar that literally runs horizontally from breastbone to side. Although I had seen scars of all shapes and sizes when assisting Great Lakes Naval Hospital surgeons during the Viet Nam War, when I first saw this one, I still steeled myself for the emptiness where there once had been a beautiful breast. I managed to mask all emotion then, commenting only that I thought the incision would heal well. She mentioned the numbness caused by the severing of nerves, and again I had little to say. Words were so inadequate, anyway, to describe the way I really felt at first sight of the disfigurement. I just reassured her that I would always see a beautiful woman when I looked at her, and we would beat this disease.

The physician is gentle but efficient in his removal of the stitches; he nods and glances at her eyes from time to time as Jody recounts the horrific experience with the minor port surgery and the lengthy, late-night emergency room visit. The surgeon openly smirks with disdain at both events and scoffs at the port under the skin.

"We almost never use this type," he says. "It isn't warranted at all unless it is going to be a very long-term chemotherapy regimen."

Jody shoots me a quick, anxious glance as if to say that nobody told us this was going to take an inordinately long time. She worries aloud that the UW oncologist's clinical diagnosis is leaning toward inflammatory cancer.

The surgeon rises up like a bear protecting a cub. "Bullshit!" he exclaims. "No way was this inflammatory!"

While Jody is visibly taken aback, I know that she must also relish the idea that he feels familiar enough with her to swear — her own typical reaction to stress. I suspect she finds comfort in the delivery as well as the message.

The surgeon isn't finished: "If it had been inflammatory in nature, we would have treated you with radiation therapy first to shrink the tumor before letting you have the surgery."

"Hey, we're just the messenger," I remind. "This wasn't *our* diagnosis."

The surgeon calms himself, then outlines the symptoms of inflammatory cancer. He reminds Jody that she exhibited no signs of the "orange peel" skin distortion.

"Well, no. But the skin was hotter than the surrounding tissue. I could feel the heat. That's consistent."

"It was not inflammatory," he insists.

She looks at me, a spark of hope evident on her face. Before I can say anything, she forges ahead: "Kevin and I have been talking and we think maybe we've come to the fork in the road where we'd like a second opinion. Do you think you could get us in to see your Dr. Frontiera?"

Apparently pleased that we are now on the right track, the surgeon himself schedules the appointment. Before he backs out of the room, he offers Jody his services should she want any future surgeries such as the port removed. That, he says, he'll gladly do for her right now if she wants, and replace it with the *right one*. She ignores the bait, saying only that she will call him when it is time to remove it at the conclusion of her treatment.

It is very evident that Jody likes and trusts him. She's told me outright that she considers him to be her personal savior; that she'd be dead without his intervention. I doubt she'd ever go to a different surgeon again, and that's okay by me.

Once again, I see the scar as she dresses.

It was only a breast, I think. I remember from Greek Mythology that Amazon warriors would have their breasts removed so they could use their bow and arrows more efficiently and be greater warriors. Jody has always been a warrior. Now she shares a kinship with other cancer warriors. She had hers removed to live and fight another day. This was an act of bravery and of selflessness. She is my warrior. I no longer see a scar. I see her courage.

I marvel at her beauty.

I stop doubting that we can beat this disease. However, I also know that we will need the very best medical knowledge available. I only hope that this new oncologist is as deserving of our trust as Jody's surgeon has proven to be.

Thursday, August 31
JODY:

A Dean Medical nurse left a message yesterday that they had not received any reports from the UW, so I should bring copies to the appointment scheduled with oncologist Michael Frontiera. So I ask the UW Clinic to copy the records again. *Does my time mean nothing to anyone but me?* I collect the materials, sign the forms, and sit in the car and read the reports. The hospital report states that I have inflammatory cancer. Next I read a contradicting UW path report stating that it is lobular invasive. The university pathologist apparently agrees with the Dean pathologist and surgeon. Hopefully tomorrow's second opinion will put an end to the misdirection. My doctors should thank their lucky stars that I'm not given to filing lawsuits, because a courtroom could at least prove to be a forum to get the facts straight.

After a reasonably productive day, I come home to Summer's phone message that she won't be able to make it to Madison tonight after all. I understand she's trying to get settled into a new class schedule, but I'm disappointed just the same. Kevin is making shepherd's pie and I bruise his feelings when I taste it and proclaim the potatoes to be artificial. I hate fake spuds as he well knows, and so I don't know why he would expect me to like them now. He growls at PJ over some silly little thing. And growls again. I know he's coming out sideways because he doesn't feel he can be directly annoyed with me. When you argue with someone with cancer, they win, so you find somebody else to argue with. PJ certainly sets himself up as the perfect target because he's at the height of teenage insolence. So now we are all three angry.

"Mom doesn't like that crap," PJ smirks. I feel like slapping this lanky kid that I love so much. I can imagine how Kevin feels. He turns from the stove to face PJ.

"Take your own crap downstairs," I warn PJ.

I just want some peace and quiet so I'll eat the damn shepherd's pie and pretend I like it. I should have kept my own yap shut; I know Kevin is annoyed when he tries to do something nice and his efforts reap criticism. And food is admittedly a sensitive topic. Just today I sent an email to a large number of people thanking them for the hot food they keep bringing to the door, but also asking them to please stop. I didn't divulge that Kevin finds this very depressing. The food and flower deliveries put him in mind of a funeral, and he just can't take it anymore. He'd rather cook night after night for people who seemingly don't appreciate it than have one more person ring our doorbell and stand on the steps with a casserole dish and a hanged-dog expression. I don't think he can gracefully accept many more hugs and words of encouragement. The more my friends try to help, the more mindful he is of the threat on our doorstep. So I asked them to stop, saying that we needed to settle into a routine that included meal preparation.

To top the day off, my chest has been hurting again, a mysterious pain, but I'm not saying anything now because I'm expecting a thorough exam tomorrow. Still... perhaps I should mail a beloved Ronald McDonald doll to Brook and give the autographed Philadelphia Eagle's football to Summer. Would Kevin know that I'd like them to have those mementoes? I've allowed a real emotional setback because my oncologist is clinging to a fatal diagnosis. The only numbers that mean anything are 0% and 100%, of course, but the word *inflammatory* drags the slide much closer to 0% than the words *lobular invasive*.

I take another bite of shepherd's pie, 100% positive that I hate fake potatoes.

CHAPTER *4:* September

A second opinion • **The one-breast dressing challenge** • **The chemo routine** • **Kissing a bald head (and other sensual thoughts)** • **"Don't call me Inspirational"** • **Family crises** • **Ghost dreams**

Friday, September 1
JODY:

Dr. Michael Frontiera enters the examination room, a big bear of a man with curly salt-and-pepper hair, intense brown eyes, and a thick mustache. In spite of his starched white lab coat, he appears comfortably rumpled and his offer of a handshake is accompanied by a broad smile. The doctor laughs aloud when I explain that I can't shake hands because of a splint on my middle finger, broken a few days ago during a family night bowling outing. I had been so determined not to hurt my chest that I sort of lobbed the ball and snapped the finger!

"Why don't you tell me why you are here," Dr. Frontiera invites.

I consult my numbered list of frustrations and count them off:

1. My oncologist said chemo would take 1½ hours. It takes three. I'd like my expert to know basic facts.

2. Although his lab concurred with my surgeon's diagnosis, the oncologist refused to change his diagnosis from inflammatory cancer to lobular invasive or to consider me for clinical research trials.

3. The oncologist said the first dose of chemo would throw me into menopause, *critical* because my cancer feeds on estrogen. Five days after chemo, a period began that lasted a week. When I called the clinic to report it, another doc said I might menstruate indefinitely and it was no big deal. The rebuke left me feeling like an idiot.

4. I was told to expect a telephone call the day after chemo to be certain I was okay and not having a delayed reaction; the call came four days later.

5. A lack of routine blood monitoring resulted in an emergency hospitalization rather than a routine transfusion – after which there was not even a follow-up phone call from my doctor's office.

6. The oncologist never mentioned blood transfusions, though the port surgeon said he ordered a specific port to accommodate transfusions, and hospital doctors said I may become transfusion dependent.

"In summary, Dr. Frontiera, I am being seen at a comprehensive cancer care center but I have not yet received comprehensive care."

"Your guy at the UW is a good man," he replies thoughtfully. "I agree it sounds like you are slipping through the cracks, but it has to be a series of honest mistakes. However, I can arrange for the transfer of your care, if that is your decision. We do this all the time, both directions."

Dr. Frontiera gingerly but thoroughly examines my chest and pronounces my surgery to be "a beautiful job." He checks the mobility of my left arm and shoulder, and then lightly touches the port embedded under the skin that snakes into the jugular vein. "We can take that out now, if you want," he says. "It looks awfully uncomfortable. You could try chemo without one, or we could replace it with a Hickman catheter, the port we typically use."

"She can't sleep with the thing," Kevin confides. "And your lab tech didn't even know how to draw blood from it. This thing has been a fiasco from the very beginning."

What he says is true but I shake my head. "Not now," I mumble, unwilling to imagine another surgery so soon. I move to a more pressing concern: "What is my diagnosis, in your opinion?"

"I've reviewed all the findings, and I agree with the oncologist. You have inflammatory cancer." With this pronouncement, he reaches over and rests his larger, warmer hand atop mine for the briefest of moments.

"All right then," I manage. "If you both think so, then I'll deal with it."

"I'm very sorry," he says.

"Don't apologize for telling me the truth. *Always* say it straight out. It's the only way I can deal with this. Now I'd… I'd like the other breast removed."

He is adamant that I do not. "Your main concern for the next year won't be a new occurrence," he says. "It will be a *re*occurrence in your chest wall where the tumor was. Your body has enough to fight in the coming months; I don't want to deplete your resources with an unnecessary surgery. I'm strongly advising against that."

"Okay… but I want copies of my blood levels so that I can chart it."

71

"Agreed."

It is settled: The established chemo protocol will remain my routine, but I will get chemotherapy at Dean under Dr. Frontiera's direction.

Late afternoon, Summer arrives by bus from Chicago. I bask in the simple pleasure of having her home, though she will sleep at a motel because she's allergic to all of the animals in our house. PJ is at a friend's house, as it seems he often is lately, but he's agreed to be home in time for breakfast with his sister tomorrow. For dinner tonight, Kevin and I take her to a 1950s-style restaurant for burgers, where I also down a vodka grapefruit to help wash the gritty metal taste out of my mouth. Summer orders a cocktail too, after I tell her that her grandmother is back in the hospital again. Although only 66, Mother isn't handling the chemo very well and, because of the bone marrow involvement, she needs a lot of transfusion support. In addition, my brother Bob gives her a series of daily shots in her stomach to help shore up her white blood count.

Summer has done her homework on both her grandmother's diagnosis and mine. Tears spring to her large green eyes and we talk of other things. We take pictures and force merriment and toast the fact that I still have hair! I'm clearly losing what little is left; there are noticeable bald patches and hair goes flying if I rub my head. The dead follicles stick like tiny quills, leaving my scalp black and blue — *why has no one told me this would happen?* I announce an impromptu decision to shave my head this weekend!

"Cool," Summer says, signaling for another drink.

"I'll help you shave," Kevin offers. He smiles at the waitress but declines her offer to bring him something more substantial than a coke.

I'm not normally a drinker either, and being on chemo, now less inclined than ever. But tonight I order a second vodka and then down it with a hearty toast to bald chicks everywhere. Here's to my cancer sisters!

As soon as we get home, I disappear into my bathroom and add a Valium chaser. I don't want to get in bed and think about any of this anymore. Taking off my clothes, I catch a glimpse of the deep scar running across my chest. No matter how much I self medicate, this isn't going to go away. Another breast isn't going to magically appear. The site is always going to look like a war wound.

Tiny scars also remain where two tubes were stitched to my chest wall to handle routine drainage. My surgeon removed one about a week after surgery but elected to leave the other in place a while longer. Naturally the second site became infected while he was on vacation. The pain quickly became excruciating in the inflamed tissue where the plastic tubing rubbed. Unable to wait four more days, I stormed into my general practitioner's office and insisted that he remove it. "All I need," I told him, "is somebody to pull out a freaking tube! How much medical training could *that* take?"

To his credit, the physician agreed and quickly directed me into a familiar little surgical exam room – the very one where I had been given the news of cancer — the room with nothing interesting to see on the walls. However, all that mattered at the moment was getting rid of the white-hot poker pain in my side.

"This is badly infected, for which I'll give you oral antibiotics, but it's really going to hurt when I pull it out," he warned as he cut the tiny sutures. When he pulled, several inches of plastic tubing were followed by several more inches of thick, stringy blood clot. Amazingly I felt nothing except deep-tissue relief. Surface nerves had been severed during the mastectomy.

I finger the tiny scar now and feel the usual aversion. The sensation of touch in the area of the mastectomy is sickening in a deep, deep way even beyond the initial creepiness of touching nerve-deadened skin. It's like picking a belly button. I can't alter my physical appearance, since I'm not a candidate for reconstructive plastic surgery due to the size of the tumor and the scarring expected from an aggressive radiation protocol. But I should buy a jell-like breast form to stick in my bra so that I can stop wearing loose clothing to mask the fact that I have only half of a 38C set.

For now, I just want to go to sleep. Here's looking at you, kid, *I think, toasting the mirror with an imaginary drink. I am either drunk or crazy, but who cares? I've got bigger fish to fry than drug addiction. In fact, drug addiction actually seems like a pretty good idea.*

Monday, September 4
KEVIN:

Kissing a bald head is a very sensual thing.

Does this make me strange? Could I develop a fetish for bald women? I didn't think so before Jody agreed to let me shave off her remaining coarse hair. Now that the last vestiges of chemo-locks are gone, I find this look attractive. I pronounce her head "perfect" and kiss the smooth skin at the crown with an exaggerated smacking sound.

She has already purchased two wigs, a short red style for work and a blonde wig cut to a medium shag style in which she resembles a female country singer or a hottie housewife. I doubt she will wear the latter one in public, but it would be fine with me if she wanted to wear it at home on occasion! She also bought a couple silly hats with fake hair sewn into them for lighter moments, and she has a drawer full of scarves of all colors. No one outside the family (which has been extended to include Joe, who continues to stay with us at least once weekly) will ever likely see what I'm looking at now. For some perverse reason, this only intensifies the attraction.

Jody is being a sport about her baldness in the safety of our home; she grins before the mirror and then floats downstairs to make a dramatic entrance with her "new look" to amuse Summer. But while she is only pretending to like it, I'm not pretending! I really do prefer the shaved head to the most recent and shortest butch haircut yet. Not that I could say much, because in a show of solidarity, I cut my own hair to *fuzz length*, accentuating my own impending baldness. Certainly my widow's peak more truly resembles a widow's arrow! *Time to embrace the upcoming hairline recession,* I think, glancing into the mirror as I clean Jody's short quills out of the sink. What would I look like if I were to shave my head, too? I could do it. I could embrace baldness. Or... maybe I'll just grow a beard. Too much contemplation! I want to grab my wife and kiss her head again.

Saturday, September 9
JODY:

I wake up exhausted from trying to find a comfortable position to sleep. I can't lie on my left side because of the surgery and the resulting damage to my left arm. And I can't lie on my right side because then the port pokes me in the neck. That only leaves my back and I hate sleeping on my back. Since I'm told to drink quarts of water a day, I also have to pee about once an hour. So I continuously wake up during the night and have nightmares when I *am* able to sleep.

I need help.

This is Day Two, Round Two. The chemo yesterday actually wasn't so bad, although they do little fringe things differently at Dean. And as expected, the staff was inept with my port. The lab tech didn't know how to needle it, so a nurse with more experience ("I've done a couple of these at the hospital") gave him an on-the-spot tutorial. In the grand scheme of things, the experience was unspectacular.

I get dressed slowly. Why is this so hard every day? The biggest decision is whether or not to put on a bra. If I do, I have to fill in one side with wadded scarves. If I don't, I look weird. I wish I had been born flat-chested or had persevered in having both breasts removed. Now I am a freak. I choose a big, loose denim shirt, over which I will wear a denim jacket. It beats putting on that horrible bra. I pull up the jeans carefully, since I have yet to regain full use of my left arm.

Mom has sent a $5,000 check because she believes she is dying and she is dividing her cash reserves between my two brothers and me. She has stated what she expects me to buy: a new refrigerator, washer and dryer, and whatever. Something for PJ or us; she is adamant that the money not be used to pay bills.

We take PJ to sign up for a bowling league at the neighborhood bowling alley. While there, we use some of the money to buy him bowling shoes and a new ball. Afterwards, we order a more extravagant class ring for him than he otherwise might have talked us out of. We eat lunch and then go to American TV and Appliance, where we buy a $2,000 fridge. Kevin and PJ pick out a state-of-the-art washer and dryer, since I have no opinion or intention of using them in the immediate future. The day has a surreal quality to it because I can't believe why we have the money. I don't want to believe it. I pretend the money was always ours and we've just been saving it for this day.

We return home and I sleep a couple hours.

The telephone ring wakes me. Summer is pregnant! I have to laugh out loud, because just yesterday I sent an email to friends saying that I would like to live long enough to hold a grandchild on my knee. Now I think I should amend that, since it isn't likely to buy me as much time as I'd hoped! We do some quick math and discover that she became pregnant the same time that Mom and I were diagnosed. She's put new meaning in the Mile High Club.

I convince Kevin to go garage sale shopping and I buy a stroller from a neighbor up the street. We splurge. Why not also get a new car seat and bath seat and some clothes for the baby? I call Summer back, excited with our finds, bursting with love for the very idea of this grandchild. I call my mother because Summer says I can break the news to Grandma, and so I tell her after thanking her for the money.

"I'd like to live long enough to see that," Mother says wistfully. "My first great-grandchild."

"So would I, Momma. So would I."

Kevin and I cook side-by-side. This is a good day. We make Swiss steak and mashed potatoes and PJ has his friend Jake spend the night. We all sit down to a hot meal together and it is almost like it was "before." Close enough for tonight. Close enough to see my husband actually relax for a few minutes.

Now I'm too tired to do anything more. I answered emails but I'm too whipped to help with house cleaning. I'm bone-tired exhausted, but I sure feel a lot better than I thought I would by now.
Maybe I can do this treatment thing after all.

Tuesday, September 12
KEVIN:

It is obvious that the reactions to chemo will get worse before they get better. How much worse, I don't know; I guess that's the million-dollar question for every patient part way through treatment. But while dressing this morning, I glance at my wife and think it is a mistake for her also to be dressing for work. She needs her rest. I'd like to remind her that she could try working from home at a reduced pace, but I know the look that such a comment would evoke.

Call me the worrier, but I am also concerned about Jody's insistence that she continue driving. Chemo-fog already is causing my wife bouts of aphasia, where she either cannot remember words, or uses wrong (though similar) words. I know she is aware as soon as she misspeaks; I witness her as she masks the mistakes in jokes. However, her driving abilities have also suffered, though she remains in denial on that score. To have her skills further impaired by the cumulative effects of chemo is not an inviting image.

Those are my concerns. Jody's concerns are to live as normal a life as *before* and to hold up her end at work. Her profession is more than what she does; it's become, in her mind, a big part of who she is, and she cares very deeply about the people she supervises and mentors. Getting her to stop is apparently not in my bag of persuasive abilities.

Still, I have to wonder about taking on a new business venture now. Bill created an opportunity for her to buy into a partnership before any of us knew about the tumor and, surprisingly, he didn't rescind the offer after the diagnosis. I alternately marvel at her ability to take on such an ambitious endeavor and question her judgment and objectivity at such a low point in her health. She's been very impulsive lately, especially with regard to spending. Her living-in-the-moment approach to life, endearing in other areas, is downright disconcerting when it comes to money. I married a financially restrained woman, which I considered to be a good thing. Thanks to automatic deposit and Jody's handling of the checkbook, I never even see our wages or the bills they pay, and I'm nurturing a dread that remaining financially blind might no longer be in our mutual best interest. We began this journey comfortable and I plan on us ending this journey (together) in a similar state.

I'm not really sure how to respond. If I gently wrest the comptroller duties from her, I'm removing her primary family responsibility, which could send the wrong message. But if I don't, we could be in some serious financial trouble in about a year. I worry about this at night when I can't sleep. Or maybe I can't sleep because I'm wrestling with this? But I keep coming back to the decision to lend silent consent to her whims. Then, when she makes it clear of this disease, we will find a way to pay off any accumulated debt. She's still *inside the lines* with her spending... as far as I know.

Maybe, when the spirit next moves her to have one of her blunt talks (the ones I avoid), I might convince her to pull in the reins a bit by pointing out that we need our financial resources to guarantee P.J.'s education. Then there is the pending grandbaby; I know Jody will want to continue helping provide for her *wee one* whether she is on this plane of existence or another. She's only known of the child for less than a week, and already she's bought a wide array of baby equipment, clothes and toys.

Paddy and Summer have decided it would be more fun for them not to know the baby's sex. Jody hints it would be easier to shop if she knew, but the young couple refuses the bait. I've urged her to tell them the truth, but Jody is equally stubborn. The truth is that she doesn't trust that she'll be around when the child is born and so she'd like to invent as clear an image as possible of the child to carry in her head. The kids love her very much; they would understand. But Jody has refused out of respect for Paddy's role, and to support her daughter's major decision. Still, the desire to know this child in any way is so keen that it shows in her face when she speaks of the pending miracle.

Maybe this is a good thing, I think, stepping aside as she gathers her briefcase and purse. *Maybe curiosity will keep the cat around longer.*

She gives Foley a big hug and kiss, part of every morning's parting ritual with the dog. Does she know how often I watch her lately, just to delight in doing so? I kiss Jody goodbye before she ducks out the door, dark circles under her eyes revealing a glimpse of the devil she's fighting, but, just as evident, a smile that hints of her determination to take on the world one more day.

The garage door opens. I can't help but sigh as I wonder what she will bring home for the baby tonight.

Friday, September 15
JODY:

Wednesday I was rushed to the clinic with a fever of over 101. After two days of fluctuating fevers and chills, I've been feeling darned sorry for myself. And there are the increasing battles with chemo fog that I seem to be losing and find quite dispiriting. Just the other day, I was talking to

77

a friend on the phone and suddenly had it in my head that I was talking to another and totally confused her with a long rambling story about her doctor husband. Her husband is not a doctor. Another friend said she'd keep a journal with my emails so later we could laugh at all of the misspelled words. Ha ha ha. I make my living working with words – why did she think that being inept at my work would be funny to me?

I'm also having a problem with well-meaning individuals who say that I'm handling this situation in an uplifting or inspiring manner. I wish they'd not say or write this to me anymore, because it makes me feel guilty. More and more often lately, my thoughts fly back to the Chicago Ronald McDonald House, where I was hired as manager in 1979. Then, the lodging facility gave first priority to outpatient children with cancer or leukemia. These little patients soon became extensions of our family, since we lived at the house on a full-time basis. There I learned that cancer often selects children who have not yet had a first kiss, a first airplane ride, a first anything. I have no special place compared to these darling children who fight with more grace than I can imagine.

I just finished reading a book wherein several cancer survivors share their reactions to their diagnosis and treatment. One woman wrote that she made a list of everyone she could think of who "deserved" cancer more than her. Did she lose her mind? I mean, I know cancer does weird things to people who otherwise might be decent folks, but.... As I am coming to realize, I'm at the best place in my life for this to have happened. I have a loving and devoted husband who takes care of me in every way he can. I have an understanding boss who gives me opportunities to heal without worry of financial ruin. I have seen Summer and Brook become beautiful, responsible young women, and PJ is only a few years away from adulthood. I am old enough and wise enough to know what is happening and to prepare my family for what is yet to happen. And most of all, I have lived a full life and I am not afraid of death, even as I work with my doctors every day to accomplish a cure.

I'm going to tell people who tell me that I'm inspirational to contact my friend Sandy Lampman at the Madison Ronald McDonald House and offer to become a volunteer. Assist families whose kids are seriously ill. That's where they'll see the real deal.

Saturday, September 16
KEVIN:

Jody has taken to wearing colorful scarves to help camouflage what she considers to be the obvious missing breast. She loops the scarf around her neck and then anchors it on the left with a brooch. She's also using scarves beneath her clothing most days to stuff the empty bra cup, although she says they move around and she's always worried that one will fall out at a most inopportune time. Nor do the scarves leave her with the most natural appearance.

While I don't feel that her surgery is overly obvious, I am empathetic and suggested last week that we visit a Victoria's Secret store to see if they carried breast forms. She was reluctant and so I made the initial inquiry of a store clerk. We were amazed at the only available small size. Jody took the box into a dressing room and soon opened the door a crack and called me over. "Look," she whispered, pulling her blouse away from her chest. She had wedged two forms inside one bra cup and still had room. She was near tears: "I don't think this is going to work. Let's get out of here."

She was not truly disheartened, only momentarily frustrated. However, the fashion clumsiness is getting to her. Short of reconstructive surgery, which is not an option, a form is our best bet. If only I could find the right store!

We stop at a little shopping center because Jody needs something from the craft store; I wander down the sidewalk searching out a window with more appeal. Most of the stores cater to women and children — no golf shop or newsstand — but there is a small lingerie shop at the far end called Intimate Hours. It appears to be one of those Naughty-but-Nice venues.

I decide to scout the merchandise, hoping to spare Jody the embarrassment of our last breast-shopping foray if this is another dead end. I explain our situation to a knowledgeable saleswoman; apparently the store does a brisk business with mastectomy patients. I demonstrate with my hands about how large my wife's breast was. She says they probably have something that will work and holds up a sample that looks to be the approximate size and shape. Bingo! I can hardly contain my hopefulness as I race back to fetch my wife. Although skeptical, Jody is moved by my enthusiasm. She lets me drag her to the other store.

The saleswoman is very kind and her approach is gentle. She shows us a couple different styles (with nipple and without, pear shaped or triangle) and offers to help fit Jody so that she might get the optimal effect. She suggests a bra that might be more comfortable and will not chafe the incision area under Jody's arm. The form is filled with a gel-like material and made to fill the concave space created when the surgeon removed the breastbone tissue. We touch it tentatively; it moves like the real thing. Jody giggles nervously, disappears behind a curtain, and reappears *sans* scarf. We give it a "9.5" — two saleswomen and one husband judging Jody's chest. A little larger form, we decide. The next size, the largest they carry, is a perfect match. We give it a "10."

"It's a little cold to the touch," Jody remarks. "Kind of a shock. Even though the nerves are cut there, it still feels cold. How weird is that?"

"It'll warm up soon from body heat," the clerk assures. "Or use a hair dryer to warm it in the morning before you put it in."

"Turn your receipt into the insurance company or the American Cancer Society," the other woman advises. Apparently Jody is allocated a breast or two per year. We will not make a claim; the expense has not been too great and others need the reimbursement more than we might. Besides, I'm calling this my Sweetest Day present to my sweetie. I *want* to buy it.

The artificial breast greatly cheers Jody's spirit. Her mood is noticeably lighter — so much so that she suggests we take P.J. bowling.

She must be kidding. "*Bowling?*" I ask. "Are you sure you're up to that?"

"My energy and strength spike and plunge," Jody reminds. "Let's take advantage of this unexpected high while it lasts."

We go home and I relay the invitation while Jody waits in the car. P.J. is actually amenable and suggests that we eat dinner at the bowling alley together. He hurries to get his paraphernalia, perhaps fearing that his mother will tire and change her mind, but we're out the door and at the alley in no time.

As Jody walks back to the ball return, there's an extra bounce to her step... and to her chest. I overhear P.J. ask his mother in a somewhat embarrassed tone how the "bounce" is possible. She laughs and tells him about our earlier purchase.

"It really looks real!" he exclaims. High praise.

A few hours of bowling and we're all exhausted, but Jody has held her own. We tease her, driving home, that the breast has done wonders for her bowling form, too, as she's scored 162, the highest score she's ever managed.

The jovial mood extends into our bedroom, where I put the breast on my head after she disrobes. "I could warm it up for you every morning like this," I offer.

Dear God, it is good to hear her laugh again.

Friday, September 22
JODY:

Everybody keeps giving me non-fiction cancer survivor books to read. I'm not complaining, for though I used to devour an average of two novels a week, I no longer have the slightest interest in fiction. When I do have the concentration to read, I pick up a cancer book. So far, my favorite is **Red Devil**. Five minutes ago, I finished Lance Armstrong's **It's Not About the Bike**, and I feel a deep kinship with him because he explains the chemo effects I've been feeling more and more. But **Red Devil** is still number one with me.

It's really getting harder to cope every day, and I realize that Kevin and PJ are denied the opportunity to see *me* at all most days. All they see is the husk, all that's left by the time I get home from work at 5:30 p.m. I actually sob, driving home, because it takes so much concentration, and I know that I probably shouldn't be driving at all, but what is the alternative? To give up what little normal life I have left?

Still, by the time I pull into the driveway, my energy reserves are completely depleted and it is all I can do to hobble to the couch and huddle under a blanket. The other night, I locked myself away in the bedroom closet in the dark and cried and cried because it was all I *could* do. The fatigue is unlike anything I have ever experienced before. I no longer have even the energy to puke … I guess that's a good thing, sort of. I also certainly do not have the vigor for traditional imagery when I do go to bed. Lie and imagine waging war against cancer cells? Who has the strength?

Imagery is very much on my mind lately, because Salli took me to a dinner program featuring a counselor speaking on this topic. (Salli offered to drive and also had pre-ordered a special bland meal because my mouth was sore. What a great friend!) The speaker pointed out that cancer patients who expect some divine intervention in the ninth inning instead of assisting with their treatment by having the right mindset are just stupid. She didn't say it exactly that way, but she delivered most of her sermon directly to me, the single cancer patient in the room of 20 or so svelte women. Easy pickings, with my bald head and surgical mask, worn because of low blood counts and increased susceptibility to infection.

Another friend later suggested imagining myself curled up in the palm of God's hand when I need comfort. And Mike, my oncologist, recently sent me to a shrink. (Actually, I asked for a referral to a cancer specialist because he's not one to willingly dwell on the darker side of chemo.) He recommended a woman who was reportedly good with people who suffered from chronic pain. Her single-minded interest in my relationship with my mother (how did she know Mom could be a pain?) only made me more upset. I had been hoping for a little imagery training; instead I left 50 minutes later with a headache. I'm obviously not ready for professional intervention yet.

I know what hurts the most. I am not by nature a patient person; I am naturally the one who makes things happen. Now, after I make it home from work, the biggest move I make is to reach for the remote to change the television station to the next program. I have to be prodded to eat because lifting the spoon to my mouth requires so much effort. And any change of the routine (say, a pre-empted TV program) upsets me tremendously; I don't have the reserves it takes to react to change. I need stability.

Chemo has become routine. Once every 21 days, on a Thursday, Romeo draws blood from the port ... and every time it's still a semi-big deal. If the blood counts are within a certain range, I'm called in to talk to Mike. Kevin goes with me. I typically have a list of questions like, "Why am I taking rat poison on the side?"

"Don't call it rat poison," Kevin sighed, *"It's Warfarin."*

"It's used to kill rats," Mike admitted. *"But for you, it keeps your blood thin, which is what we need with the port. Keep taking it."*

I read that the average consultation with an oncologist is only seven minutes. Frightful! Mike answers every question without regard to time. I give him a big hug whenever I see him and he either pats my shoulders or touches my hands when he answers me. He mostly teases Kevin. He understands my need to challenge him with Internet research, and the nurses have told me that he's the most aggressive at Dean. He'll treat when others would postpone.

The only thing Mike does that irritates me is that he is forever pushing me to be positive, be positive. It pisses me off. He asks how I'm doing, and I start to say something negative and he hushes me right up. A nurse confided that he can't cope with anything negative at all. "Nobody hurts more for his patients more than Mike, but he believes he's helping you by not talking about it. We've told him that he shouldn't refuse to discuss painful symptoms but he is downright stubborn on this point."

I'll say. If I could change one thing about him, I would change that, because having to seem much braver than I am could get me into trouble. I need to have this one person be the one that I can share the dark with as well as the love, medicine and miracles buzz. If we don't really look at what's happening to me or why I'm being treated, I think it could sneak up on all of us and kill me.

Why didn't his therapist ask me about how I feel about chemo or Mike? Is everybody afraid to ask what it is REALLY like to have cancer?

But back to chemo. I'm then sent to another waiting room for the 15 minutes it takes the oncology nurse to prepare the solutions. She always gives me at least one warm blanket, usually two, because chemo cocktails feel like they're served on the rocks, and I get chilled very easily. The port is flushed again, and, like at UW, I get the steroids, relaxants and anti-nausea medication.

After the Adriamycin push, I have a pretest for iron, which will be delivered an hour later. I have shown an iron deficiency that pills aren't addressing, so this is our compromise. The sample is delivered into the IV; the bag of fluid looks like rusty syrup. After the sample, that line is closed, another is opened and we begin the Cytoxin. Drip, drip, drip into the vein. Then the iron line is opened, which takes another 20 minutes. Last treatment, I arrived at 1:30. We left at 5:30.

The nausea is continuous regardless what or when I eat, with the exception of the first few days following chemo, when it is handled pretty well by an anti-nausea pill. However, the prescription is only good for three days. Mike says this should only last the first week or so, but he is wrong. The chemo taste doesn't go away, and that's what's nauseating.

Every cancer patient should know about Biotene gum. I buy an extra pack of 16 pieces for a couple bucks at Walgreens and hand it to women in clinic who've found no relief from common chemo side effects. It is amazing for dry mouth. When you can't talk because your tongue is stuck to the roof of your mouth, Biotene to the rescue. Every clinic visit, I share it with someone new.

On the rare days that I'm able to do something by myself that's a little extra, like grocery shopping, it feels like some gigantic high. I'm so emotional on those wonderful days that my battery carries a little more charge and I want the day to last forever! I try and channel that energy to my family, because hope and love are two-way currents and sometimes you have to give some positive energy back so that they can keep on keeping on, too.

Today is not one of those days. It is just another "Groundhog Day," like in the Bill Murray movie. I have chemo blisters all across my face. I wonder what I can do to make today *different*, to create some meaning for all of this. I have to do this for my children, because they are watching, regardless where they are. And for Kevin, who cooks my meals and washes my clothes and tells me I'm beautiful and always finds something to compliment about me every day, even if it's so lame as my choice of television programs to stare at.

If there was just me to consider, I'd quit treatment. It would be so easy to say, "Stop!" Stop the damn treatment and let me bank more than three good days in a 21-day cycle. And then, when the heart attack comes or the cancer moves to the bones or lungs, it'd be time to lie down and find some peace and let it be over. Everyone dies, after all.

But what if this thinking is just chemo depression? What if… if I wait it out a few more days… what if then I'll feel good again? Mike said it *could* happen that I could be cured, or at least it is possible to buy one "good year" for every "treatment year" invested until they come up with a better drug. Maybe in a few more days, I'll be strong enough for the next cycle. It's just that finishing eight cycles seems awfully far out there, with radiation waiting to tag team the chemo.

I'm still in here, foggy or not. Fatigued or not. In a slightly different body with a different look to it as my eyebrows and eyelashes fall out. This weekend I'm hoping to do the things that might give Kevin and PJ a glimpse of the old me. Go bowling or to a movie, perhaps. Things we used to do without thought.

"You're so brave to come out," a woman said to me at a luncheon the other day. I wore a scarf on my head, my face was so sore that I couldn't tolerate makeup, and I was slumped in a chair feeling anything but brave. I was too tired to stand to network but longed to be part of what I used to take for granted. I didn't know the lady, but I wondered if that was supposed to be a compliment? After all, in polite society not so long ago, I would have known to stay out of sight.

I am not so brave. I'm just like everybody else. I don't want to stop living before I die. And I don't want to be half-dead while I'm alive.

Thursday, September 28
KEVIN:

Same bed, different night. Two months have passed since Jody and I have made love. Although we've been assured there is no danger to me ("Wait a couple days just after chemo, but then everything should be fine"), there are other reasons for celibacy.

The mastectomy was painful during the healing stage, as was the port site. Then Jody began chemotherapy even before her stitches had been removed. Now the cumulative effects of the curative poisons have drained most of her energy. And what she does have, she's necessarily chosen to expend at work rather than in the bedroom. I know she would be willing to have sex (very quick, very superficial), but I'm not looking for a quickie.

Despite everything, I still strongly desire this woman in every way. Our marriage bed was enjoyable for us both before the diagnosis. Now Jody has put her sex drive in park and shut off the engine, and mine is idling in neutral. Still, I find it hard not to touch her, lying next to her every night. But I know that even a gentle caress will not bring a responding caress, but rather a muffled cry because it causes her such discomfort. I want to show her that I'm okay with the scar, to touch it and reassure her that it is no big deal to me. But I dare not approach the incision because she's already warned me that the

84

slightest pressure there nauseates her.

I wonder if I am weird for wanting to touch my wife's scars, to kiss her there. I wonder if other men think about these things. I worry that I'm selfish for wanting to be intimate with my wife. I've been celibate for long periods of time before when out to sea, but this is different. I love this woman and not being able to even give her a deep hug or sensual kiss on the mouth is getting to me. Every night I have willed myself to sublimate such desires and just go to sleep.

I wish I had someone to talk to about this; preferably someone who has been through it himself and could give me some real advice. I have searched the web for support groups and even created one myself, but am receiving no response. I considered going to a hospital-sponsored support group, but realized that I'd likely only end up being the supporter and not the supported. Therapist? I analyze myself out of this option by confessing that I know what the problem is. I just need to find a reasonable rationalization to effectively hide it.

So much of what Jody and I do now demands changing paradigms, looking at things differently. Chemo has brought her to her knees and put her on a couch rather than in her home office, where her many varied projects once kept her happily occupied most evenings. We say things to each other like *Isn't it nice we have time to watch television together now? Isn't it nice that I get to drive more often? And isn't it a great opportunity for me to cook? And isn't it damned nice that we are learning to express our love in different ways?*

That's what we say aloud, but inside myself, I hope she soon develops a tolerance for the drugs. I wish she wouldn't work so hard. I wish she had more time for me. I wish I could concentrate when I'm at work. I wish P.J. and I had been able to develop a closer relationship before this happened instead of it being forced upon us now.

Waaugh, waaugh, waaugh. Okay, pity party over.

I look at her, where she lies lost to me in a sleep brought to her by the makers of Ambien, her favorite sleep aid. The familiar stirring rears its head. I look away, roll over to the other side.

I always slept well when out at sea, despite a constant sense of seasickness. Despite the rolling ship. What was it about being at sea? With no friendly port in sight, drifting, drifting, drifting... off to... sleep.

Friday, September 29
JODY:

Just when I thought the rest of my body parts were safe, my fingernails began showing signs of ridging and discoloration. "That's normal,"

Mike assured. "Your fingernails and toenails may actually fall off. Many patients lose them. It's not uncommon." I was in high school when Uncle Gene, a career Air Force man, was sent to Viet Nam. I was frightened that he might be taken prisoner and tortured. I'd lie in my bed at night and worry that he might have his fingernails pried off, or have wooden matches stuck under them. It seemed like a far worse thing than death. Can't say that my view has much changed in 35 years.

Our own present-day Air Force girl Brook called the other night and cried and cried because she was so far away and couldn't be with the family, specifically with her sister. "I never realized how dependent I am on my family, and you are way too far away when all our lives are going to hell," she sobbed.

Prior to calling me, she learned that Grandma was again in the hospital for blood transfusions. So she called Summer, who was unfortunately in a Chicago emergency room with a tear in her uterus and bleeding, which caused the ER doc to project a 50/50 chance of miscarriage. And so Brook called me. Kevin warned her that I had an infection that left me on antibiotics and forced bed rest. Poor Boo-Bear had called all of us looking for a little comfort because she had the flu with a high fever, but had worked a 13-hour duty shift, thanks to an unsympathetic sergeant. After returning to a lonely bunk, she wanted one of us to mentally tuck her into bed. Or tell her everything would be all right.

Hearing that she was sick didn't do anything for my own mini-depression. The only thing that helped lift it even a little was learning a couple days later that Summer was deemed *fit to carry to term*, Mom was released from the hospital, and Brook's flu ran its course.

The experience of watching my family collapse made me more mindful of missed opportunities lately with PJ to create more "normal time." And so I've decided to leave work around 2:00 every day so I can see PJ when he gets home from school. I'm not going through all of this treatment to lengthen my life so that I can sleep through all the time with my family.

Not that sleep is coming easy, because the nightmares are incessant. No one told me that I would have bad dreams, but I suppose they couldn't have predicted how often I would wake myself up with my own crying. Unspoken day fears become night terrors. The other night, I dreamed that Bill treated me like a ghost at work. He talked right through me to my staff, as if I were just a mirage. I realized that he wanted to demote me from vice president to manager because he was losing confidence in my ability to lead. I knew I would quit rather than take a step backwards because it was the final insult, when I was trying so hard to be at work every day that I could. Did he have any idea what it took just to get dressed? It was just so unfair!

I woke up sobbing.

Then I wondered if my subconscious was picking up signs that I was too tired to recognize during my "normal" waking state, and I worried all night that it wasn't a dream, but reality. By morning, I was worried that reality might really be paranoia caused by chemotherapy poisoning my brain now, too. What if Bill is just trying to help, which is likely what I need right now? This, of course, is exactly what I need! But what if it isn't help, but an ambush? I went to work exhausted and confused.

My oncologist pointed out that being too tired is hindering the therapy. Mike reminded that I'm at great risk of opportunistic viruses when my counts fall, so I have to get more rest. So I'm changing time slots at work to end my day earlier for the first two weeks after chemo, reverting back to the full-day schedule for the third week, when I start to recoup in terms of energy. I've told PJ and Kevin I want more quality time with them when I DO have energy. I don't intend to spend this precious time listening to petty arguments in the other room. And I'm trying to shore up little Brook, and reassure Summer through her fears of losing a baby, and be with my mom daily via phone calls as she plummets into despair with her own situation.

I wonder if Bill will think that my leaving the office earlier indicates I can't hack it anymore? I'm just being crazy... but if I'm crazy, wouldn't that give him reason to fire me? I am *not* a ghost. I am struggling to go to work every day!

I am struggling with ghosts. That's the problem.

CHAPTER 5: October
Mom visits, shares oncologist • Kevin looks for answers • *Footprints* & Faith • Family bowling outing • Neighbor Bill announces cancer

Wednesday, October 4
KEVIN:

Jody sits at the kitchen table waiting for dinner. P.J. is eating with a friend tonight so I'll be cooking for only two. I take a quick inventory of the food in the cabinets, wondering what she would find appealing. Probably nothing. I move to the refrigerator.

"Mom would like to fly in from Denver," she announces out of the blue. "She'd like to stay with us a few weeks in early November while Bobby goes hunting." I glance her way, where she is absently pulling apart a paper napkin, piling the fine strips of paper onto her plate like so many chicken feathers. She adds, "I know it's a lot to ask of you right now but I called Mike and he agreed to be Mom's oncologist while she's here."

"If that's what you want." I turn back to the fridge: "I'm going to scramble some eggs, get a little protein into you for a change. No mashed potatoes tonight."

"Whatever," she mutters, disinterested.

As I cook, I recall Joyce's visit last Easter when she and her adult son Bob visited with us for a week. I was intentionally nice to her and though she remained wary, she responded in kind.

The interaction between mother and daughter was much more complicated. One minute Joyce was very critical of Jody, the next minute she asked Jody for kisses, and it was apparent that Joyce needed much more affection than she was able or willing to return. I don't know if that's always been the dynamic because Jody is resolute in not talking about her childhood. What little I have learned is the result of drawing her brothers into private conversations or by listening carefully to her mother. I tuck away any puzzle piece unwittingly divulged; from these separate bits, I've reconstructed an out-of-focus picture of a single mom with a couple of kids living in abject poverty and I'm pretty sure Jody and Bob spent some time in a foster care situation arranged by a Salvation Army pastor before Joyce remarried and had Kurt, Jody's younger brother.

Although I believe the family's financial situation improved after the marriage, I have deduced that Jody's adoptive father was an alcoholic and that her mom never quite succeeded at anger control. Later, they divorced and Joyce married another alcoholic, Jody's stepfather for more than 20 years. I suspect there is much more to know but Jody remains secretive.

Regardless of what happened in the past, Jody's bond with her mother is real. My wife isn't blind to the fact that her mother's treatment of her often borders on insulting, but Jody will not confront the woman in any way. I offer no advice though I've been tempted to point out that I historically cut ties to such toxic relationships. My wife embraces — even clings — to this one.

"You know that I don't get your relationship with your mom," I comment aloud.

"You didn't order it," Jody quips, borrowing one of my jokes.

"You're right, I didn't," I answer pointedly. She looks away and shrugs her shoulders, sparking a flash of guilt. *She doesn't need my approval to love someone.* She has made quite a mess of the shredded napkin. I tidy up, give her another napkin without comment, spoon her eggs onto her plate, and kiss her forehead, a peace offering.

I eat while Jody plays with her food. My mind wanders and I realize that I don't quite know how I feel about Joyce, whom I met while we were on our honeymoon. We were called to Denver because Jody's stepfather was losing his battle with cancer, and sadly he died while we were still about four hours away. It wasn't the best circumstance under which to meet new family members, and added to that was the fact that I'm not at all comfortable with the funeral ritual. I had never attended immediate family viewings or funerals, and the ones I later attended were obligatory, such as the one for Jody's stepfather. There was no feeling of loss or expression of grief expected. To be honest, I'm not really sure what acceptable behavior is at such services.

My earliest memory of a wake is mired in the shock of my brother's death and it is a hazy recollection of wailing mixed with laughter and lots of food being brought into the house. I have a vague recollection of being relegated to mixing drinks for my parents and relatives. I never saw my brother in the coffin and so, having seen no proof to the contrary, I thought Michael might still be alive. I didn't easily let go of that hope.

To this day, I don't know the reasoning behind my parents' decision to keep their children from the burial but, as a result, I really can't clearly recall the chain of events following the knock on the door the night my parents were told of his car accident. The knock itself triggers a clear vision of climbing out of my bed and watching from the top of the stairs as first my father, and then my mother, approached the door. From the other side we heard a muffled, "Police. Please open the door."

"Don't open it!" I called out, but too late: the unthinkable words of my brother's death were already forced through a crack.

The second most vivid memory of that horrific time occurred after the wake visitors left, when my father fell to the living room floor, completely wasted, and cried like a baby. While I'm sure she must also have wept, I don't carry the image of my mother's tears. I know I didn't cry, though, and I know I *still* feel guilty for my long-ago ineptness with emotion.

When my parents died (Mother first, and then, little over a year later, Father), I was overseas. Following Mother's death, I could have taken leave of duty to comfort my father and siblings but I rationalized that Naval operational commitments required my presence. I didn't go home. Later I was informed that Father privately handled the disposal of her cremains because she had "donated her body to science." There was no burial.

When he later died of cancer, my dad's body was also "given to science," after which my sister made arrangements to recover his ashes. My sister's intent was to scatter Father's ashes alongside Mother's; the only problem being that none of us knew where Father had put Mother! It was a family mystery until a local Kentucky funeral home director telephoned to report that Mother's ashes were stored in his basement. He said that Father had never bailed her out despite repeated requests from the funeral home. My sister could take custody of the cremains for a nominal fee.

I did not cry for either of them. So as I said, I don't do well at formal services.

I'm not looking forward to Joyce's impending visit. Jody is visibly weaker every day, and my life is consumed with caring for her, parenting an increasingly uncooperative teenager, and trying to stay on top of my own demanding day job. I've already no time for me. I'm now to also care for my mother-in-law, who apparently is sicker than Jody? I wonder what Joyce's moods are like lately, and if she'll extend her critical eye my direction.

Maybe Joyce and Jody want to spend some quality time alone together. I hope so. Otherwise, this is a stupid idea that could have a negative impact on everyone involved, including innocent bystanders like P.J. and me.

Finally Jody eats the food on her plate and I clear the table. I assure my beautiful bride that her mother is very welcome in our home and, furthermore, I'll take good care of them both. Nothing to worry about. I bring her the phone and invite her to call her mother and let her know we'd both love to have her stay. She stares at the phone but doesn't move to take it. I put it back in the cradle; if she's too tired to push buttons, then she's also too tired to talk. I want to hurry and help her to bed before she's too tired to sleep. It happens.

Let Joyce come. Anything to ease Jody's burden, I think. Our quality time will shrink dramatically with Joyce in the house, but I quickly sublimate that selfish thought. Apparently I'm not coping much better with cancer than I do with funerals.

Thursday, October 19
JODY:

I bought a cheap ($2.99) *Footprints* bracelet forged of some stiff metal, wide enough and deep enough to have an abbreviated version of the religious story etched on it. *When you look back on the most sorrowful events of your life and see only one set of footprints in the sand, do not believe that I ever abandoned you. It was during those times that I carried you.* Admittedly it was an impulse buy and I had to paint the inside band with fingernail polish because I'm allergic to cheap metal.

I bought the bracelet because I'm enamored of the idea of a guardian. Sometimes I look back at recent weeks with wonderment that I was able to talk to my son's teachers or listen to my husband's work-related stories, because certainly I was too preoccupied with fear or too tired to absorb much. The answer is that I was carried. *There was one set of footprints in the sand.*

I know this because I have had the same experience in the past. The night Daniel died, I held three trembling, sorely frightened children where I sat on the floor in a kind of stupor. Finally I surfaced long enough to call friends out of their beds. Then I went outside and sat on the steps to wait for Amie and Pastor Hazel to come. With their arrival, I was calmed sufficiently to be able to bring the kids into a circle on the living room floor. Our friends gathered pillows and blankets and I read aloud until the children fell asleep. Except I knew it wasn't me caring for my children, because I lacked the focus and the strength. Christ spoke to them and kissed them and comforted them through me.

Then, when they were asleep, I was returned and I fell to my knees and wailed, a pillow to my mouth so as not to wake anyone. I cried until daybreak. They woke and I stood ready to answer their questions as best I could and to help however I could. Because, again, there was one set of footprints where I walked. In the odd moments, I lost it — times when the children were outside my sphere of influence or I was in the car alone. Even now I'll hear a song on the radio that was played at his funeral and if I'm alone in the car, I may dissolve into tears. But if someone is with me, I change radio stations. I am strong when it is required of me. If Christ carried me through everything, I would never know my own strength, mission, or purpose.

I saw a new counselor today, and she said that's what I'm doing with the cancer now. I'm waiting for a safe time to express myself when it won't distress my family… a safe time to mourn what is happening to my body and to my energy and to my very spirit. And that's why I still cry in the car on the way to work or in the closet in the dark. She's offered her office as a safe place and perhaps I'll continue to see her every couple weeks. I'm undecided.

In the interim, I'll wear the band to remind me that I'm not alone in this. Even though I might not have purchased the cheap bracelet (let alone worn it) a few months ago, I don't believe people become more religious in times of crisis. But I do believe they become more aligned with who they really are, more attuned to what is true and what is not, and more clear about their faith.

I am a child of God. He is with me and He carries me back into the light.

KEVIN:

Good things come to those who wait. In this case, an almost good thing has happened – my sex drive has waned and so I am no longer feeling sexually frustrated. It's probably due to increasing weight and lack of exercise and, though I hate to admit it, it might also be attributable to my age. But who knows? The men I know don't talk about this kind of stuff, and at this point in time, I'm not too thrilled with doctors either, so forget asking them. I'm not sure I'd get a straight answer from anyone.

When this is over, I'm going to start taking better care of myself. Maybe I'll take vitamins. As for the added weight, I'll just buy bigger pants. Yeah, that's the ticket.

I just hope the sex drive returns at the appropriate time.

Friday, October 20
JODY:

The cumulative effect of chemotherapy has dropped my hematocrit to an all time low. The result is a suspension of therapy. Go sit in a penalty box!

Mike says that the next standard protocol for my stage of cancer is Taxol for four cycles; each cycle followed by 20 days to absorb and recover before the next. Because of my depressed bone marrow response to the first drugs, he is considering a tailored protocol of one-third the usual dose administered every week so that the effect is cumulative.

Red facial acne makes me look like a burn victim. How could I hope that Kevin would be interested in me physically? I make no overtures, even when I have the energy or mildest interest. I don't want to put him on the spot... to make him *try* to be turned on. I've noticed already that there is little response if I snuggle into him, and who could blame him? I don't.

Recently my gums bled profusely after brushing my teeth, leaving dark, crusty dried blood all around my mouth. The outline of my eyes disappeared with eyebrows and eyelashes. I'm a ghoul! A grooming guide for cancer patients suggests wearing big earrings or extravagant necklaces to draw others' eyes away from your face. I hide my medical alert necklace but I adorn jackets and dresses with Sari scarves and even put butterfly decals on my bald head. What could I add to make flannel pajamas more alluring?

Kevin looks like Ringo Starr now, with his new beard and clipped hairstyle. I feel like a teenager with a crush. I am still here. Still in love.

I only wish my husband could feel that way about me again.

Saturday, October 21
KEVIN:

No matter how poorly Jody feels, we still get up very early every Saturday to accompany P.J. to his bowling league. Last year was P.J.'s first foray into team sports and we watched his bowling improve to the point where he was averaging in the 100's almost every game. We bought him a new ball this year with a finger-tip grip and the improvement has been phenomenal. His game average has jumped to 135. Of course, the improvement might also be due to the fact that he is maturing by leaps and bounds. He must have grown six inches in the last year and put on 20 pounds! Soon I'll be teaching him to drive.

His eyes flit to his mother between his every turn on the lane, seeking her encouragement. She applauds, I coach. He is genuinely glad that she is here and this makes me proud; I think perhaps he really appreciates how hard his mother strives to bring a semblance of normalcy into both his life and mine, when we all three know that she doesn't really have any desire to sit on uncomfortable plastic chairs. Her uncomplaining presence gives P.J. implicit permission to act as if everything is all right.

In return, he ignores the fact that she remains bundled up inside a loose-fitting sweatsuit with a stocking cap pulled down to just above her eyes. She is also wearing a surgical mask to protect her from strangers' germs. In the not-too-recent *normal* past, P.J. made it no secret that he was embarrassed to be seen with us on a good day. Now he's just happy that she's able to be with us, regardless of how she looks. This is a quantum leap in maturity.

More and more often, I notice P.J. teetering between boyhood and man-hood, and there are days when manhood wins. Today is one of those sweet days when he is older rather than younger, selfless rather than selfish. He takes his time, slows his approach. He bowls for his mother. He bowls a 212.

The drive home is abuzz with much good humor. As soon as we're inside, P.J. calls first Brook, and then Summer, to share his highest-ever score. I hear him excitedly rattling off his statistics and other teen-life events. It is obvious that P.J. loves both girls. He hands the phone to his mother, who begins each conversation with loud kisses into the receiver.

This is a very loved and loving family I have joined.

Tomorrow, if Jody doesn't feel up to it, perhaps P.J. and I might go bowling by ourselves. If she has the strength to watch again, or perhaps even to roll a ball or two, so much the better! I'd just like two days in a row like this one.

Tuesday, October 24
KEVIN:

A very small, frail woman tucked in a wheelchair is pushed into the airport arrival area. I barely recognize Joyce. Is this the vital woman I played golf with just a year ago? Unlike Jody, she has lost a lot of weight, at least 40 pounds. I am extra gentle with my welcoming hug, fearful of injuring her by touch alone. She and Jody seem equally joyful to lay eyes on one another, a good beginning. They lower their surgical masks for a quick kiss.

We quickly get Joyce settled into the guest bedroom, a short hallway from our own. We will hear her if she gets sick in the night, as is her worry. Still, my wife and her mother have been chatting away since the airport, neither show-ing the usual signs of exhaustion. I linger in the dining room though it is obvious that they are content alone, and so I announce intentions to watch TV in the family room. Before I go, Joyce tells me that she needs a daily injection in her stomach. Her son does it for her in Denver, and although she says she is willing to administer it to herself, her hopeful glance says she really doesn't want to. I offer to do it and she accepts without hesitation. I go downstairs to the couch, not thrilled to be doing such a personal thing for my mother-in-law.

Before she goes to bed, Joyce asks about the shot. To be honest, it is no big deal, a subcutaneous injection delivered underhand. The only tricky part is drawing the medication into the syringe. It is slow going until I remember to put the same amount of air into the vial as liquid I wish to draw out. Her stomach is bruised from past shots and I'm surprised to find that I'm genuinely happy to be able to ease her mind about the shots. I can't help but feel sorry for her.

Jody seems better. She is trying to be the primary caretaker for her mom and this has somewhat energized her. Joyce is not faring as well by any means. I think this will be her last visit.

I think that she thinks so, too.

Friday, October 27
JODY:

Brother Bob's only request this year is to go deer hunting in his beloved mountains, and so we made arrangements to assume Mom's care. She arrived looking like a ghost. Have I not noticed before how her back is bent? She's only 66, but she looks to be 80 with her patchy snow-white hair and bruised skin.

However, I don't dwell on her downward spiral at this moment, when I am preoccupied with thoughts of my neighbor. Bill Ferguson likes to dress in a kilt and play the bagpipes and sometimes he stands in the garage and I get the full effect. Sometimes he plays in his living room with the windows open. I know his name because he introduced himself the day we moved in, but we never really got beyond that so I don't know his wife's name, a pleasant woman in her 50s who waves in her comings and goings. And honestly, what I knew about Bill was scarcely more than that... before yesterday.

Mom and I had just returned from the clinic and she went upstairs to nap. I took off my cap and shoes (a hot flash makes me want to be cooler) and without thinking, threw a leash on the dog and walked Foley in the front yard. Across the street, Bill started to approach us, then paused. I realized I probably looked like a bald lunatic with no shoes and – since I was dressed in jeans and a comfortable shirt of Kevin's — he probably had no idea who I was. I waved encouragement to approach.

He slowly crossed the street. When we came face to face, he announced, "I had chemo yesterday. I have lung cancer. I get treatments every week and I just finished my fourth one."

I must have looked as stunned as I felt. "I still have my hair," he added quickly, following my eyes to his lush white beard and crop of thick white hair. "I had a mass in my lungs and tumors alongside. I was in the hospital for five days and they punctured my lung accidentally during the biopsy. Now I'm getting chemo. I left my job and I don't think I'll ever be able to go back."

"Did you smoke?" Immediately, I regretted asking such a dumb question. What difference did it make?

"No," he said. "But I did the pipes." A weak joke, but I smiled. "I don't ask my doctor the hard questions," he added. "I don't think I'm ready to know."

But Bill was ready for a few books on increasing survival chances and the phone number of my friend Marty, who made the 2% survival odds with small cell lung cancer. As Bill left, he turned to add, "Well, I'm home all day now if you need anything."

I think I'm beyond the shock of diagnosis and treatment and I've gotten my mind around the enormity of my prognosis. Or I could be kidding myself about my own mental toughness.

Ironically, Bill's trip made me glad I occasionally walk the dog without a hat. Otherwise I doubt very much that my neighbor would have recognized our shared kinship and trusted himself to approach a stranger with that startling statement: "I have cancer."

Dr. Susan Love, guru breast cancer oncologist, wrote that empirical studies with double-blind experiments at major cancer centers indicate that regardless whether they are personally religious or not, prayed-for people fare better with their treatment than people who go it alone. Prayer is powerful, even when one isn't aware anyone is praying for them. I'm going to add a prayer for a proud Scotsman with a love of the pipes and a dread of his illness.

I'm sorry for the quiet that has muffled the neighborhood lately. Bill's treatment has left him breathless at a time when my Irish soul would most appreciate hearing *Danny Boy* as it was meant to be piped.

CHAPTER 6: November

Mom reflects on past • Actively seeking *The Lesson* • The stash of pills • Another lump! • Florida family vacation • Belly drumming • Cancer *sisterhood?* • Insurance game • This new chemo named Taxol

Friday, November 3

JODY:

Lately I'm fixated on the idea that I have Lessons (with a capital L) to learn and that is why I was put on this earth. Perhaps the Lesson is Humility. Perhaps Patience. I don't know WHAT the Lessons are, only that I'm supposed to be learning them, so I keep my eyes open for opportunities. It is an exhausting process … having embraced the idea of reform, I've noticed a lot of potential areas to work with.

This week I have listened to Mother's Life According to Mother. Some of it I didn't know. My recollection of much of our shared history is different than hers and I almost tell her so, but I'm mindful that this is her story, not mine. My Lesson is to not edit, but to let her tell it her way. I bear some responsibility for the telling, since I prompted the unhappy monologue with a few key questions about her childhood, something I had instinctively known to avoid in the past. I thought I might weave together family stories and pictures in a book and present it to her for Christmas. But my mother isn't sharing the type of story that others might want to read. Her stories are fragments of pain rather than smooth paragraphs of complete events or happy holidays. She gives me bits and pieces and then becomes quiet and withdrawn. I recognize her reluctance to talk for what it is — it is how I deal with Kevin's forays into my own personal history.

We sit at the kitchen table. She takes a checkbook out of her purse, turns it over, and draws on the cardstock backing. I pull closer, curious in spite of myself. "This is a rough blueprint of my house when I was a little girl," she explains. It was a big house where she lived with her mother, grandpa, and two brothers. She points to a little box on the diagram. "This was where the coal stove was, in the warm-up room that heated the house. There was nothing else in it." She draws an "X" behind the coal stove. "I tried to kill myself sitting right here when I was 13," she says. She skirts my gaze, finished with that story.

Another day, she is in a St. Marys Hospital bed. We're in a mass blood transfusion area divided into tiny cubicles for privacy, though a large woman across the way repeatedly graces us with shots of her bare ass. The poor lady crawls in and out of her tiny gurney bed, always exiting in a most unusual manner that leaves her backside totally exposed. I am alternately repulsed and mesmerized. (Maybe there's a Lesson here about charitable thoughts.)

Admittedly, I'm not feeling very charitable about anything. I have spent the day sitting on a hard plastic chair by Mother's bedside, decidedly uncomfortable in the tight quarters. My chest hurts. My back aches from sitting in the same position, but there isn't space to move around. I had the forethought to bring a Christmas needlework project to finish, though when I put it down, Mama gets quiet. When I begin to stitch, she starts talking. It is becoming annoying, this game that she won't confess to playing.

Mother describes herself using colors. She is *a blue* with *a hint of gold* and *a little orange*. She learned this in a half-day seminar just before becoming ill. I am tired. I have no idea what she's talking about. We are both blue, I think, dressed alike in our matching denim shirts and jeans and even denim ball caps. Hers has *Rocky Mountain Cancer Center* stitched across the crown. Mine proclaims *Cancer Sucks*.

"You are not blue," she informs me. Her tone has taken a superior air: blue must be good to be. "Blue people are fastidious about where they live and like things tidy and neat."

I want to tell her that my house was tidy and neat before I had cancer, and to remind her that I have a dog and two cats and an adolescent son adding to the current clutter, while she lives with my neat-nut bachelor brother. But I hold my tongue. The truth is that a clean house is about the furthest concern from my mind. She is right, I am not *blue* about my house. Still, I say, "The last thing you and I need to worry about right now is dust bunnies."

"That's one way to look at it," she grouses.

It would be better if mother's life story didn't overlap the edges of my own life story. Or if only one of us was thinking about it. But we both are privately reflecting on Lessons learned or not learned, trying to figure out where to shore up, where to let go. I bet aloud that we are the only mother-daughter team diagnosed with cancer on the same day. We are unique. Our story is weird. The oncology nurse agrees; she says she's never encountered it before. We could be on Oprah. Or Jerry Springer. My mother beams as if this was a great accomplishment.

We are lying on facing couches in the living room. Despite all the books available to her in our home library, Mother has chosen to review my medical records as a backdrop while again reminiscing about people who hurt her feelings or made her do things she didn't want to do. She is fascinated with the fact that I chart my blood levels and track all the clinic visits and medications. "You were a little down here," she says, showing me the bar chart I created. "You should rest more."

"I'm trying to do that right now."

"I bet if you checked what you were doing on the day your levels were down, you'd see you were doing too much. You've got to slow down, Sissy. And certainly you don't have to go to the bowling alley every Saturday – PJ is old enough to go by himself. He has to understand that you have cancer. And why do you still go to Chicago to see Summer? Can't she come here instead of you having to go there? She's pregnant, for chrissake, not sick. You baby these kids way too much. Always have, but now you've got to stop it for your own sake."

She has hit a nerve, and the emotional reaction leaves me soaking wet as a sudden flash of heat radiates up my neck and into my face. I have to escape the hot cocoon of my leather couch. I get up but quickly kneel beside her sofa. My face must be a deep red; her eyes widen and she burrows deeper into the cushions, uncertain what is coming. She has no reason to fear I'll hit her, but even she must know she's gone too far. I surprise her by gently taking her hand. "Listen to me, Mama," I say, "You and I need to remember that we aren't sick, we're in treatment. There has to be a difference or treatment will become a self-limiting condition. And it's just silly to imply that loving my kids is wearing me down because you know I feel better when I'm with them, just like you said you're feeling better because you're with me. Besides, Summer and PJ need to believe I'm someone strong enough to beat this – what message would I send if I gave up my usual activities? You know I'm right not to change to accom-modate cancer. The blood levels show the effect of chemotherapy; they aren't a reflection of self neglect or overdoing anything – especially lov-ing the kids."

"Thank you, Jesse Jackson, for that inspiring sermon." She adds a theatrical mighty sigh though only mildly offended. She dismisses her cattiness by saying she doesn't mean it as a criticism; she's just worried about me. Besides, the only complaint she has ever really raised with regard to me is that I have no common sense when it comes to men. Of course, she loves Kevin, but…

I bite my tongue and return to my own couch. Look for the Lesson! So I do not argue aloud that her taste in men has proven to have an astonishingly strong aftertaste of abusive alcoholic. But once I start thinking that way, I'm on a runaway negative horse of my own and I remember, flying down this familiar path on this sorry nag, every stinker she has ever dragged home.

One Thanksgiving long ago, my last stepfather regaled my young children with a horror story of throwing kittens into stop signs while driving 65 miles an hour – a memory of a fun time shared with boyhood buddies. The kids cried all through dinner despite my false assurances that their grandfather was…teasing. Wayne then forced drinks on my easily intimidated brother until Bob became drunk enough to pee his pants. Then Wayne made fun of him in front of the rest of the family.

Wayne was also known to give Mom a shiner on occasion, yet he remained her knight in shining armor. My brothers and I could see what she could not – that he was addicted to the thrill of getting one over on somebody. Everything was a con game, everyone a potential sucker. He was a loudly self-anointed family man and also a gambler who drank too much and a thief who forged my mother's name to withdraw her retirement fund – which he quickly lost by day trading. He then bequeathed his life insurance benefits to a daughter by a prior marriage, triggering a family feud of immense magnitude when he left my mother penniless following his death last year. My mother was so incensed at his beyond-the-grave betrayal that she publicly threatened to throw acid on my stepsister's face, forcing me to intervene with the very real threat of locking her up in a mental institution and throwing away the key. I imagined Wayne laughing in hell. I cried with a broken heart at his funeral but I refuse to visit his gravesite. I believe I am somewhat *conflicted* about my own tolerance for his hurtful antics.

"You really don't want to discuss our menfolk," I warn, wondering why either of us ever loved Wayne, the man I called *Dad* even after I knew his true character. Was there a Lesson there as well?

I'm totally caught up with this Lesson thing, to the point of editing my thoughts and making myself take back the *bad ones*. It's become compulsive, this desire to be in truer alignment with my highest potential.

I have had cruel thoughts during my lifetime and I am sorry for every single one of them. I have Lessons to learn about humility. My mother's visit has brought that home in a big way, as I listen to her own review of events in her life.

In many ways, my childhood eerily replicated Mother's. She reproduced what she knew of family — how it should be, how kids should be reared, steered and disciplined. In fact, she was still a girl herself when she ran away from home with a baby (me) at 18. She's had struggles and feuds and out-and-out fights, each one remembered aloud this week; each one dredging up my own memories, and I can honestly say that most of them were better left packed away.

Mama and I both were raised in houses without running water, with out-house toilets by the back alley and with wells stained with typhoid. She was briefly married to Bob's dad and when I was two, we moved to a run-down farm where Bob Sr., only 19 himself, worked bringing in the crops for the owner. Bobby was nitrogen poisoned from the well water, run over by the landlord's car, and has lingering medical problems from eating lead-based paint chips. Mom and Bob Sr. divorced and we moved to a little shack in town, but little changed. Bobby and I stole pears from the neighbor's tree to eat for breakfast; when pears were out of season, we went to school hungry.

When I was five years old, a 16-year old babysitter became mightily frustrated when my mother forgot to come home one Friday night. All the next day Mary Jane beat and tortured three-year-old Bobby and me, leaving us bruised, cut, swollen, and burned. The mentally-ill girl was long gone by the time Mom resurfaced, but Mama took one look at us and tore out of the house saying she was going to kill the bitch, which terrified me more than the ordeal I'd just gone through. When the hunt proved fruitless, Mom came to her senses long enough to summon our pastor for help. She was afraid that if she took us to the hospital, she'd lose her kids to the county foster system.

The kind pastor arranged for a doctor to do a home visit, and he also arranged a six-month placement for Bobby and me with another parishioner. Bessie Lou Jackson agreed to take us into her home in return for church assistance with her groceries. It was unorthodox, placing white children with a black woman and her six children in 1957, but her kindness was all that stood between Bobby and me being placed in an orphanage while our mother got her life straightened out.

I was seven when Mama married an older next door neighbor. Living with his abusive tirades was no picnic, either, though he legally adopted me and provided for me until I was old enough to set out on my own. Likewise, mama's financial situation rose from dirt poor to lower middle class and she would stay married to Lawson until their son Kurt was 16, at which time she divorced, dated a string of losers, moved to Denver, and met Wayne.

During her lighter moments these past few days, I've tried to remind Mom that she's had impressive successes and reasons to be amazed and grateful. Mama has worked her way up from squat, taken college courses, and risen to professional positions and salaries once beyond her reach, abilities, or even her dreams. She's done it all herself, without anyone's earthly help, and yes, it took damn hard work, but she's successful! She has a six-bedroom house with three bathrooms and ample food hoarded against any emergency. She's safe… aside from having cancer, of course. But so what if she does have cancer? She's lived long enough to experience the birth of four wonderful grandchildren and she's held each in her lap and watched them grow. However, those aren't the stories she's interested in telling (or hearing) now.

The experience of listening to her life's darkest moments replayed has convinced me not to put together a family story. My children are free to forget or even to not know. I don't want to decide what color they are… or aren't. And I don't want to revisit the scenery of my childhood again through anyone's eyes, especially theirs. But I will be here to listen if Mother chooses to talk because, as I said, it's her story told her way. That's my Lesson for the week.

Monday, November 6
JODY:

Mom is refusing to submit to another blood transfusion, although her clinical evaluation indicates that she should have at least one and possibly two units of blood. Nurse Pam lobbies a little harder, saying she can schedule it within the hour at St. Marys.

"Maybe you didn't understand my phraseology," my mother says to the oncology nurse. "I'm not spending my last day with my daughter in another damn hospital bed." She winks at me. "I'm not sick. And we have plans to go to a bookstore and to have a nice restaurant lunch like normal people. I'll get the transfusion back in Denver in a couple days."

Pam's deep frown conveys her disapproval and concern but I feel good about Mom's decision. I understand her willful disobedience and seeming disregard for her own well-being because this nut didn't fall far from the tree. I have a secret stash of pills… more than enough to kill myself. I've squirreled them away, though occasionally I pull out the prescription bottle and pour the contents onto a clean washcloth. Last count I had 97, surely enough to overcome whatever resistance my brain stem could muster. I liken having my stash to having a window to the Great Beyond. The pills offer at least the possibility of escape and that is helping to ease my depression.

Like I said: The nut doesn't fall far from the tree.

Tuesday, November 7
JODY:

I put Mother on the plane today, a little woman hunched over in her wheelchair, a white surgical mask tied across her face. She looked so vulnerable that it broke my heart. "Please take good care of her," I asked of the boarding stewardess. Then I went home and laid myself down on the couch and puzzled over the fact that the pain I've been feeling in the good (only) breast is changing from a general sensitivity and diffuse soreness. In this past week, it has become a localized, focused ache. I am scared. I feel as if the cancer is back in a new host.

I touch it with my fingers, a large mass that wasn't there last week. It feels warmer than the rest of the tissue. It feels too large, too familiar, too deadly. I want to ignore it but it throbs like a toothache. Tomorrow I will call a nurse. *Look, I've been down this road before and my doctor told me to wait until he could face up to the fact that I had cancer. Test the hell out of it and tell me what it is, please. And please do that NOW.*

That's my fantasy of standing up for myself, but more likely the nurse will whisper with Mike and within minutes calm my anxiety over the phone and tell me that I'm on chemo, remember? Chemo kills cancer. It couldn't possibly BE cancer. Maybe the dog jumped on me too hard or I hurt myself and don't remember. But I cry most of the night, first in secret and then finally I take my angst to Kevin. He says all the right words to comfort my fears... until he feels the lump himself.

"Jesus," he whispers. "Don't go without me to see the doctor this time. I mean it."

KEVIN:

There's another lump!

How can this be happening? Jody has been begging the doctor to remove her other breast and now we find an all-too-familiar lump! Is the medical community so arrogant — does it hold us mere mortals in such contempt — that it refuses to consider our requests or ideas? This is not good, not good at all. I can't lose her, don't they understand? The anger and frustration that has been slowly building is now starting to boil.

This better not be cancer!

Wednesday, November 8
JODY:

I call the clinic and am told to have it checked TODAY. Mike Frontiera is off duty until tomorrow, but they'll fit me into another doctor's schedule. "With inflammatory cancer, time counts," the nurse said. *No kidding, Sherlock.* (I didn't mean that in a sarcastic way, so I don't have to take the thought back.) I call Kevin; if it's to be bad news, they won't take me by surprise and turn me loose alone. Kevin will drive the basket case home.

Dr. Prendergast is openly concerned about the size of what appears to be a tumor. He excuses himself, promising to return in a few minutes. Mike Frontiera shocks me when he waltzes into the tiny examination room five minutes later. He whispers, "I'm not here" and I nod. *Things must be very serious indeed*, I think, *to have Mike paged on his day off.*

"I have to see this for myself, what is happening," he tells me. So I strip again and he prods the very same spot, which feels like a drill hitting an exposed nerve in my breast. Within moments, Mike orders more tests. My surgeon will interpret the results and determine what his role is to be.

"I'm very concerned," Mike confesses, touching my hand.

I can't talk.

"I don't think it is a cyst or hematoma," he adds. "It feels like exactly what you fear: a smooth, round tumor. But we can't be sure until we see the tests."

I go to the water fountain and down two Valiums. Kevin volunteers to call Bill to say I won't be back this afternoon. We wait for appointments to be made. The nurse calls from the phone in our room: "But we have to get her in right away," she says. "We *don't have time* to wait until next week. We want her to see the surgeon this week too, if at all possible."

It is not. Tests Friday, surgeon Monday. The surgeon is on vacation. Fuck, fuck, fuck! (And NO, I will NOT take that thought back!] We consider getting another surgeon but... I want the one I trust. The Valium begins to work. Mike gives me a new prescription for pain pills which I'll save for later, after I make calls to Mom and Summer and Brook, after I spend a little time with PJ, after I try to figure out if I can make it to Florida for our conference/family vacation next Tuesday. Will my surgeon let me postpone the other mastectomy? Will the tumor stop growing for one damn second?

What am I up against here?

Thursday, November 9
JODY:

The pain pills produced waves of nausea all night. Every time I turned over from a hot flash, I almost threw up. My tolerance for narcotics appears to be shot. This is confirmed this morning when I vomit for two hours. I email the staff that maybe I will be in later. I tell Bill what is going on, tell him I feel like a little girl on the scariest ride at the carnival and I can't make the evil carny dude let me off. Despite lots of cool water and soda crackers, I throw up two more hours, purging my system of any pain medication and making my throat sore in the process. Finally I can take some Lorazapam, prescribed for nausea as well as anxiety. It melts under my tongue. I call Bill asking for a ride to work. I can't drive while on narcotics. I call back moments later saying I've reconsidered. I had better sleep it off.

I sleep on the couch fitfully. Foley kisses my face, wanting to be taken out. I get his leash and walk him barefoot, a quick trip on the frozen snow. I mistake brown rice for white, cook it, smell it – more nausea. Finally I manage to keep down a small bowl of dry Cheerios. By noon, I drive to the office. I don't want to stay home and dwell on being sick, yet there are cancer-related things at work to face as well. I tell Carrie, the company Conference Coordinator, that I might not be going to Florida, though I dearly wanted to pair a business trip with a family opportunity to see Brook. Carrie nods; she's already formulated a Plan B to cover my assigned tasks *just in case.*

I call Summer and then Brook, trying to gently warn her that we might not see her after all. Although I struggle not to, I burst into tears. She cries too, telling me not to cry and we both cry together. She's homesick but can't leave the base. She feels guilty she hasn't seen me since the diagnosis. I can't comfort her. This is so unfair!

The despair and anxiety are no better controlled at home. I'm at a loss what to do, how to make the time go by more quickly. Then Phyllis calls and asks if there is anything that she can do to help. I tell my friend, "I have this box that I've been trying to mail to Brook since before Halloween with stale brownies and things she really wants. I just can't do it, can't get it done. I don't know why. But I want them in the mail in case we can't see her." And I start to cry again. Phyllis swoops in like an angel and takes the box with her; she'll buy fresh brownies, repackage and mail it.

Kevin eventually comes home but we don't say very much, nor does PJ, who earlier was very mature about the prospect of losing his vacation. I offered to stay behind with friends and send them on to Florida, but PJ assured me that he didn't want to go if I wasn't going. Which Kevin seconded. We all go or we all stay home. Kevin busies himself with making dinner. Mashed potatoes. I've been asking for them every night, or noodles with butter. But tonight he adds fried chicken and corn bread. I eat a lot, not because I'm hungry but because it fills time and my hollow stomach.

Now it's late enough that I can feel guilt-free opting for two Valium and bed. Not talking about it is as hard as talking about it, but if we talked about it, we'd have to talk about it. I wonder how much longer two Valium will suffice and think that I should refill the prescription before I need to. I may want to squirrel more away in case the tests are positive.

Friday, November 10
JODY:

Kevin and I go together to clinic. My lumpy breast is throbbing, but a technician shows no mercy and flattens it between clear plates until I fear it will burst.

"Here's the tumor," the tech points out, showing us a huge area that we thought was actually the breast. We need to redo the tests. Then we're sent to ultrasound for a look at it from inside out. The new tech is careful what she says, but then slips: "There are actually three," she says. "Here's a cyst hiding between the other two."

"What did you just say?"

"I have to go see what the radiologist will let me say," she hedges. A few moments later she returns, smiling. "The masses appear to be cysts that your surgeon can drain with a needle on Monday. They don't appear to be a tumor when we go inside them."

I can barely stand to button my blouse. Kevin has an amazed look on his face. "It isn't cancer," I whisper. "We're still okay with the chemo."

Kevin doesn't know what to say, really, and I'm unsteady from the Valium and relief. Suddenly euphoria washes over me like a warm waterfall. "Take me to work!" I announce gaily.

Kevin rebounds more slowly; he still has a dazed look on his face. "I.... I'll get some things to fix that leak under the floor and stop the knocking in the furnace," he finally says.

Good plan. I go to work and give Bill the good news and then take a half-hour nap in the conference room. Still, the drugs are with me. I'm high on narcotics, I'm high on life. We're going to Florida instead of surgery! My greatest heartbreak will be boarding Foley. I can live with that! I still have a chance to live the five years I've been bargaining for with God. And thank heavens, I'm not a medical freak, growing cancer while on chemo!

KEVIN:

Whew! I am so relieved that I dare not show any emotion, lest I jinx the determination that this is not cancer. Still, I would prefer that the 'cysts' be drained TODAY to prove the radiologist's verdict. Jody is so happy and animated on the ride to work. She is excited that the trip to Orlando is still on and makes plans aloud for last-minute activities.

Suddenly her face becomes somber. In a quiet voice, she states with great resolve that she wants the remaining breast removed. I promise that when we see Mike again, we will discuss it, though privately I wonder if this truly is the best course of action. I am painfully aware of the alternate numbness and feelings of revulsion elicited by any contact with her mastectomy site. I have not touched it yet, as I don't think she wants me to. If the other breast is removed, will the surgery cause the same sensations? What would that mean to our sex life, when the urgings return for us? What long-term impact would removing both breasts have? These questions are not easily asked or easily answered, but I'd like them at least considered before the deed is done.

I guess this is one more situation for which I cannot properly prepare. One more in a long series. I expend far more energy reacting to situations than planning for Jody's care. No matter how much I plan for it, the worst-case scenario can get worse. I need to be able to steer this roller coaster we are on but I can only hang on and try very hard to keep us both in the car. Sometimes I find Jody with her hands in the air and not holding on at all, so I hold her with both hands and brace with my knees. At these times I am most afraid that I can't ease her worry, her pain, her suffering. What if my faith is not strong enough? If she doesn't make it, will it be because I didn't make the right decision at the right time for whatever reason, selfish or not?

I hate roller coasters.

Tuesday, November 14
Disney @ Coronado Springs, Florida
JODY:

I can't believe that Kevin, PJ and I are really here and that I will soon be able to see Brook and her new boyfriend and his son! I really have to pinch myself to believe we pulled it off.

My surgeon, of course, remains my hero. He was his typical no-nonsense self ("No need to numb first, right? You just want this over with.") He drew many, many cc's of beautiful, clear liquid out of my right breast. "No problem," he said. "Nobody knows why these develop or why so quickly sometimes, but this definitely isn't cancer." His treatment was far from painless, but a sore boob is a small price to pay.

While I have great reason to celebrate, I'm not exactly carefree. I have always traveled with the conference division and I really want to help with registration and workshops, but I'm not confident about putting myself on public display, bald with a face full of chemo acne. But I'm feeling secure in the hotel room now and we're calling Brook to come right over. Patrick Air Force Base isn't so far away, and this will be the first time I've held my daughter in my arms since the diagnosis. I may never let go! We could go to the Boardwalk for dinner and we're planning a boat ride for her and *her boys*.

PJ is ready to run off to the pool but promises he'll be back before Brook arrives. He's a bundle of activity. This trip meant so much to him! I am so very, very thankful for this opportunity to spend some quality time with him.

"We'll be there in about an hour," Brook promises over the phone.

Kevin comes over to the bed and takes me in his arms. "I can't believe it," I say over the lump in my throat. "We're really here. Brook is really coming. Summer's pregnant! I don't have a new occurrence of cancer! Good things are really starting to happen to us again."

Thursday, November 16
KEVIN:

Although she says she's feeling better, it is obvious that Jody's last whacking (as she calls chemotherapy) is still having a pronounced effect. She's worked every shift she's been assigned at the conference, but she is winded climbing half a flight of stairs. When she thinks no one notices, she sits with her head in her hands, trembling with exhaustion. I notice. I notice everything about her. I am ever watchful because that is my role now and I've taken it to heart.

While not as fatigued as she is, I'm nonetheless tired, too. I could use some downtime and frankly would be happy just to lounge around the pool or even our hotel room. However P.J. has decided that we are to be joined at the hip. He is reverting to his annoying-teenager-in-search-of-a-target persona and I'm convenient, since he knows I am trying to appease his mother and keep her centered. It gives him an edge that he's quick to take advantage of when there is nowhere for me to escape to.

He accidentally bumps into me repeatedly. One taunt follows another until he gets me so riled up that I threaten to withhold his spending money, the only leverage I have. Even then, he manages a smart-ass final comment.

Although we're staying on Disney property, it came as no surprise to me when P.J. stated his intention to visit Universal Studios, a non-Disney venue, as often as possible. I bought a packet of tickets to Disney shortly after we booked the trip, not that P.J. considers a family budget to be his concern. We've compromised so far, but only because a co-worker's spouse accompanied him to Universal all day yesterday. By that time, it was worth the additional admission price for some respite.

Today P.J. returned to Universal and I made plans to enjoy a leisurely, solitary Disney day before Jody invited the son of Brook's enlisted boyfriend to accompany me. They now live together on base as a family, a decision made quickly after the couple met. I warned Brook that nothing is quite so desperate as military love, with the threat of separation always there to fuel the passion, but any advice to slow down has fallen on deaf ears. As have my comments to my wife about this *sudden family* that she has adopted without pause. ("You're a fine one to talk about sudden love," she noted, and the point was well taken.)

Jody has been talking to the seven-year old on the telephone weekly over the past couple of months since Brook and his father began dating. He calls her *Grandma* and she's very happy referring to herself that way, too. It worries me how quickly she gives away her heart. This young lad may never be her grandson; his father hasn't married Brook and the couple may never marry. We are not his grandparents. Maybe Jody doesn't believe that she will live long enough to ever hold a true grandchild and she wants the experience, even borrowed. But this is too fast. I should talk to her about this again, say something that will get through to her. If Brook and the young man separate, the child will feel like he's lost a grandmother, too, after this visit. But what can I say that won't upset her?

For his part, the boy is lapping up the attention. His birthday is today, and Jody has bought him several gifts, hidden in a drawer. Yesterday she suggested that he spend the night with us in our hotel room. She told Brook, who had to return to base to work a night shift, to come back for him late this afternoon, when we might all have a little birthday party together. Meanwhile I could play grandpa and take him to Disney today while she works, because he's never been to the theme park. Wouldn't that be fun?

Actually, I thought it might.

He gets to pick and he chooses EPCOT. However, once there he is afraid to go on even the tamest of rides. We barely walk through one of the amusements before he announces that he's ready to go back to the hotel to swim. EPCOT was not inexpensive to enter, but I take him back anyway. Once in the pool, he clings to the side wall or to me. I feel sorry that he has so many phobias and issues. I also feel sad for Brook, though I muse that we have more in common now than ever before as we both struggle with our assigned parenting roles.

P.J., however, does something surprising and even endearing after returning from Universal. He plays with the boy without being asked and without insisting on a bribe of extra spending money. I am relieved of duty and P.J. takes over with uncharacteristic good humor. P.J. is great with the child. I am astonished as I watch him with a little boy who now appears to be anything but fragile. The child is positively gleeful as he twirls in a hyperactive frenzy, practicing judo kicks and running up from behind P.J. to tackle him.

At home, P.J. often displays this same gentleness when he plays with Foley. In turn, the dog is nearly as devoted to P.J. as he is to Jody, which says a lot. I feel a pang of regret that it is so seldom lately that I recognize these traits in my stepson. Has the stress of the situation blinded me to his positive attributes as much as I believe his mother is now blind to his insensitive side? Has his own grief and worry fueled his need to test me and try my patience? Does it give him some sense of comfort to see that no matter how hard he pushes, I stay? Is this what he needs to be reassured of on an almost daily basis? Why must I so often respond with anger? It almost seems as if we are both spoiling for a fight, although neither of us will own up to such desires because neither of us is the real target for all of this frustration. It is the cancer we are angry with.

Now, watching P.J. sidestep our young visitor's latest charge, I can't help but admire his patience. At this moment, he certainly has more than I.

Jody finishes work and Brook returns to the hotel. There is a commotion of activity including dinner in a Disney restaurant, complete with cake. And presents. Lots of hugs from Grandma. Lots and lots of pictures snapped. And then it's time to bundle up the gifts. How did they all fit in the drawer? Does anyone want the extra cake? Where is the boy's shoe? *Has anyone seen his other shoe?* P.J. finds it and I breathe a sigh of relief. I am really tired. I need to go to bed. But first, Brook wants us to come to the parking lot and see the hot car she is driving. It's a red Trans Am with personalized plates that announce that she is a Chicago Cubs' fan. Cool. I remember when I have bought sports cars, though those days are long past. Then I realize that this is the car that Jody and I bought for her. I catch a glimpse of the expression on Jody's face now as she watches Brook touch it. It was a good buy.

It is nearly 11:00 p.m. and Jody will have to get up at 6:30 a.m. to have enough time to dress, apply her makeup, and report for her shift at 7:30. I need to get her into bed. P.J. sprints off ahead of us to get a soda from a vending machine; we walk back toward the hotel room hand in hand, then arm in arm as *Grandma* needs more and more assistance. Jody is developing a pronounced limp when overly tired, and now is listing pretty severely to the left. I slow our steps. A noise above my head catches my attention; P.J. is whistling at us from his vantage point up the three flights we have yet to climb.

He slips his key in the door and brandishes an offhand wave over his shoulder before the door shuts behind him.

We are just approaching the stairs, which Jody would likely tumble down without assistance. Her balance becomes very precarious when she outpaces her energy. I make the decision to walk her down a longer aisle, seemingly away from the room, but one that will lead us to a corner elevator. I notice and memorize such things lately. She yields without comment, understanding.

Finally we settle into bed, say the last goodnight, turn off the last light. My relief is almost palpable. Then a voice carries from the next bed: "We're going to Universal tomorrow instead of to baby Disney, right?"

"P.J., knock it off," his mother mumbles.

I could really use a vacation.

Monday, November 20
JODY:

Having cancer has changed me. My relationships with friends have changed and certainly things are different in our family. We've done some things that, honestly speaking, we might not have without the cancer push.

Just yesterday, while PJ was over at Jake's house telling his friend all about his wonderful vacation, Kevin and I basked in the pleasure of a rare afternoon alone. After a cuddly nap, we invented a new coffeehouse act featuring a bald poet dressed in a white robe playing bongos on her husband's tummy. Kevin let me practice for half an hour before pulling his red belly out of the act. It was okay, though, as I had already finished every line of Muriel Rukeyser that I knew and I even snuck in a little Sylvia Plath: *You do not do. {Drum, drum, drum} You do not do anymore. {Drum} Black shoe in which I have lived like a foot for a year. {Drum, drum} Thirty years, if you want to know the truth {drum, drum, drum}.* The cadence was groovy, man.

Kevin and I have created unorthodox ways of loving each other since treatment started because I have no authentic interest in sex. In fact, I find the entire enterprise somewhat repulsive. And having sex takes so much energy! In past relationships, I have faked an interest when I didn't feel up to making love, but now I'm more honest about being turned off or afraid. Despite Mike's reassurances, for example, I fear that since my cancer is fed by estrogen, having sex might jeopardize the treatment. I'm also less likely to pretend things don't hurt when they do and so I say it does *not* feel good to be touched *there.*

I suspect that my attitude is further compromised by a moderate depression. I can't honestly get past the Internet prognosis I found when I

111

first started researching my illness: *Inflammatory breast cancer is an advanced stage tumor due to cancer invading the lymphatics of the skin. Despite improvements in outcome, the five-year survival remains at 35 percent. Inflammatory cancer of the breast has the worst prognosis of all breast cancers.*

My college minor was statistics. The 35% only means that 35% of the women diagnosed with this cancer on such-and-such a date are still alive five years later. It does not mean they are cancer free at that marker and it does not mean they have not had reoccurrences, aren't presently in treatment, or are expected to be alive at seven years, the more truthful mortality marker for breast cancer.

I'm also learning that despite all the hype to the contrary, there is not a true *sisterhood* of women with breast cancer. We may believe we have the inside track on what having cancer is: We've heard the diagnosis, felt the shock, and lived the treatment. But our experience is unique. Our symptoms differ, our regimens differ, our stages differ, our types of breast cancer differ, and our supports are different. We like different comfort foods and have different tolerances for information, assistance, and pain. Some of us can't work; others can't be convinced to stop. Perhaps the cruelest and swiftest sword we have is the ability to invalidate another sister's experience by saying dismissively, "It didn't affect *me* that way." At best, we might listen to others' experiences without adopting them as our own, judging them, or denying them. Ideally, if we don't use painkillers or anti-anxiety drugs on *Days 10-14*, we don't feel superior, but only fortunate that we didn't experience another sister's pain. If I were ever going to preach anything after this experience, this would be that single message.

Oh my gosh! Is this The Lesson I was to learn? (If so, can I stop being schooled and get back to my *real* life?)

I am most curious about my next chemo regimen, which begins this Friday. Mike prefers the relatively new protocol of a one-hour injected dose of Taxol every week for 12 weeks to reduce the side effects. I've read of clinical trials in which it killed outright when not properly monitored. It can be a bugger.

Journalist Katherine Rich's book shares her roller coaster ride of beating cancer, then getting it again and again and again, in bones, lungs, etc. She suffered *ten reoccurrences* and treatment protocols, including the one I most fear having, the high dose chemo bombs followed by a bone marrow transplant. A cyst is the best she hopes for when she feels a lump and I certainly identified with much of her story, even while very cognizant that her story does NOT have to be my story. Still, she had the same weird catheter sewed into her juguler vein and the same reaction: *I was completely unprepared for what felt like a space station embedded in my chest. Each bump made me groan in pain and worry that the thing might come dislodged. It was a few weeks before I lost the stiff Tin Man pose.*

Her first protocol also mirrored my own. She began with Cytoxan and Adriamycin (or "Red Devil," which is the title of her book). We've had similar experiences of chemo fog: *Reality became slippery and once or twice I lost my grip. At a lunch, I became sure that the other diners had hair because they knew how to grow it. I used to, but I'd forgotten the technique. No, that wasn't right, I wasn't trying hard enough. I was lazy or just dim. I concentrated on willing my follicles to bloom. I willed them so hard, my head hurt.*

She also describes Taxol: *For weeks after the injection, you can detect its path as it trails through the body, destroying cells and stamina. Four days later, bone pain. Ten days later, exhaustion.* She speaks of being unable to walk and being completely bedridden for days. Likewise, a coworker of Kevin's warned that her husband had to carry her up and down stairs when she was on it; her hips were in so much pain that she could only manage baby steps. Others report discomfort that is handled by medications ranging from Tylenol to MS Cotin to morphine. I'm more willing at present to limp than to medicate, but we'll see how brave I am after I'm on it.

I hope that I end treatment like the cancer survivors who refer to themselves as *the lucky ones* because they were able to blend the treatment experience into the rest of their lives rather than treat it like an isolated occurrence. My plan to integrate the two now is to drink plenty of water and kiss a dog. To don a white robe and beat a belly drum. To cradle my adult daughter in my lap and to search out some wondrous quality in my son every day. To find countless ways to thank my husband for his undying support.

The monster-riddled journey I am on is not without incredibly beautiful scenery.

Wednesday, November 29
KEVIN:

Jody's cancer diagnosis is affecting my work, although not in the way I expected. Our new division boss is a devoted family man who sees no problem with my taking Thursday afternoons off to take my wife to get whacked. He also understands that I may have to leave abruptly, should an emergency arise.

113

That is not my concern at the moment.

Part of my job is to assist Lori in the negotiations of employee benefit contracts and, of course, our most important negotiation involves choosing a medical insurance carrier. The current insurance representative informed us that our rates will be adjusted upwards by 52%, an untenable jump. However, insurance shopping is no problem; we are soon courted by our current provider's largest competitor. Negotiations proceed along a better path and soon a much lower rate is offered.

Then, two weeks ago, Lori received a call from their rep asking about the medical history of all of our employees and their families, whether insured through my employer or not. Both Lori and I found this strange. I am insured through Jody's employer, as is she. Why should her medical condition be exposed to this new company? If exposed, would it become a pricing factor? A bit annoyed, I advised Lori to only divulge such information for all employees insured through the company, not those who aren't.

"They want everyone," Lori insisted. "I tried the other approach but they said it wasn't enough."

Although exasperated, I know the deadline for employee enrollment is fast approaching and we have to get a contract in place.

"Fine, give them everything," I told her. I filled out a special form but omitted the particulars. Days later, Jody received a letter asking very personal medical questions.

"I don't have this insurance," she fumed. The letter had arrived at a low point, making a bad day worse.

I stormed into the office the next day and handed the form to Lori. "Remind them that I am the employee, not Jody," I said. "Any correspondence in the future should come to me. And also remind them who the decision-maker is in these negotiations. Tell them that they have pissed him off, and warn them that they better not use Jody's condition against us."

They do. Three days ago, a new proposed rate increase arrived showing a significant hike over their first offer. Obviously they realize that I have every legal right to sign Jody up for their insurance coverage. Although I have no plans to do any such thing, my wife's cancer diagnosis is affecting my fellow employees' wallets.

I contacted the representative, who denied that Jody's condition had any impact. I didn't believe him, so yesterday I asked Lori to find out how low they would drop rates if I signed a waiver that neither Jody nor I would request their insurance during the open enrollment period.

The reduction was significant.

Thursday, November 30
JODY:

Bill is being given a lifetime achievement award from the Madison Advertising Federation and Kevin and I will be at the awards dinner this December to see Bill blush, though the date is going to be challenging for me. It is a Monday night and it is already apparent that I don't do well on Mondays on this new chemo.

When I went to get my first injection of Taxol last Friday, I met a woman who had just completed her *106th chemo treatment*. To date, she's had 16 different chemo cocktail combinations. Two years after being diagnosed and treated, she had a re-occurrence, and she has been in treatment now a total of *six years*, four of those bald and seeking some relief of the chemo and radiation symptoms, as well as a glimmer of hope that she would ultimately survive.

She, too, has inflammatory cancer.

"You're the third one!" she lisped when I revealed that it was also my diagnosis. "Dr. Frontiera has three of us; I was the first, and I know the second one. I wondered who the third was, and now I know."

Oh boy, I thought. *I really do get to be in a club of three,* the number of "inflammatories" most oncologists treat in a lifetime. It reminded me of the classic college orientation speech: "Look to your right. Look to the person on your left. One of you won't be here four years from now." So, Mike has us all at once. Is this a blessing for him or a curse? Was he learning anything from her failures that could help me? Would I be a test for a treatment for her? Could I stand being bald for FOUR YEARS instead of 14 more weeks?

In the *Before days* I would have thought the odd woman had a speech impediment, but she'd just had chemo. A couple hours later, I would also be slurring, barely able to walk out and certainly not able to carry on a conversation, as I'd had 500 units of Benedryl to prevent an allergic reaction. The sedative hit me hard. I went home and crashed after treatment. When I awoke, however, I was *different*. For one thing, I didn't have that gross taste of sweet metal in my mouth. And I wasn't nauseated for the first time in months. In fact, I wanted a turkey sandwich and corn and Waldorf salad and pie! (Steroids affect appetite.) I could even drink coffee and Pepsi again!

Saturday, I was the best I'd felt in three months. Not well enough to tackle cleaning my home office or to pay bills, but well enough to make a big family breakfast, take care of lunch sandwiches, and make a huge pot of chili for dinner. Well enough to feel like I had a purpose for getting out of bed.

Sunday I made a roast with all the trimmings. "This Taxol is a piece of cake!" I marveled and then went in search of pie. I even paid bills on Sunday night.

By Monday morning, I couldn't lift my arms over my head. I felt like I not only had the flu, but also arthritis, sprained ankles and wrists. The bones deep inside my ears ached, and continue to. It hurt to sit, to lie, to extend my legs. My knees throbbed. This was supplemented with chills and complete disinterest in food. I could not imagine leaving the couch. I couldn't read, couldn't really think, and basically spent the day trying to figure out if taking the pain pills with the Lorazapam could be done without another episode of nausea. In the end, I decided to stay clear of the pain pills until Kevin got home, and resigned myself to the most uncomfortable afternoon spent to date in treatment.

I watched Nelson Mandela on television, hoping to salvage something to account for my lost day. I didn't answer emails, didn't listen to phone messages, didn't feel connected or even as if I really existed. The pain was real and that was enough to know.

Tuesday, back to work. The site around my port where they inject drugs into my chest has become dark, and the chemo stain has spread across my chest and up my neck, making it look as if I don't own a washcloth or soap. Nothing can change it; it's the pigment referred to as *chemo toxic*. Every week I have more reason to wear a blouse that buttons higher and higher. Pretty soon, it'll be turtlenecks only.

Back to work Wednesday. And Thursday. Budgets to do. Staff to direct. A magazine to proofread and release to the printer. It makes me feel useful. It makes the time pass. Pain flares worst at night. A solitary pain pill won't make me sick. I crash nights and don't do much of anything.

Tomorrow, I start the new chemo cycle all over again.

But the pain now is not unbearable or excruciating, just a constant companion, making me think that this is still a piece of cake in many ways. I'm still having hot flashes, but not crying jags. I've convinced myself that I am cancer free and just have to survive treatment. I have enough visits with other specialists to check the damage done by the oncologist and I'm determined not to miss a sign or lose a chance for full recovery. I am getting further and further away from the influence of the drugs that were poisoning my brain and really posing a serious toxic threat to my sense of hope.

The next side effect of Taxol is fatigue. It should appear very soon, but then be overshadowed by the pain again next Monday. Fatigue is an old friend of mine. I've found that I can hand sew Christmas stockings while lying flat on my back. I won't be rendered useless much longer.

Life goes on, thanks to celebrations like Bill's achievement award, and I intend to be there when they hand out those sticky name tags. *Congratulations again, Bill, and thanks for giving me a reason to celebrate — even if it will be on a Monday.*

CHAPTER *7:* December

Taxol horrors • Holiday stupor • Mom's remission • Taxol crash & Dr. X • Medical wrestling match • Hospital birthday • Toby's story • The Angels: Crystal and Morphine • Friends take over

Wednesday, December 6
<u>KEVIN:</u>

Last year, the house was in full holiday splendor by the day after Thanksgiving. Not only is the house not yet decorated, it is a mess. Typically I tidy up or push back the clutter somewhat or slip P.J. a little something extra to pitch in, but I stopped really cleaning or dusting shortly after Jody went on this new chemo protocol. We all have, really, because she can't stand the roar of the vacuum cleaner, can't abide the god-awful smell of cleaning agents, can't tolerate very much activity around her after she stumbles into the house after work. In response, I've opted to spend most evenings holding her feet in my lap as we watch whatever she wants to see on television.

We watch TV a lot. I'm astonished at the number of shows broadcast *daily* featuring breast cancer. I have watched only a few from start to finish, believing that our reality is not so easily summarized in a one-hour docudrama. I also don't find the material to be particularly helpful. Conversely, my wife has seen them all. I suspect that she's searching out some explanation of her usually cruel side effects of late. If so, she doesn't find any answers today.

We both hate the new drug. We were lead to believe that it might be easier to handle than the Red Devil, but are finding the opposite to be true. It's one more glitch that has affected our ability to plan, to prepare, to cope, and now maybe even to celebrate. It's hard to pretend holiday cheer when what I really feel is fear (how much more can she take?) and anger (I hate this!).

P.J. saunters into the room. Jody looks up and tilts her head expectantly and he immediately comes to her side and lightly kisses her cheek. Foley, ever present with his mistress, is now lying along the full length of Jody's body on the couch, his head on her shoulder. The dog whines for a pat and P.J.

rewards him with a kind word as well. "Do you want me to make you some tea?" he asks his mother.

She is grateful for this gesture. I follow him to the kitchen, where I take him aside and ask how he would like to surprise his mother even more by helping me decorate for the holidays. His eyes light up and I realize that he's missed the traditional trimmings as well. We make a pact that we will put up the Christmas tree together early one morning this weekend while his mother sleeps.

My stepson and I have certainly traveled our deep valleys, our divergent paths. But sometimes we come to an intersecting higher purpose and have a meeting of our better selves. The smallest miracles are the most potent. I feel the first stirrings of holiday reverence, for which I have P.J. to thank.

Thursday, December 7
JODY:

For the first time in my life, words fail me. I want to be uplifting and yet I'm falling on my face. The medical community is poisoning me in ways that I never imagined. But everything is yin and yang, joy and pain, a step backwards into the black and movement forward, toward the light. *Right?*

I'm desperately trying to change my perception of what is happening to make it more endurable. Tuesday, I was ambushed at my desk with a flare-up of new symptoms. Deep earaches and jaw pain were followed by a serious bout of chest pain. The heart is a muscle, and muscle pain is standard for this treatment. By afternoon I was hanging on at work by fingernails that also ached. I tried not to walk more than necessary (shin bones on fire) or sit too long (hip pain). Or move an arm, either one. And who was so cruel as to take a cheese grater and rub it up and down my back? Surely someone did. There is no being blasé about it, since the pain still continues to snipe.

Wednesday I woke up determined to fare better, as if I could just will it. I took the analgesics and steroids. By the time I got to the office, I had to lie down and close my eyes. Two hours later, I became conscious again. Meanwhile, the earache worsened and something odd happened to my feet to make them feel like I was wearing oversized clown shoes. I could barely walk. Soon my fingertips hurt too much to type and my eyes ached and my peripheral vision failed. By 2:30, I threw in the towel and drove home, arriving just moments ahead of a migraine. I slept in the bed until 6:30 p.m., then counted hot flashes to get my mind off the mastectomy incision site, which felt like it was on fire. There would be no more sleep.

Today a friend drove me to work, as my feet are still feeling too weird to drive. Tonight Kevin and I are scheduled to ring bells for the Salvation Army for a couple hours. I have to do something that matters again. I just have to.

Tomorrow I have chemo again. A friend accompanied me last week, another will this week, and then Kevin will go the week after when I also have the doc's review (once every three weeks). The pre-cocktail is providing the best sleep I have all week, so I don't let them cut it back as they suggested after realizing they were *snowing* me. My friends help me home and I sleep until 7 p.m. without dreaming or moving. Then I wake up and we are well into *Day One*. Still, I watch PJ bowl Saturday mornings, so that is something on my meager list of accomplishments. And last week I made it Christmas shopping and got Brook's presents mailed.

I realize that I am low functioning and that I'm mad at my doctor, who continually downplays expected side-effects. Doesn't Mike know that I can deal so much better with the expected than with the unknown? Does he really think that if I expect something, I'll have it – that I'm a hypochondriac? It worries me that either Mike doesn't know what the hell he's doing to me, or my body is over-reacting to a substance that other women can better tolerate.

Kevin's Christmas party is coming up and he typically hosts the event. I remember last year's gala event and how much fun we had. I am thinking we will not be doing these things this year and I feel sorry for Kevin. He deserves so much more, so much better. I have to learn how to better cope, though I am doing everything I possibly can think of. I hung a chorus of angel dolls in my office window and put friends' names on slips of paper and attached them to the halos. It represents my choir, the community I have created of friends and colleagues. Ringing bells will also bring me comfort because I need to turn outward and the Salvation Army is my favorite charity. I do remember my blessings, which include Mom's recent release from the hospital, so that she can return to her home for the holidays. Thank God for the women friends who are accompanying me to the treatments, and for Bill, as always, and his patience when I need to quit early.

Still, I'm fearful of receiving Taxol tomorrow.

Thursday, December 14
JODY:

When everything seems to be going against you, remember that the airplane takes off against the wind, not with it. Supposedly, Henry Ford said that.

This week brought with it a Christmas miracle. The airplane took flight.

Only two weeks ago, Mom was near death in a Denver hospital bed following her chemotherapy. Her counts were not low; they were *non-existent*. NO white blood cells. NO platelets. For five days she remained hospitalized as they pumped in antibiotics for a completely depressed immune system (chemo kills bone marrow cells as it kills cancer cells), and they gave her shots to boost her white blood counts. Platelets were pumped in, along with red blood cell transfusions. Meanwhile she had stress fractures in her bones and a constant fever.

Her protocol called for one more chemo treatment, but after being released, her doctor had a serious conversation with her about her likelihood of surviving another treatment. So it was decided to stop and evaluate her by proceeding with painful bone marrow extractions for analysis. There were more bone scans and blood tests. The idea was to make a determination about if this was even helping curb the cancer and worth one more near-death treatment, or if it was time to stop and make her comfortable with whatever might follow.

Our hearts were in our throats as she made her way through the testing phase. And then Monday she called, crying on the telephone. "All the tests were positive," she babbled. Positive? DAMN! "No, I mean positive for me! There's no sign of cancer anywhere!"

My mother is in full remission. Her treatment is concluded and she is free to return back to work on February 1, following a convalescence period appropriate for the level to which the chemotherapy has weakened her. Her doctor was so surprised with the findings that she had another oncologist review every test result and they are trying to get the insurance company to agree to testing with a new experimental machine that looks for sugar levels on a cellular level, indices of cancer. A PET scan. But she appears to be cancer free at this time.

My relief is immense. And, of course, I think that if they can cure her, after beating her down like a dog over and over, then I can better bear my beatings. Meanwhile, Taxol continues to amaze me but I am no longer afraid of it. Last week, I was becoming convinced that it would soon trigger a life-threatening situation and, in fact, it appears I have a sensitivity which quite likely could result in my becoming increasingly disabled. I know this from my own research, not from any helpful insights from a well-informed doctor, but regardless of how I learned of the hyposensitivity reaction, now that I know, we can respond appropriately.

I've learned, for example, that long-term side effects are unknown since the drug Taxol is relatively new. Morphine is often needed since pain caused by nerve damage may be disabling for several months. In addition to having critical blood counts and accompanying fevers this week, my toes are numb but the bottoms of my feet burn. I likely will be using a cane soon. I can't differentiate colors very well (blacks and blues) and I've had a migraine every day and sudden stabbing pains in my temple. I bite my cheek so often that I get used to it. Then all of my teeth are loose, every nerve exposed. Breathing is hard and there just isn't enough juice to push the engine any further. I believe I will be reduced to home care soon. In fact, Kevin is already providing that level of care.

Another morning, I eat breakfast and dress for work. This is the paradox of Taxol: It teases me into thinking that I'm past the worst. I decide to make dinner as a surprise, so I take chicken out of the freezer to thaw before driving to work. Within an hour, I hit the brick wall. I stop moving around the office to conserve strength so that I'll be able to drive home later. I read editorial copy that I've saved for this time of the day. Perhaps Kevin won't mind cooking again.

I am learning flexibility and to let go of expectations without letting go of hope for a better day the next day. I am learning how to sail my ship. We have nine more Taxol voyages to make.

Today, I am dressed in my best holiday business dress. The company is hosting a party for 400 people to celebrate our new magazine. I even put a wig-hat on my head, topped off with a Santa hat. And makeup! I look almost normal! I feel good today. Steady, if I don't hurry. Bill is driving the 90 miles to Rockford; if I get too tired at the party, I can sit in a corner at Ramada Suites and rest.

My mother is cancer free. This is what I am taking with me to the party. This mantra is my holiday gift to myself.

Taxol eventually will return me to my family. It may have me like a rag doll in a dog's mouth at the moment, but I am not a rag doll. I am a person with a light from within, and I am going to keep the flame lit.

Friday, December 15
JODY:

Instead of seeing Mike, who is away at some convention, I get handed off to a substitute oncologist – who I will refer to as Doctor X, though he does not deserve the gift of anonymity. I am disappointed, but okay. It happens. After listening to my very detailed and lengthy list of side effects and pains, he smirks and says, "Other than that, how did you like the play, Mrs. Lincoln?" Perhaps he finds himself amusing, but what I am describing was not intended to be taken lightly. Something is wrong with my reaction to this new Taxol drug and I am afraid to take it again.

Dr. X considers this. "You can refuse any more Taxol if you want to," he agrees. "It only buys you a couple extra survival percentage points, anyway."

Well thank you, fuckhead, I silently fume. *In case you haven't noticed, I don't have any extra percentage points to lose!* I say aloud, "I'm not comfortable dropping a protocol that Mike Frontiera thinks best without conferring with him next week."

"The second option is to take a whole dose versus the third you've been taking of Taxol, but I'll hold back the steroids because that might be aggravating the symptoms." He glanced at his watch… we must have passed his seven-minute mark. "Which is it going to be, Ms. Patrick? None — or the preferred full dose? Personally, I'd advise you to just start a bonfire and get through it, versus starting smaller fires and then continuously putting gas on them. At least you won't have to do it again for three weeks."

The drip takes three hours.

I come home to hell. I cannot even stand to relate the details. HELL.

Saturday, December 16
KEVIN:

I am powerless to stop Jody's downward spiral. I've never felt so utterly helpless in my life. Nothing brings her any joy anymore, not even the upcoming celebrations that she has so dearly loved in the past. She is turning away from all talk of holiday plans, a very bad omen.

I understand that Taxol is kicking her butt. I wake up every time she hobbles to the bathroom in the night, though I pretend to be asleep, knowing that if she thought she was disturbing my sleep, she'd feel sorry. She doesn't need any more grief right now. The relief drugs prescribed for her are ineffective and certainly not sufficiently potent to abate her continuous pain, yet she won't complain to Mike between visits.

To make matters worse, I'm starting to feel guilty about work. I've missed more time in the past five months than in the last 30 years. I'm trying to make restitution by going in earlier and staying later, and hoping that my actual performance isn't suffering. Add that to the 50-minute commute each way and it makes for a long day.

Jody says little, but I can tell that she resents my extended days because she suddenly is actively lobbying for a job change to a Madison firm. And even more upsetting, she appears to be very insecure about my late hours. I wonder if she thinks I'm fooling around? The men in her recent past weren't the most trustworthy or faithful, so I understand her frame of reference, but I don't think anyone else has loved her as much as I.

Perhaps I should share with her that my sex drive has changed to more of a *sex park*. Maybe she thinks that we're not having sex for the sole reason that she is not interested. I'd tell her that I just don't have the desire myself lately if it would ease her mind, but on the other hand, I don't want her to feel responsible for my own waning libido.

My wife is often described by her friends as a superwoman, but they have no idea how fragile Jody's ego is right now. I see it in a hundred tiny ways. I try to compensate by telling her constantly how much I love her. In some sense, maybe the spouse of a rape victim would understand my hesitation to move forward with a more physical demonstration of my affection. Perhaps only he could really understand my reluctance to jeopardize a long-term relationship for a short-term romp. I just can't do it.

To my way of thinking, I'm still at sea. There is no one waiting in another port. I'm celibate, plain and simple. I'm certain that I willed the desire out of my psyche, and remain confident that when she survives this, I will be able to will back the craving. She need not worry about me. I wish I could say these things to her, but I don't know how. There is so very much that I don't know how to tell my wife lately.

But the more pressing concern: how can I remind her, without making either of us feel guilty, that my present job is the best I've ever had in the corporate world? I see only one way to address the conflict between my duty to Jody and my duty to my employer, a conflict which is escalating on a daily basis. I've begun the process of checking Madison job postings on the Web. I know that in the not-too-distant future, I'll be making the change. *Sacrifice or reasonable accommodation?* It is what it is. There's no point in belaboring it or pretending otherwise. I begin to pull away from my peers and co-workers.

Missing the annual Christmas party is my first step.

Tuesday, December 19
JODY:

I am dying. Not in the abstract, but in the immediate present. Kevin has rushed me to the hospital, and the emergency room physician has called Dr. X., insisting that I be admitted to the oncology floor.

I know that I am dying. The reaction to Dr. X.'s treatment was akin to creating a serum poison in my body that has compromised my skeletal, muscular and nervous systems, all three. I am suffering. The bone pain is indescribable. Every muscle feels like it has been pounded and punched.

My skin is rashed, welting, raw. I have a pronounced hypersensitivity to light, sound, smells. My lips are numb, tongue is swollen and scored with tiny lacerations and ulcers, and my throat is covered with sores. My blood pressure, normally 80/65, is now 186/130 and climbing. I have to get out of this body that is drowning in a sea of pain. Tooth pain, ear aches… bleeding sinuses… stomach problems, burning toes. How can I fight something that causes *fingernails* to ache?

I want to kill myself. If I can get Kevin to bring my stash, I will. It is time.

Dr. Foley returns. Can you believe it? He has the same name as my dog. It comforts me to have a Foley looking over me, but not nearly enough.

"We're going to put some drugs into an IV to help with the pain, and we're giving you a shot, too," he says. "This will be very, very fast acting."

I am woozy. The room is spinning. Now I'm nauseated. I need to throw up. But at least he has managed to take the edge off the pain. My right knee is on fire! I can't sit up because my spine feels broken, like splintered glass. This is not enough help.

"Please kill me," I beg the good doctor. "Please!"

Kevin touches my hand and I pull away. That hurts, it hurts, it hurts!

Dr. Foley leaves but soon returns. "I can't believe this, but your doctor doesn't want to admit you," he says. "He's a little angry that you're even here."

"Dr. X. is not our actual doctor," Kevin says. "He's a stand-in, and a poor one at that since his own answering service told us to come here! What the hell do you mean, he doesn't want to admit her?"

Dr. Foley says that he will refuse to release me from the emergency room. However, he lacks the clout to admit me to the oncology ward, and so we have a battle of wills going on here. *A wrestling match*, I realize, and almost laugh aloud because our dog Foley was named after the WWF wrestler Mick Foley.

Dr. X. comes out of the corner fighting. My protocol causes pain, he expected pain, and this is just part of the treatment that can't be made better by putting me in a hospital bed. A second phoned request for admission is denied.

Dr. Foley rebounds off the ropes saying that my level of pain is having a pronounced effect on my blood pressure and this is the worst chemo reaction he's ever seen, and he's seen plenty. He will NOT release me. No way.

Dr. X. announces that he will then come into the hospital and release me himself.

"I obviously don't think your wife should be released," Dr. Foley tells Kevin. "I believe that she clearly needs to be in the hospital where we can at least make her comfortable. We certainly should help her through the next 24 hours."

"I am not comfortable yet," I whisper. "Please, please help me."

"She's not going anywhere except here tonight," Kevin says. "And I'll see to it."

When Dr. X. shows up, he is very agitated that he had to drive all the way to the hospital. He can't believe that his service told me to go to the hospital. "If you had gotten through to me, I would have told you to meet me in the parking lot and saved us all from this hassle," he fumes. "Now you're in the hospital system and you have to be discharged." He thinks he will send us home and be finished with this nonsense; I think he does not want to have done something so stupid as to have overdosed me with a medication to which I have shown a marked sensitivity. I think he might not want my hospitalization on his record. I suspect he has screwed up and he knows it, but I don't intend to die at home so he can pretend he has not.

"She's not going anywhere," Kevin says. His voice is low and calm and very scary. I realize my husband is very close to physically attacking this pompous oncologist.

Dr. X. is not so sure now. He sighs and looks at me. I begin to cry. "This hurts so much. Please, please let them help me. I can't do this at home."

"I believe you are anxious and that is making things worse," the patronizing shithead tells me. "So we'll keep you here for pain control and monitoring, but I think you would do as well at home. But stay tonight, if it makes you feel better, and I'll see you tomorrow."

I do not sleep one minute the entire night. The pain pills he has prescribed are most likely placebos. At least, they have no effect on me. "Why aren't you on morphine?" the attending nurse asks. "It should never be allowed to get this bad."

They call the doctor and ask for stronger drugs. He decreases the time between doses, but the pain medication remains the same. I watch the clock through the night. *Please, please can I have something yet?* Is there to be no relief?

I can't do this anymore.

Wednesday, December 20
JODY:

The pain crests and wanes and is finally endurable, but just barely. An aid brings Cream of Wheat cereal. I like that but my tongue and throat hurt too much to eat. And I can't hold the spoon in my fingers.

Kevin comes early in the morning. "How are you doing?"

I shrug.

"Happy birthday, honey," he says. "This is really the pits, I know, but it'll get better."

No, it won't. "Don't leave me alone," I beg. "I have to ask Dr. [X] for stronger pain medication and I don't know if he'll give it to me."

"Oh, I know he will," Kevin warns.

A quick rap on the door is followed by a familiar face: *Mike!* He's still supposed to be out of service, but he heard of the hospitalization. I sob with relief at the sight of my very own oncologist – the real deal!

Mike sits on the hospital bed and hugs me gently. "I'll be honest with you, hypersensitivity to the drug occurs in less than one percent of patients, but you certainly have the most severe case of it I have ever seen, and even more severe than I've found in the literature." He asks if I want to go or stay. I say that I'd prefer to be home, if I knew I could stand the pain. I tell him that the medicine given to me through the night is crap. I have yet to get over the top of the pain.

Mike writes a script for morphine on demand; we're to get the prescription filled and take the first dose before we leave the hospital. If one does not work, I can take another 10 minutes later, up to 10 or more pills. Mike says he is also prescribing antidepressant pills to slow down transmissions between nerves to help depress the general nerve symptoms; this should help with the skin welting and rash. He suggests a heavy-duty sleeping pill at night for some badly needed rest. And more Lorazapam for anxiety and nausea caused by pain. He promises to get me through this reaction, which could take a month... or even last indefinitely.

Mike's voice is gentle: "Don't be a hero, Jody. You could have called me well before this. This reaction is out of control now. You should have been on morphine for a long time already. I would have gladly given it to you."

"I was holding out until our appointment, then you weren't there, but I did tell Dr. [X] about the pain," I protest. "I told him absolutely everything. He made fun of me and called me Mrs. Lincoln. He—"

"Well, I'm back now and we'll just look ahead," Mike interjects. "Let's not dwell on the bad stuff so we have energy to keep going."

The first morphine pill makes me seriously nauseous. It is bitter and horrible tasting as it melts under my tongue. It doesn't help. It will take five more before I can sleep after climbing into my own bed.

Even as I sleep, our friend Salli has rallied my business and personal friends for a *Jingle for Jody* day in honor of my birthday. Although there is a blizzard raging, they are standing in the freezing weather ringing bells for the Salvation Army. Every two hours, new friends relieve others and take up the bells. Still others, like my friend Bob Oyler, will match the donations put in specific kettles. Salvation Army Major Paul Moore emails: *It is a rare thing when friends give such a personal gift as yours are giving you. They will be matching your passion for the humble work of the Salvation Army with their own self-sacrifice, giving time to others.*

I know nothing yet of this, however, when I wake. I know only that Kevin and PJ are sitting gingerly on the bed. They smile, present me with a beautiful crystal angel with face uplifted beseechingly and hands palms up. She is my prayer angel and certainly a wonderful birthday gift. They kiss me, then leave me to get more rest. I lie in a morphine haze, holding onto my beautiful glass angel. Although Kevin turned off the light, she continues to shine in my hand.

I stare at the angel glowing in the night. She becomes surreal. I realize that I am not afraid to die, though this doesn't mean that I now have a great faith. Great faith, like great love, takes great effort. I learned this particular Lesson long ago, when I was manager of the Chicago Ronald McDonald House. I can remember everything so clearly. My faith wavered during day-to-day encounters with serious childhood diseases – it was sorely tested by the harshest reality of all: Children die. With each final goodbye, I found it more difficult to separate the death of a child's body from the demise of existence. Belief in Christ's triumph over death and the promise of eternal life was within my grasp… but standing next to grieving parents, I couldn't *feel* it. All I felt was a stinging loss. I comforted parents with the right words as best I could, but my faith was a flickering hope at best.

Now the morphine takes me further adrift from my physical body and I noticed that God comes in mysterious ways. His visit takes the form of a true memory. The scene plays behind my closed eyelids and I am spellbound watching it again, living it once more:

"Goodbye" chirps a small, bald, chipmunk-cheeked boy. Toby is leaving the Ronald McDonald House for the outpatient clinic at nearby Children's Memorial Medical Center. He flashes one of his rare smiles.

"Hello," I say, returning the 10-year-old's grin.

"Why do you always say 'hello' instead of 'goodbye'?"

"Because you're coming back, of course! I don't say goodbye to kids until they go home for good. You and me, we'll be seeing a lot of each other."

Toby leaves hand-in-hand with his mother, a short walk to Chicago's Children's Memorial Hospital. The morning is bright and warm. I sit on the porch steps and watch until they are out of sight, knowing I can't say goodbye. Not to him. Our lives are connected. Toby eats dinners with my children, plays ball with my husband, listens to my stories. Goodbyes are reserved for the time when children are successfully treated or for when they can't be saved. With no way of knowing which ending will separate us, I simply refuse to say good-bye. Goodbye means forever.

The doorbell chimes. Toby returns from clinic exhausted and ill. His mother says they are in the last of a series of experimental chemotherapy treatments. She doesn't know if it will reverse his symptoms or make them worse. Toby qualifies for the trial because his leukemia has been deemed terminal and barring a miracle, there is little hope.

Suddenly it is Thanksgiving. We have made arrangements to transport Toby from his hospital bed to the Ronald McDonald House for dinner with family and friends. He sits in his wheelchair, too exhausted to play, too sick to eat. We speak of better days, when Toby participated in House-sponsored events.

Toby speaks, his voice soft and high pitched, the words spaced by lack of oxygen, about his trip to Walt Disney World. He remembers summer adventures at the One Step at a Time Camp. His face flushes as he describes attending a Chicago White Sox game, loudly dedicated to him by none other than then-announcer Harry Caray. Toby has two years worth of stories to tell, two years full of hellos. This day it seems evident that a miracle isn't to be. It is growing nearer the time to say good-bye.

Too soon... too soon it is December. Outside Toby's private hospital room it is snowing, the day cold and gray. Leaden, like my heart. As I watch Toby doze, I try to memorize every feature on his face. When he rouses from morphine-induced dreams, his mother mops perspiration from his face and I help him take small sips of juice. Both his mother and I seek ways to comfort the child and to draw his attention from the constant pain. Every movement is agony for Toby; his moans wrench our hearts.

He announces that he wants to speak to me alone. His mother stands, but there is a measure of anguish in her voice as she agrees to leave the room only for a few minutes. When she steps out into the hallway, Toby *opens his eyes and stares directly into mine.*

"I have to ask you something," he whispers.

I offer up a silent prayer that he not die before his mother returns. I promise to do anything he asks.

"Take care of my mom," he says with great difficulty. "She's gonna miss me terrible. I'm all she's got."

I lightly kiss his forehead and promise.

His mother is again by his side, holding his hand.

"I'm so tired." His next word is mimed, but I can still hear his sweet voice in my head as he mouths the thought: Sorry.

"I love you, baby," his mother answers, fresh tears running down her cheeks. "You have nothing to apologize for. Ever."

He looks at me and I tenderly caress his free hand. "Don't tell me goodbye," he croaks. "Tell me hello, like always, 'cause we're gonna see each other in God's house. Promise."

When I am able to speak, I nod, whisper, "Hello, Toby."

"Hold my hand tighter," he says to his mother. She, too, does as asked, and whispers to her child that she will always love him.

"Say it," he urges.

By prearranged agreement, she begins reciting the 23rd Psalm.

I startle awake, but this changes nothing. Toby did not live through the recitation.

I lie in bed marveling that the day Toby died, I was shown God's promise. "Goodbye" is just a word after all. No sermon had or has since ever moved me as much as Toby's last instruction, because I heard truth in his words in a way I hadn't been able to before. The child's simple faith allowed him to let go of life, to embrace the One he was certain waited for him. His example was a gift that allowed me to internalize this crucial tenet of faith.

I tried to pass along Toby's gift in my work at Ronald McDonald House and afterward. Toby's spirit was tapped every time I ministered to bereaved families, helping them say goodbye to a beloved shell, and hello to the truth of an afterlife.

I know that I can say goodbye when I am called to do so, because I am certain death is merely a doorway to a new life. However, I'm grateful not to have to take any more Taxol in the interim, and I'm grateful for my earthbound angels – including the crystal figurine in my hand, and the angel that goes by the name "Morphine."

Monday, December 25
KEVIN:

I'm so thankful to have this Christmas with our little family! I watch my bride as she sleeps and, in a rush of good cheer, I decide to begin the day with a gift to P.J. I'll not only let him sleep in, but I'll also relieve him of the chore of taking Foley out for his morning constitutional.

The shepherd/Aussie mix sniffs from place to place, suddenly finicky about where he will poop. Although the yard is buried beneath a foot of snow and the temperature is well below freezing, he will take his time. I suspect this is a silent recrimination for not exercising him any other way; he has come to understand that as soon as he finishes his duty, I'm going to yank him back inside the house. So we walk and he sniffs and we walk some more and he sniffs some more.

I think to remind Jody that it can't be good for her to be outside in her condition, even if she bundles up, and so I don't want her walking the dog today. I know she will, though, because Foley is pathetic in his whining and she's an easy mark. Also, chemo-brain has stimulated her already naturally impulsive streak and reportedly causes her to *forget* logical instruction. How can Jody handle him, when I struggle just to stay upright? Yet she does. I've watched her hobble across the yard, taking halting steps until she gets to the epicenter of our property, Foley at her heel. Then she stops and lets the dog run in circles around her. Somehow she keeps her balance on the icy snow, switching the lead from hand to hand as he races in circles in all his glory. It makes me dizzy, and yet their private ballet is bewitching to watch.

A strange dog and his owner pass our corner lot. Foley lunges, nearly pulling me off my feet. Should I drop the leash, our puppy would take off like a shot with me not so close behind. Obviously he and I still have some choreography to work out because I'm easily tangled in his leash. Foley continues pulling. The snow has glazed over, making the ice more treacherous. He cuts back to me and just as quickly runs the distance of the 25-foot lead and then pulls, tugging for more play. No artistic circles with me, just a straight tug-of-war.

In many ways, Foley reminds me of P.J. Just another inch. And another. They both enjoy challenging me. Last June, Jody and I found a local dog park where the puppy could run unencumbered by a leash. Amazingly, Foley would stay near us, always within sight. He would also come when called, opposite his behavior when he slips loose at home. This also reminds me of P.J., who wants to be independent and yet not too independent. Both boy and rescue puppy have abandonment issues and like to keep me in their radar. And they both have good souls.

It's Christmas, after all, and I'm feeling generous. I want to make today special. Foley finally does his *happy dance*, a kicking of his hind legs in celebration of a successful outing, and we return to our warm nest. The dog shakes off the cold and races upstairs to snuggle with Mom. I hear Jody stir and murmur to him, her youngest baby. Chances are good that he might hop into bed with her and the two of them fall back to sleep.

There's no reason for her to hurry out of bed. We have no special plans for this day, not even a meal planned. I have no expectations at all for today, although I do expect to cook bland food for Jody and whatever type of food P.J. wants.

I turn on all the Christmas lights in the house; it's a gray day and the lights make the house look so inviting. The counters are literally covered with holiday cookies and candies and food gift baskets dropped off by caring friends. I like this. This feels good. Last night, we also lit up the house and the tree before we opened all of the presents. From outside our windows, looking in, we must have seemed like any other family, caught up in ribbons and wrapping paper and presents carefully selected.

P.J.'s gifts were easy to buy. Gift certificates from the mall, Best Buy, Circuit City, Old Navy. Snow pants, rabbit-lined gloves. But it was tough to buy for Jody. Due to the chemo, standard *lady gifts* were cut from the list: perfume nauseates her; she doesn't need a razor or hair products; she's adverse to the idea of sexy lingerie; and by her own choice, the only jewelry now worn is her wedding rings and a medical alert necklace. She isn't feeling really good about her appearance and her weight is fluctuating, so clothes weren't a great choice, either.

I opted for spiritual items and one special piece of jewelry. Although she likely won't wear it soon, I gave her a delicate gold cross that seemed to mean a great deal to her. Jody has told me that she feels much closer to God lately. When I gave her the cross, I reminded her that she got about as close to God as I want her to get on her birthday. God can wait; I want her around next Christmas.

Is that her now? I hear footsteps and paw thuds as the sleepyheads make their way down the hallway. It's about 10:00, but already she is walking tentatively. Before braving the stairs, she goes into her home office to check her email.

There is always email.

I want to make her a special Christmas breakfast. I will fry her eggs hard like she likes them. I try not to break the yokes. Usually I'm not successful, but today is different. Today is Christmas. I round out the menu with soft bacon and butter-soaked toast and privately congratulate myself for being diligent in her meal preparation despite her recent bout with mouth sores. Lately she's struggled to even be able to swallow water, since the ulcers coated her tongue and blistered her throat. The food may not be the most nutritious, but it is very important to my psyche that she not adopt the emaciated form that we see so often at the clinic. In fact, Jody has actually gained weight on chemo, which I think is a good thing. I make her warm tea, not too hot. She can't have orange juice because of the acid. There is so much now that she can't eat or drink.

Jody smiles and shakes her head in either amusement or amazement as I present this small offering to her in her office, a token of what I would like to give her but can't. She makes room on her cluttered desk for her plate and cup of tea.

"This looks good," she says. If she is lying, she's getting good at it, because I believe her.

I hand her a mixture of liquid Benadryl, lidocaine, and antacid that she drinks straight from the medicine bottle. Although we lacked faith that the prescription Dr. Frontiera wrote would help, it actually *does* temporarily numb her throat. Amazing! She swallows it with difficulty, but manages to keep it down. Ten minutes from now, she'll be able to eat.

She has some wonderful responses to her Friday Updates; in fact, she has overwhelming community support in her battle. She draws strength and energy from these responses and reads them aloud. Soon she is reading between tiny, tentative bites of food. When she has had enough to eat, she absently sets the plate on the floor for Foley to lick clean.

She follows my glance: "I didn't give him a lot."

"That's okay. It's Christmas."

"Thanks for taking care of me," she says. "I don't know what I'd do without you."

This far into treatment, we have the *what would I do without you?* script down pat. I give my standard answer: "You'd just hire a butler and a pool boy."

"But we don't have a pool."

"Exactly," I reply playfully. "However, a beautiful woman like you can always find some use for a pool boy." I kiss her lips very softly, careful not to put any real pressure on her tender mouth.

She coos her line: "You can be my pool boy."

"Me in a Speedo. Now that is an awful visual," I remark, laughing. She laughs aloud too. "Besides," I add, "you don't have a pool."

She smiles: "Exactly."

It's Christmas and no matter what the rest of the day brings, it will include holding my bride, albeit very gently. I also know that our next Christmas will be even better. When I selected her cross necklace and held it in my hands, I renewed my faith that we will see it together.

It's at the top of my wish list for next year's gifts.

Wednesday, December 27
KEVIN:

Due to the holidays, the plant has shut down for the week. I update my resume and float it to local recruiters, a traitor to the company that has shown me such kindness. I expect to get a few bites from Madison employers, but holiday hiring isn't usually very expedient.

Jody seems to be just going through the motions in her daily life. What most worries me is that her mental attitude is slipping, even to her friends — those she usually snows with false good cheer. Her latest *Holiday Update* email was very dark with veiled goodbyes. So much so that I wonder how her friends can stand to read it.

She has stopped searching the worldwide Web for other survivors; a lack of ones with her diagnosis is more depressing than helpful. Reading posted *success stories* has brought her no solace, since the majority of them are later reported to have passed on by their survivors. I'm secretly glad she's turned away from this avenue, since I find it even more depressing than she.

I don't want to be thought of as a *survivor*.

We don't talk about death, and I wonder if this is a mistake. I wonder if she is considering ending her own life. I wonder this because I could imagine it for myself, if I was in her shoes and dealing with all she is dealing with, and this frightens me more than anything. I have to count on her being stronger than I know myself to be. I'm glad we don't own a gun because committing suicide by use of a firearm seems to be more spontaneous than premeditated. Jody and I are spontaneous people. Now, I have to rely on her logic and reasoning to save her from her own spontaneity.

I'm not so sure that is a good bet right now.

Friday, December 29
JODY:

Although on formal *vacation* to recover from my Taxol experience, I've still been able to work on both magazines by doing a little final proof-reading, writing columns, etc., and today I even vacuumed. Considering that a week ago I was barely able to walk, this is a vast improvement. I could tell that I could have knocked Kevin over with a feather when he walked into the room and saw me cleaning! *Surprise!*

Apparently my reaction to Taxol was unique to the way I process some enzyme. The hospital visit was followed by an emergency clinic visit. The rash continued to consume my body, for which I was given steroids but finally the *maintenance drugs* seem to be helping suppress the reactions.

The down side is that I've lost two treatment cycles. Mike doesn't feel the chemotherapy was able to do what it was intended so we have to find another chemotherapy agent, which he will discuss with me on January 5. Meanwhile, morphine keeps the pain in check, the antidepressant slows nerve synapses, Lorazapam is handling any nausea reactions, and Ambien helps me sleep. Warfarin makes sure my blood doesn't clot and Rantidine prevents ulcers. I'm forgetting something, but mostly it just feels good to walk again and be looking forward to a more *normal* week next week.

The kindness of friends has been a real blessing. Julie and Don, Joey, Abby, so many! Ruth Ann and Paul brought over Chinese food, cut into little bitty bites so I could eat it. Ruth Ann made natural, unscented soaps for my sensitive skin, and their family later surprised ours by singing carols on our doorstep at night, a delightful reminder of Christmas. As was the beautiful huge poinsettia plant that Bob sent which hangs in our living room window.

I managed to have tea with Ruth Ann and Salli. Then Salli and Phyllis brought a special evening to me, a very quiet and loving get-together. Tracy took pictures of people ringing Salvation Army bells during the *Jingle for Jody* day and presented me with the pictures after my birthday. What a wonderful thing for her to do! My friend Beverly has been in touch by phone and email, Lynn's cards arrive every couple days, and Rich sent a most welcome email. Barbro's emails are always uplifting, and Leslie is standing by to take me to chemo. Bill drove me to the clinic and then brought us home-baked goodies from wife Nancy. Marty stopped by for a couple hours and, of course, my staff has been wonderful. Summer, Brook and Mom have been vigilant with phone calls and PJ is helping dear Kevin clean.

God bless you, every one.

CHAPTER 8: January
Mom's cancer returns • Sex... possible again? • New puppy • Kevin's anger • Chemobrain
(Is my husband poisoning me?)

Friday, January 5
JODY:

I could rant and rave or cry a river, but I'm helpless to change the fact that mother's cancer is back.

Mom has been waging a solo battle with her multi-layered insurance company this past month because her doctor ordered a Positron Emission Tomography (PET) scan. The insurance company stalled until her doctor appealed. (Perhaps some research dollars should be diverted to advocacy programs to help cancer patients access the technology already sitting in our cancer centers.) Finally she was injected with a drug that emits signals measuring metabolic activity. Because cancerous areas are more metabolically active than non-cancerous cells, such sites are clearly shown on the scan.

She lit up like a Christmas tree.

The miracle test detected cancer in her arm, shoulder and back. She was declared Stage Four, handed off to another doctor at the Rocky Mountain Cancer Center, and scheduled to have yet another bone marrow test to determine if the cancer was still the original type (lymphoma) or whether it was a new cancer. According to her doctor, preferred treatment is high-dose chemo in preparation for a bone marrow transplant.

Mom's doctor relayed all of this information to her during a three-minute conversation. Mom had the bone marrow test Thursday; she's still waiting for someone to call her and tell her what this all means.

My oncologist, having also treated my mother, declared that there is no way she can survive high-dose chemo. Mike insisted he would *never* have suggested it because there are other, more viable treatment options to prolong her life indefinitely. Mike also questioned that her cancer would show remission at the original site while growing somewhere else, and he added that the PET scan may indicate cancer where there is actually arthritis. He felt strongly that the PET scan is not designed as a screening tool, and said that he would not consider one at any point of my treatment for that purpose. Literature posted on government news sources and on medical Internet sites disagrees with his position and, in fact, Medicare just approved payment for PET scans. But it's good to know where he stands.

Mike put me on antidepressants just in time. This is incredibly dispiriting. Even medicated, I am so angry with Mother's doctor for suggesting something that I, in much better health and spirits, am frightened to consider. A bone marrow transplant is *my* best chance, should I have a reoccurrence, but one in ten recipients dies during the procedure. High-dose chemo is also very risky, and mother's heart already shows damage and she's being treated for high blood pressure. Of course, I say nothing of this to Mom. If she ever believes it to be a death sentence, it will be.

My heart is breaking.

In the midst of this melodrama, Kevin and I are working hard to create as normal a life as possible. We bought a puppy and named him Micky, again in honor of wrestler Mick Foley. (I only agreed because "Micky" has an Irish lilt to it.) The adorable pooch has a Beagle face and a hound dog body and he's totally irresistible. PJ tried to ignore him but the mutt eventually won him over, too.

I pet both dogs absently now, where they lie under my desk. I have just come from chemo, an almost 2-hour drip of yet another anti-cancer drug, Taxotere. Rather than kill cancer cells outright like Cytoxin, Taxotere works like its cousin drug, Taxol, to paralyze the skeletal structure of the cancer cell so that it can't replicate. If I can't tolerate the one-third doses each week, we go back to the Red Devil. And I have to admit, I'm somewhere between the devil and the deep blue sea with this medication.

But there is no time for whining. Kevin has admitted to feeling a bit neglected lately, so I'll pull him away from the television set for a cup of tea at the table. And Summer and Paddy are coming home this weekend to celebrate Christmas (I didn't want Summer on a crowded bus over the holidays and I wasn't up to making the trip either). Now I want her – *need* her – to come home; I want to see her pregnancy for myself again because the promise of her child is a beautiful anti-depressant. Given my mother's diagnosis, I need all the help I can get.

137

KEVIN:

I'm extremely ticked off! This time it is with Jody. Since returning from chemo, she's prattled on about a new friend who also has breast cancer. Jody has formed a kinship with this lady after only a few visits, my heart-on-her-sleeve bride. Not only do they share cancer, but this woman is also a professional person, very well educated, very worldly. A *nice* woman, Jody stresses. Jody adds that the woman is divorced. A sad story; her partner left her. The lady, Jody says, now is in full remission. Then Jody states that if she (Jody) dies, this woman would be perfect for me.

Okay, first: Jody is not going to die. Second: I don't need her fixing me up — from this life or from the beyond. I do not intend to marry again because I have met my soul mate and married her and if God takes her to be with Him, then I'll just wait to join her. I will not love another woman after Jody. Third (and I realize that this is the most selfish reason even while I'm thinking it): why would I knowingly go into a relationship where the chances favor the other person to get sick and die?

What I do for Jody, I do out of love and devotion. If I can ease her suffering and help improve the quality of our lives, I have lived up to my marital vows and to all that she has a right to expect. But I have absolutely no desire to do this for another. Stepchildren yes, of course I would care for them, too, but I draw the line in the sand right there.

I know Jody is thinking of my welfare but I don't want her thinking about dying and I don't want her playing matchmaker. If she worries about me being alone, perhaps she'll hang around longer. My goal is to precede her in death (after all I am the older and a male). After a long life together.

"In case you haven't noticed, I'm pretty pissed off at you," I tell her. My swearing catches her attention because I seldom curse. I make her hear me out, where we sit at the table, and I tell her why — or at least most of it, leaving out the part about not wanting to be somebody else's caretaker. A man deserves a private thought or two left unexamined.

She smiles. She knows. And at this moment I know, too, that she was just feeling insecure and wanted to hear how much I love her.

"Come on," she says, leading the way to the family room. Television remote control in hand, she flips to *Jerry Springer* and I can't help but laugh out loud. We watch it when we want to feel better about our lives. Even with everything we've faced so far, we're grateful not to be among his guests or even in his up-close audience. We've made a pact that we'd rather be dead than have our lives sink low enough to be fodder for this program.

Jody settles into a chemo-daze, napping on and off. The show ends and I get up, kiss her head and return to the kitchen to start dinner. I'm no longer angry. Things could always be worse: We could be on Springer.

Wednesday, January 10
KEVIN:

Finally! The return of my desire for sex, a spark further flamed by my wife's own flicker! Jody's condition isn't yet conducive to prolonged love-making and we have to be inventive to find a position comfortable for her, but hallelujah and praise the Lord, there is interest. That I take as a good sign that we might both have a complete recovery!

I'm not expecting to seduce her with any regularity in the immediate future, since the drugs have forced her into menopause. But then again, this is just one more aspect of the disease and treatment that we will have to learn to manage. Technically, I guess, this sailor is still out to sea. But how much easier it is to drift along with the promise of an occasional harbor visit. The upside is that I will be able to love the same beautiful woman in every port and she will more and more often want to make love to me.

Friday, January 12
JODY:

Before I get whacked again this afternoon, I'd like to accentuate the positive. I've had a very good week. And after today, I'll have only four more treatments before radiation!

I've been able to work a complete schedule, go grocery shopping by myself (first time in months), spend time in Rockford, and attend a company party last evening. This has been a very full week, indeed, despite continued reliance on morphine. But my physical complaints are *manageable*, reducing the amount of energy needed to fight pain and increasing the stamina available for much more productive activities.

Last Saturday, I was atop a ladder most of the day to decorate two boring walls of my home office. I cut out the backgrounds of family pictures and made a huge collage of faces, transforming the walls into a photo gallery with over 1,500 pictures of various sizes. It took several hours of cutting, stapling and arranging. Interspersed with the photos of family and friends are notes of encouragement and tickets to events we've gone to in the past year or so.

When Summer and Paddy came home late Saturday night, they spent the most time in front of those walls. Summer traced her life back to her first baby pictures. Even PJ stood in front of the pictures for the longest time, grinning at his memories and telling stories.

I am feeling more and more like me! Since morphine, I am better able to snatch back pieces of my old life, of familiar behavior. While there still is breakthrough pain, there is more and more often breakthrough ME.

Monday, January 15
KEVIN:

I just did well in a job interview with a multi-location company based in Madison. This one makes baby animal food. I'm told that a second interview will be forthcoming.

"Great," I lie. I leave knowing I could do the job, but also certain that I would be bored silly. My only hope is that the next interviewer realizes what I'm unwilling to disclose: I hope they don't offer me the job.

The position would be a serious step down the financial ladder from my current job and not the direction that I normally would want my career to travel. But this is not a normal situation. The job meets my single criteria: location. This is the most trapped I've ever felt in regard to my career. I've always been able to go where the job was. I no longer feel that this is an option.

I tell Jody about the interview. She watches my face closely and so I try to muster enthusiasm. When I finish going on and on about the benefits of working for an animal food manufacturing plant, she says simply, "Don't be an idiot. Location isn't everything. Stay where you are until you find an area job that you want."

Now this is the woman I married!

Saturday, January 20
JODY:

The first issue of *In Business: Rockford* magazine hit the stands today! Our new business publication is launched and I'm a partner! I can't believe we did it! What a high this is!

And what an equally low downer it was to learn this past week that Mom was told that she has three choices in regard to her medical situation. The first option is to do nothing, in which case she'll be dead by July. Or she could agree to see how long they can keep her alive with standard *salvage* chemo that probably would involve several hospitalizations. Or she can choose Door Number Three — have the high-dose chemo and bone marrow transplant using her own stem cells. This, her doctor claimed, would actually give her a 30% chance of complete cure versus an expected 20% chance of death during the procedure. Assuming she could also survive the period where her stem cells were still maturing and she had no immunity. She would be hospitalized for several months before and after.

She was too depressed to make the decision, so she told her doctor *I'd* make it. Then she called me, gave me the info and her doctor's phone number, and hung up.

I poured over reference books to learn more about the chemo involved in the pre-bone marrow transplant, the procedure itself, the recovery period, and cost ($200,000 for the operation alone.) Then I called her doctor, who repeated the 30% cure rate. Then I called my mother and gave her the complete report before handing back the final decision to her.

When I later met with Mike, he said the 30% was completely false. That is the popular number for lymphoma, but only for those who relapsed and then were put back into remission and were doing well before the surgery. Conversely, my mother's cancer is extremely aggressive in the bones (in the last two weeks alone, spread to ribs, back, skull, and left arm). He repeated that she was by no means a candidate for the surgery.

"This is not a viable option. It is a death sentence," he stated flatly.

I telephoned my mother and repeated Mike's assessment. I didn't want her to be taken aback in the event the one marrow specialist turns her down for the procedure. The waiting games are so cruel, and she would spend all this time thinking 30%!

"I'll keep that in mind," she mumbled. Mom's doctor increased her anti-depressants and added another pain patch. She is more comfortable and claims to have finally achieved an acceptance of her condition or what she calls *a lack of emotionality*. Although Mom still refuses to tell her brother Gene in Illinois, or my brother Kurt in Missouri, about the relapse. I called both so they would be in a position to support her when she does call.

If this was another down time in my own therapy, I don't know if I could keep juggling her situation and mine. As it is, my thoughts often stray to Mom, regardless of where I am or what I am doing. I find myself needing to shut my office door for a few minutes, or find a quiet place in the house to cry.

As if all of this were not enough drama, I received a voicemail message this week instructing me to contact a special agent with the Department of Justice in reference to an unsolved murder for which I had been the responding crisis intervention counselor when working for the police department in Cudahy. The Department of Justice was stepping in at the request of a police detective because the case was stale.

We connected by phone the next day, when he asked me several questions about the case. I clearly recalled the early Sunday morning that I was called from home about 9 a.m. to provide crisis support for the death of a four-year old — a death likely caused by one of his parents. The special agent said the police log of that day confirmed the many details I was able to remember. He then asked for my resume to establish my credentials with the court as an expert witness so that I might offer direct testimony should he bring his suspect to trial.

Although I mailed a resume the very next morning, I have a nagging concern about what a defense attorney could do with someone who has experienced chemo and radiation. Since on this new drug, I'm experiencing real mental hurdles. As of late, I am particularly challenged by the English language, struggling with both verbal and written word choices. It's getting harder and harder to hide. I had to look up "pesky" when re-reading a column, suddenly unsure of the meaning of the word I had written myself!

Add to that a growing difficulty accessing recent memory. Upon waking each morning, I can't clearly recall the day before. I eventually come up with the general sense of what I've done, but only by really concentrating and creating a chain-link memory which attaches each activity to the one just before or after it. Mechanical functions are trickier; I am suddenly blank as to what key to hit on the computer to do a simple search-and-replace function. Or I forget how to open an Excel spreadsheet. I have to stop and think, though within a minute or two it comes to me.

Chemo-brain is real and it is humiliating and frightening.

Boy, could a defense attorney have a field day with me! Should I have mentioned cancer treatment to the special agent? Kevin rightfully raised the question of alerting the agent to the full story. Instead, I asked my doctor if this would be an ongoing brain trauma, like the permanent nerve damage already attributed to my feet and fingertips. Would I make a fool of myself searching for words in the witness box?

Mike asked when the trial would be. Beats me. No one is even charged yet.

"Good," he said. "You'll be fine in a few months. It's just the drugs."

My relief felt like a warm bath. I've always known the hair would grow back but I wasn't so hopeful about brain cells or synaptic connections. I gave Mike an extra hug.

Kevin, thinking part of my cognitive problem to be exhaustion, let me sleep late this morning while he took PJ to league bowling. PJ bowled a 175, 180 and then his more typical 130. Kevin was a proud papa when they came home and PJ was uncharacteristically chatty about his accomplishments.

I too was beaming, having correctly followed the directions printed on a can of cherry pie filling and recalled how to properly operate the oven. For my efforts, there will be cherry pie with dinner!

Monday, January 23
KEVIN:

A job recruiter just called. The animal food people want to hire me. Fortunately their offer didn't match my current salary. Why the recruiter thought I might be interested in taking a serious reduction in pay is a mystery. Did I project such desperation?

"Location be damned, compensation counts, too," I said. "There will be other opportunities in Madison."

Jody knew that I would like to find a reason to decline the offer. I think we're both somewhat relieved that it makes sense to do so, because she understands the monetary consideration. Beyond medical bills, there looms the financial investment behind Jody's new venture with Bill. *In Business: Rockford* magazine hit the streets. Typical of a new magazine launch, it was published without a lot of paid advertising. A *loss leader* as they say in the business, necessary to generate real dollars later. Gotta have a product upfront. Meanwhile, we both understand that it is very possible that much more money will come out of our bank account before the business reaches a level of solvency. So we really can't afford to have my pay cut in any substantial way. But I don't flaunt my relief before my bride. We both act like this is a setback.

"There's always a next time," she sighs.

"Yep," I say, thinking, *Thank God, they came in low.*

Saturday, January 27
JODY:

Dear Diary,

(God, I feel stupid writing "Dear Diary" at my age, but the only place I feel safe writing *these* words is *in* a diary.)

Here's what's going on: Monday evening we enjoyed seeing Bill get his award, and Tuesday I had a wonderful impromptu tea party with my friend Barbro! However, by Wednesday I was bleeding from my throat and nose and I had to leave work. Thursday was the same, and, though I went back to the office Friday morning, the symptoms persisted.

My friend Leslie took me to chemo today. I showed Nurse Dee my mouth and she made a hasty exit to confer with Mike. Minutes later, she refused treatment. "You would feel like your mouth was falling off your face," she said. "We can't do anything with you like this." Dee ordered me to go home and take enough morphine to get over the top of it. "Get as comfortable as possible for a few days while we ride this out," she advised.

Mike might yet reduce the chemo dose or even suspend Taxotere because I'm showing signs of the same horrid sensitivity I had to Taxol.

With a free afternoon suddenly looming before us, Leslie and I decided to have a cup of tea at my house. She has a fascinating profession in forensic reconstruction and has even worked with the special agent who contacted me last week about the murder. I'd much rather hear her talk about her cases and how she figured out who did what to whom than listen to her story of survivorship over cancer... though her hair is so great looking that it inspires me to imagine growing my own again. She's so cool, with her life all orderly and all her hairs growing... I even happened to later mention to Kevin that if I died, she'd be a suitable replacement. I thought he'd be appreciative of my generosity because Leslie is so smart and funny, and she makes a good living. I thought he perhaps might even be grateful that I was *not* trying to match him up with a screwball so that I would always come out ahead of his next wife.

Yes, I realize NOW that was a dumb thing to have said. Apparently it's another one of those major "sore subjects."

Turning to a sore subject of my own, Mom is to have three-hour high-dose chemo treatments on Monday, Tuesday, Wednesday, and Thursday — even though Mom is 66 years old, weighs less than 120 pounds, wears three pain medication patches, and sucks a morphine lollipop. This procedure is contraindicated by everything I know and feel, but I need to be a strong, positive force for her now.

Ha, that's a joke – the idea of me being positive!

How could I be a positive force for *anybody* when I'm consumed by a secret suspicion that my husband may be poisoning me? He's lucky I didn't tell Leslie – or anyone else – my doubts about him. But how can you even begin to say – without sounding crazy – that you think your husband is poisoning you? Even if it makes all the sense in the world, people would look suspiciously at *you*, not him, and they'd think about locking *you* up.

But this is fact: Leslie said that Taxol was a breeze for her. A walk in the park. So why couldn't *I* handle it? And now Taxotere is kicking my butt. ... *Or is it?*

The real irony is this: even if my husband *is* poisoning me, everybody would think it's just a complication of chemotherapy! The fatigue, purple fingernails, and difficulty breathing could *all* be signs of arsenic poisoning. CLUE! They ARE signs of arsenic poisoning! But would YOU think of that — without reading THIS?

I have taken steps to protect myself, like cooking again. Kevin acts pleasantly surprised by my sudden interest in house chores – I dust and stuff so he won't think I *only* want to cook. Then, when he "surprises" me with dinner, I secretly spit the food into a napkin. And I've hidden my pills so he can't switch them.

Sadly, I'm distressed to report that I'm actually feeling better, since I stopped eating his food. But if I confronted him, he could say it's just the "okay space" between chemo infusions. Which it could be, in all fairness to Kevin.

I've thought a lot about this, and I don't WANT to be suspicious, but what do I know about Kevin? His parents were conveniently dead when we met, and I've never even met one single person from his past life, like an old friend. *My* friends can't say enough good things about him. But what do THEY really know about him?

Paranoia is NOT paranoia — if somebody is *really* trying to kill you!

I understand that I may have some toxic stuff in my brain, so I looked on the Internet. Hmm. Only passing mention of chemobrain — and not a word of warning about husbands poisoning wives! I thought *everything* was on the Internet. Or... the gatekeepers keep it off. Men control the Internet, and they probably wouldn't approve of other men killing their wives for no reason, but they might think it's okay if a husband used arsenic to speed things along that were likely to happen anyway. They'd see it as a mercy killing. Which it could be a mercy — for HIM!

I'm tired of these crazy thoughts. It's a scarier world since I'm locking myself up with these ridiculous worries, but I can't get loose. I sure hope this is over soon, because I miss trusting my husband. And if Kevin EVER found out that I thought he was plotting my murder, it would probably make him a hundred times more upset than the suggestion of who he should marry after he kills me.

Which reminds me... If anybody finds this diary and I'm dead, have Leslie Eisenberg do tests, okay?

CHAPTER *9:* February

Job decision • Taxo-*tears* • Kevin joins family business • Last chemo infusion • Pre-radiation expectations

February 5
KEVIN:

Jody is stressed because the Rockford venture is likely months away from showing a profit. This is made more troublesome because she has an open position for an advertising sales rep and is finding it challenging to recruit a qualified candidate. Night after night, she's talked her way through different scenarios in hopes of finding a solution. Tonight is no different. If anything, she has increased concern over the possible failure of the new business. She is petrified of letting Bill down when he has done so much for her.

Something has to be done.

"You know, Hon, I was given pretty serious sales training when I was a recruiter in the Navy," I muse aloud.

"That's a nice thought," she responds. Her dismissal is followed by a bemused, affectionate pat on my head.

"I'm serious. I'd be willing to go to Rockford for a short time to help get it up and running."

Her eyes narrow and her tone changes abruptly. She is short-fused lately, and I've unwittingly lit it. "You're in management now," she says, piqued. "I already have a sales manager. I need a sales rep. You'd be taking a major pay cut."

I'm suddenly cognizant that she believes my comments to be patronizing rather than sincere. I am not so easily put off: "How far away is Rockford?"

"About 90 miles." She sighs, unbuttons her pajama top and tugs off her clothing. *Hot flash.* She flips her pillow and rolls over, trying to find a cooler spot on the bed. Her cheeks redden and a thin sweat moustache appears on her upper lip. She smiles. The hot flash has diverted her attention; she forgets that she's angry. Her emotional flashes are nearly as quick and unpredictable as her physical ones.

"I'm serious about this," I tell her.

Jody rolls over again and slips her hand in mine. "I really appreciate the offer but I don't think it's practical." Now she's the patronizing one.

She soon is asleep. While she may reject my solution, at least the mere offer of it has relaxed her. I'd do about anything to reduce her stress level, since stress can be a real killer in our situation. Becoming a salesperson and driving to Rockford every day is about the last thing I want to do, but I know how important the new business is to Jody. I can't just stand by and watch it flounder if I have the skills to help. But it's her game and she's the coach. I've indicated I'm willing to play and she turned me down and gone to sleep. I'm left lying awake with mixed emotions.

Friday, February 9
JODY:

"I'm putting you back on Taxotere," Mike says. "There is no other drug to substitute. You need this, Jody. It has to be this way."

After the week off to recuperate from the first two doses, Mike worries about separating doses, even though he agrees it was all we could do. "I hate to say this, but instead of having two more chemo sessions as expected before ending chemo, I'd like to schedule three, if you can tolerate it at all, spread over the next three weeks."

"Three?"

He encourages liberal use of morphine but there's nothing he can do about the toenail I lost, the ones I'm losing, or the fact that the skin between my toes is rotting because the toes are swollen too close to one another. There's really little he can do for anything.

I ask why my eyes tear almost constantly, one more than the other. It looks like I'm always crying, always emotionally unstable. I hate this. I can't read and I look like a fool. Sometimes I can barely drive.

"You don't have any eyelashes," Mike answers. "Your eyes are easily irritated."

I haven't had eyelashes for months. This is a new complication, nonstop, and I can't feel any irritation. But okay, whatever he says. I go from his cubical to a back room for chemo. The nurse takes one look at me and says, "Oh, you've got Taxotere eyes now too, huh?"

"Eh?"

"Yeah, two women had to change meds recently because they couldn't stand this side effect, the constant tearing. It was too much for them to handle."

"So this chemotherapy has a reputation for this?"

"Sure does, though you won't find it listed on the literature we get from the drug company."

I have had it! I am positively enraged. "Is there any litmus test for what the docs actually fucking know?! I mean, these guys see women with all these side effects every day! Once a drug is brought to market, don't doctors ever poll patients about what the fuck these drugs do? Don't they ever then share the goddam information? Or do the docs just acknowledge what they read in pro-med literature initiated by the drug companies?"

"Good question," she says, nonplussed. She deals with upset women all the time and her manner indicates that she deals with them *calmly.*

"Pretending they don't realize what is going on just creates a sanctioned denial system for those who don't want to take responsibility for being the catalyst for chaos. But they sure take personal credit for healing when they prescribe drugs that *do* work!"

"And you'll give it to them, too, with gratitude," she teases, winking. *Touche.*

Monday, February 12
JODY:

I put Kevin on a plane to Manchester, England, where he'll attend a two-day program for work. Accompanying him was not an option.

Things could easily be worse. Our neighbor Bill-the-bagpiper was just told that his chemo isn't working at all for his lung/liver cancer and his doc had no idea what to do. That would be the hated Dr. X.

Bill's wife (I've come to know her as *Linda* during our many recent snippets of conversation at the edges of our yards) told me all about the visit the next day. There was silence as the couple tried to grasp the situation. Then Bill suggested a second opinion. Dr. X. reportedly replied, "Oh. Good idea."

Apparently it is now up to a stunned cancer patient at their lowest point of treatment to come up with the good ideas. Dr. X. told him to make an appointment with another oncologist in two weeks to allow sufficient time for the paperwork to clear. Linda ignored him and called right away. Bill will see a specialist this coming week. Linda does not like Dr. X. either. She says Bill liked him okay in the past, but she says that Dr. X. never cared about her opinions or questions. She finds him to be cold and abrupt.

I tell her how he *treated* me in Mike's absence: paramount to malpractice. [*Www.rxmed.com: Patients receiving paclitaxel (Taxol) should be pretreated to minimize hypersensitivity. One of these reactions was fatal in a patient treated without pre-medication. Patients who experience severe hypersensitivity reactions should not be re-challenged with the drug.*] I alternately refer to him as *The Iceman* or *That Fucking Idiot*. TFI for short. I instructed Mike to write out orders that TFI is never to see me again, even if he's the only doc on the premises and I've just passed out and can't be resuscitated. I asked him to have it tattooed on my forehead. He thought I was kidding. I was only half joking.

The third one of our little cancer trio has been hanging in there with high-dose chemo, though Mom had a scare during her first treatment, which had to be suspended until she could tolerate it. Tuesday and Wednesday the chemo cocktails went right to the cancer and started killing it, which actually reduced her bone pain. When I check in now, Bobby puts her on the phone after warning that she's a little *out of it*.

"I see bright colors and I'm having hallucinations," she says.

"Are you enjoying them?"

She giggles: "Yes."

"You know even while you're having them that they are caused by drugs, right?"

"Yes. I tell myself that when I see them, or I'd think I was crazy."

"Then just keep enjoying them. They're better than pain jolts."

"Actually, I kind of like them."

Thank God she didn't discover this in the '60s. I mean that sincerely: she was goofy enough without grass. Though I'm hardly one to talk, with those silly thoughts about Kevin poisoning me. Good thing no one checked *my* sanity as the effects of Taxol continued to make themselves known! The wheel was spinning, but the hamster was dead. The porch light was on, but nobody was home. My elevator didn't go all the way to the top.

I can't help but wonder, however, having had that confusing paranoid experience… if mother's trip to Madison last fall came at a time when she was fighting the same effects. She was uncharacteristically bleak, suspicious and even downright paranoid. Now I have to honestly wonder if that isn't a much more prevalent side effect than doctors know… or patients are told. And if so, a little support and education would have been much appreciated by at least two patients I know. Another Lesson learned.

In Kevin's absence, PJ is making our dinner. Egg noodles and a little butter. I join my son in the kitchen, where the bigger dog Foley is cleaning the floor by dragging little Micky around like a dustmop. Micky apparently was playing *dead dog* and Foley loped up and captured Micky's collar between his teeth. I think how this sight would freak my mother out about now. I laugh at the dogs aloud even while tears drip off my chin. No, I'm not crying. Blame the waterworks on Taxo-*tear*.

Thursday, February 15
KEVIN:

The new magazine still needs another salesperson. While she has a sales manager to oversee revenue initiatives, it isn't Jody's nature to delegate worry. As a result, she has warmed to the idea of my help. The only remaining stumbling block is our willingness to trade an initial loss of approximately half my income during this start-up phase. And are we willing to invest the miles and wear on our car, as well as the greater consideration of travel time?

On the other hand, we're putting our personal wages right back into the business; why not make one of the checks out to me? Fund Peter to pay Paul. This could be financial ruin... or a necessary investment. Seems we're always shifting paradigms lately. Why should this be different?

I float the idea past Lori at work. She is none-too-thrilled but understands my commitment to Jody. I say that nothing is certain, for we are still crunching numbers to see if it is workable. I leave her a bit more stressed than I found her.

Jody calls. She has set up an appointment with Bill a week from Saturday to discuss the possibility of my joining their firm. This is moving pretty fast, but then, what doesn't in our lives?

Friday, February 16
JODY:

When the company declared a snow day for the blizzard, I actually slept 16 hours straight! But now the roads are cleared, I'm back at work, and Tracy will drive me to clinic for chemo. Kevin will pick me up after he gets off work. I pack magazine proofs and manuscripts needing a final edit.

Mike is off duty, leaving Dr. X. as a poor excuse for a stand-in. I am thankful this is not my week for a doctor's review because I would refuse to see TFI and we'd have a scene. Nurse Deb gets me situated but leaves before starting the drip. She soon returns with word that I am to be denied treatment AGAIN, this time because the skin on my fingers is peeling off. I have blisters, some covering entire fingers, others just spots which appear frayed and unraveling. My frayed skin becomes almost instantly yellow and hard, almost brittle, and the new skin under it looks burnt.

I hold a hand before my face incredulously: "You're really denying me treatment because of *this*? It's just ugly shedding and it doesn't even hurt! It looks revolting, but I can handle it!"

"I checked with Dr. X. and he wants no part of treating you in this condition. This is serious. If we give you more Taxotere now, with you already sensitized, the new skin will split open and you'll have open sores that could get infected. You'll likely have very painful sores on your feet, if you don't already, and you might not be able to walk. We can't give you anything this week, and Mike will need to see you next week before we can treat again. I'm sorry... I know how much you want to finish your series and be done with it."

I fight back tears. "I told Mike my feet were rotting last week," I tell her. "The skin was coming off between my toes and he didn't say anything at all except to agree it wasn't a fungus. He never said anything about this being a side effect. I bet Mike would treat me if he were here."

I have judged this doctor guilty of giving a previous infusion when he shouldn't have, then of denying treatment at the hospital when I thought he should give it. Now he refuses a treatment that obviously would be risky, and I am distressed once again. Would I be acting in so juvenile a manner if he were Mike? This guy can't win with me ... nor I with him.

The nurse is kind but firm: "We can't help you if we make you any sicker, Jody. We must stop for a week or we'll be compromising your health further. It's hard, but that's what we have to do. If you want to talk to Dr. X. yourself, I'll be happy to take you to him."

No way. I leave quietly, a beaten dog.

I don't bother calling Kevin away from work early. I can wait. I take my creepy little fingers downstairs, where I sit in the patient sitting area and work. I carve out a little workspace where I sit huddled in an outrageous leopard fake-fur coat. Suddenly it occurs to me that I don't look artsy enough (I cling to the belief that people will excuse baldness if it is in any way connected to art) and so I buy a gold turban in the gift shop and cover up my greatest insecurity – or call even more attention to it. Whatever. Resettled, I force myself to review art compositions and text breaks. I'm not going to feel sorry for myself.

Kevin is surprised with the unexpected break in treatment, since this has been the first side effect that hasn't really hurt very much. Now that he's here, I admit that I do feel a little sorry for myself. I mean, I still am having trouble with my eyes tearing, little rivers constantly running down my cheeks. I know he is looking into just a moonshadow of a face with red eyes. It is most pathetic, I think, allowing my bottom lip to quiver just a bit.

"Since you still feel pretty good," Kevin says, ignoring my obvious invitation to a pity party, "let's go to Chicago and visit Summer and Paddy in their new home. We'll have a nice brunch, listen to some Irish Music, maybe even catch a movie."

That's a possibility. I wipe my eyes with a tissue from the cache in my pocket, an acquired necessity. "But I have this celebrity-server charity dinner on Sunday I'd really like to do, if we could cover my hands."

"We'll buy gloves, little white ones appropriate for a server," he offers. "We'll be back in plenty of time."

Saturday, February 17
JODY:

Summer is tight lipped when I remove the bandages and let her peek. She helps me tape up the worsening blisters. "It doesn't hurt at all," I assure her.

"Yeah, right," she says. "It looks like you mistook Drano for hand cream."

While cleaning a counter top, I pick up a knife by the blade instead of the handle. Because my fingertips are numb, I don't feel it slide down over my taped thumb. Soon the bandage is dripping blood. Summer brings out her first-aid kit another time. "Finally, a cut deep enough that I can feel it," I tell her, smiling. "It actually feels good to have some sensation back."

"Maybe you'd like to play with my lighter later," she mutters.

I try to tease a little smile from my grim-faced daughter: "You're lucky that I have so many interesting symptoms to share with your nursing class."

"You're nuts," she says. "Nothing about this is lucky. Or funny."

Kevin bans me from the kitchen.

The blistering quickly spreads like a wildfire; within an hour I am thinking I must be at the height of the worst of the reaction, feet and hands engulfed in blisters. There's no wriggle room; I'm forced to agree with Kevin and Summer that I'm in no condition to participate in a charity event tomorrow. I call Bill and ask him to cancel my spot as a celebrity server. I don't want to spill hot coffee on someone and get the charity sued.

Time now for a spot of tea, though I'm not allowed to brew it. Summer brings it to where I have been parked in the living room. She drinks her tea and chatters, her eyes flitting from my eyes to my fingers the entire time. It is wearisome, all the attention it takes to steady the cup between numb fingertips. We both pretend everything is *normal* as I dribble tears and tea all over the little saucer.

The telephone rings; it is Brook. She's just spoken to P.J. in Madison and learned we were in Chicago. "When did PJ's voice get so deep?" Brook asks. "He sounds like a grown man all of a sudden. Are you slipping him your steroids to get him out of the house faster?" This brings a hoot from Kevin.

We also laugh with our little Boo-Bear over her latest military police stories and agree that if things aren't right with her boyfriend, she might be better off living at the barracks again. I will miss his son, but that is not Brook's burden. If she is this unhappy, the relationship can't be working for the boy, either. The phone is passed around the room; everyone has a little advice and a little love to offer the lonely soldier. Kevin and she have forged a wonderful rapport now that they have military miseries in common. I hear her laughter over the telephone as he launches into a Kentucky soldier persona. Then Paddy takes the phone with an authentic, thick Irish brogue that drives us all to giggling fits.

Thank God my daughters don't have breast cancer....

It is as though this very thought is powerful enough to reach out and startle Summer, who casts an anxious glance my way. Suddenly her eyes brim with tears and she looks away. I am racked with swift guilt for even imagining such a horrendous possibility.

The conversation ends with Brook, and I force my voice to be light: "Let's go out to dinner tonight, and then Kevin and I will treat for a movie. We could see *Hannibal*. How's that for a plan?"

"Are you sure you're up to it?" Summer asks, doubtful.

"Honey, chemo is the only currency that can really buy time," I say, not caring if it sounds maudlin or not. "Nothing that remarkable comes cheap, and nothing that precious should be wasted. Let's have some fun with it."

Let's spend our time together making memories, not wallowing in regrets.

Sunday, February 18
JODY:

One chemo left to go! I had one just this past Friday, and Mike expects to assess me on Thursday of next week, as he's gone Friday. But he said that he would like to personally see this through and evaluate how I'm doing at that point. I had 13% less dose – his decision. My decision was to take extra steroids to try and make sure I don't have to lose another week to low counts and weird side effects. If I'm okay Thursday, I get my final whack!

Kevin and I deemed Valentine's Day a *no go* night and cancelled plans for dinner. The tearing eyes were too distracting. We pushed our celebration to Thursday, complete with a very nice dinner out. Kevin bought me a beautiful Irish ring with a diamond, matching necklace, and gold earrings. Surprise! I had managed to shop by myself and presented him with a couple suits and dress shirts – required clothing for our sales-people.

Today, I'm making *thank you* gifts for the oncology nurses who have been so compassionate and helpful, and, of course, lab tech Romeo, who still hates the process of drawing my blood through the port. He always brings me a fresh, hot blanket halfway through chemo and we talk about his days as a medic in the Gulf War, his wife, his mom, anything to fill the time. He's Filipino and my name always sounds like *Judy* when he says it. But I answer by any name to get finished.

I went shopping yesterday for materials to make Summer a personal-ized baby book. Today was a sleep-in-and-watch-a-movie day, but now I'm back on the computer with very few complaints. Either I'm getting used to chemo seven months into the regime, or this lighter dose is a Godsend. We'll see what tomorrow brings.

Kevin's decision to leave his human resources director job to join *In Business: Rockford* magazine follows many conversations with staff, but surprisingly few with each other. I think people become a magnified ver-sion of their true core when there is some threat to their family. Some would hunker down and study stock portfolios and play it safe with their income. Not us. We're risk takers and believe very strongly in intuitive responses to situations and then seeing those responses through. He suggested it and I agreed, if that's what he wants to do. He begins with us the first week in March.

Mom continues on her chemo – another round begins tomorrow. She's sleeping today and wishes not to be roused. *Sweet dreams, Mama.*

Thursday, February 22
JODY:

Mike agrees to a final chemotherapy infusion today, *a day early!* Three nurses come around the corner on cue, one holding a latex glove blown up with a face and "yeah, no more chemo!" scribbled on it. Mike hugs me tight and advises me to not let this final dose get to me, to take on the side effects and manage it just one more time.

The last one! I have waited so long to hear this! I ask how I can ever thank him and *chocolate chip cookies* springs from his lips. Next week I'm going to bring back the biggest plastic bucket of cookies he's ever seen!

He adds that, barring anything unusual, I'm not to see him again for follow-up until mid-April, when we set up the Tamoxifel regime, which is a form of pill chemo that I'll be on for the rest of my life.

Before he lets me go, he pulls me to a side wall for a last piece of advice. "You think that you'll be happy this is over, but the period after chemo is the most difficult for many women," he cautions. "Right now, you're being actively treated. Don't let your imagination run away with you after you finish. Don't look over your shoulder. You're doing great. You're going to be fine."

It is time for the last infusion of Taxotere. Hook that baby up and open the line!

Friday, February 23
JODY:

I go to the radiology clinic to be examined by a radiology oncologist to determine the next phase of treatment. Mike has prepared me to expect 33 radiation treatments. I've explained to both him and the radiologist that I have a Magna conference in DC in April, and I'd really like to be there. The airline tickets are tucked away in my purse. I am to leave April 5.

"I can give you higher doses for less days," the radiologist offers. "Perhaps just 16 or 17 treatments. You'll come back Monday for a simulation, and to have the guides tattooed on your chest to guarantee accurate placement for treatment. Because you're so close to chemo, we're going to wait a couple weeks to let it run its course. Chemo can multiply the effects of radiation. But I still think we can get your treatment completed in March."

Radiation doesn't sound too bad, certainly not compared to chemo. They will make a *form* on Monday so that I'll lie in the same position every time. The radiation treatment will be a 90-second daily electron beam over my heart and lungs, first over the entire incision area and then narrowing to a smaller and smaller beam. It will be delivered at about the same time every day. I'm to get as much rest as I can before and during radiation, as the dosage will cause marked fatigue; this should start to dissipate a couple weeks after radiation, but may last up to six months or longer afterwards.

Within two weeks of the treatment, there may be some skin burning and blistering, because the chemo I've been on most lately causes increased sensitivity to radiation and I'm fair skinned. However, they have special dressings for that. If there is any redness in the area under my left arm which could then cause lymphodema (swelling of that arm due to

155

lymph node removal), I will lose a few treatment days to let it clear up. Meanwhile, during treatment, I'm to wear only cotton fabric and nothing tight over the radiation area. No bra. That should make dressing for work easy — not! There could be some scarring in my lung from the radiation, but the doctor doesn't expect it to be problematic now or later.

The most amazing thing he said is that he is upgrading my diagnosis from inflammatory cancer to "undefined." The radiologist agreed with my surgeon and disagreed with the two oncologists. He said the surgeon followed the right course of treatment. He asks me if I understand what would happen if oncologists inflate the number of cases they say are *inflammatory*.

"Death rates will artificially fall," I answer. "Because other forms of cancer are easier to manage or keep in remission. True inflammatories would think their chances of survival are greater than they really would be."

"Exactly," he says. "But every oncologist wants to claim saving inflammatory patients these days."

I am mildly taken aback because his clinic is aligned with Dean Medical Systems, and it was Mike who referred me to him. I would expect him and Mike to be playing on the same team. But then, the rules change every day in this game, a game I never wanted to play in the first place. I have had poison in my system every day since August 17 of last year and during that entire time, I've had a reason – indeed, *encouragement* provided by other medical professionals – to doubt nearly every word uttered. This is my experience, the sad saga of an articulate, affluent white woman with a list of questions and access to the best medical practitioners in the United States. What have less connected sisters had to put up with?

Mike tried to keep my spirits up during the weird side effects we've gone through together, but he was clear last Thursday that he expects that if this cancer is to come back, it will likely be within the first year and in the bones. Inflammatory is vicious that way.

So today I'll choose to have invasive lobular or *undefined* cancer, not because I believe it, but because it better suits my needs. Why not? I have things to do, like Summer's baby shower next weekend. I have a conference to help with, a division to run, a grandchild to help welcome into this world, a son to finish raising, and a husband to thank. I may be slow moving through March, but I'm on my way back.

I hope that Mom is someday this close to survival. This week, her chemo had to be delayed due to blood transfusions and low counts. Why am I not optimistic for her? For the same reason I think I'm going to make it. I trust Mike.

"This is a mistake with your mother," he said. "A serious mistake." Her doctor called it her *best hope*.

Saturday, February 24
KEVIN:

Today presents a far more hectic agenda than I am comfortable with, for my wife's sake. We have the meeting with Bill and then a drive to Rockford, where we'll check into a hotel and dress in formal attire to attend the Addy Awards, a competition for advertising design firms. Tracy, Jody's sales manager, was responsible for putting the program together and I suspect that Jody's insistence on attending has more to do with lending emotional support for a nervous Tracy than interest in who wins what. Still, it's a crazy schedule.

Bill proves to be cautiously receptive to the idea of my joining the company. His gravest concern, he says, is that this business venture could have a negative impact on our marriage at a time when it already has so many challenges. I don't laugh out loud, but I do tell him that this is the least of my worries.

Still, he listens for whatever words will make this make sense to him. I, in turn, want something from him. I need him to say that he is convinced that the new magazine will be successful whether I join the company or not. If he has faith in the magazine, I'll give him reason to trust me as well.

More words, the right ones, are exchanged and the deal is struck. The marked change in Jody's demeanor has been decidedly positive since we've personally committed ourselves to this direction. Bill and I shake hands. The next hurdle will be to convince Tracy that this isn't a move on my behalf to take her more attractive role of sales manager, or to monitor her performance in the second city. I know I would wonder if my boss brought in their *overqualified* partner to work *for me*. However, I genuinely like Tracy and really have no hidden agenda. I feel that we had a meeting of the minds to this point in the process. Tonight I will meet my new partner sales rep in Rockford and get a feel for any potential synergy. I fervently wish that we might work as well together as I have with Lori, but am not overly optimistic. I imagine that being the boss's husband will create some artificial distance in the equation.

If this doesn't work (or more importantly, when it does), I can always return to a human resources position. For now, I resolve to get a quick start to buffer my family as well possible from the initial loss of income.

I also resolve to keep my ego in check.

The trip to Rockford passes quickly enough, with much discussion about the market. There is so much I need to know to hit the ground running. As it is, we have trouble enough locating the Holiday Inn off the main drag; two strangers in a strange land that we'll have to navigate and conquer.

Jody has purchased special makeup and takes care to pencil in eyebrows and to position a blond wig beneath a gold turban. She slips into an evening gown and emerges from the tiny hotel bathroom absolutely stunning! This is the most "Jody-ish" she has appeared in months and the very sight of her brings tears to my eyes.

The Mardi Gras-themed dinner and recognition program is to be in the same building as our suite of business offices. We arrive at the office building at the same time as Tracy and her husband, and I accept her offer of a quick tour. I am ushered into a small office about two-thirds the size of the one I will leave for this job. As I look at the small desk and chair separated from the other work area by a partition and bookcase, I mask my disappointment, thinking, *this was my idea. Where I sit is no big deal because I'll be out on appointments most of the time.*

Patti, my new associate, seems genuinely glad to meet me. I assure her that I'm just coming in to sell magazine ads, adding that I'd prefer our clients not know that I am married to the publisher. She merely nods. An hour later, as we network together, it quickly becomes apparent that Patti has already told many people who I am in relation to Jody. I wonder how small a town Rockford is and how fast news travels.

Jody pretends to enjoy herself even while becoming visibly fatigued, but the night drags on for me. I watch her, fetch her glasses of water, and attempt to make her more comfortable. Because of persistent mouth sores, my wife isn't able to eat a single bite of the highly-spiced Cajun dishes. Without a word, Abby, the editor, leaves the party. She soon returns to our table with a plate of steaming, buttered noodles, made special for Jody by the restaurant staff upstairs. I hug her for her thoughtfulness.

To say that Jody is very beloved by her staff just doesn't do justice to the relationships she has forged; I see evidence of it on a daily basis. Tonight, as she begins to limp with exhaustion, Tracy and Abby do everything they can to make this social event easier. They hover over her and invite people to her table, where she continues to hold court in a queenly fashion. A television station owner tells her that he has cancer and he begins a long story of all the details of his treatment. Her eyes meet mine and she winks. This is becoming a ritual, everywhere she goes. Cancer story after cancer story. But she will listen and offer encouragement.

Finally it is over. As I drive through the downtown area, I make a mental note of the businesses in my sales territory; those with odd-numbered addresses. Patti has the even-numbered locations. There are a number of good prospects on the *odd side* of the street.

Jody needs help removing her dress; she simply can't do it. I unzip it, hold her up as she steps out of the gown, hang it up. Help her into soft flannel shorts and a button-in-the-front pajama top. Slip off her turban, her wig, kiss her bald head. Wipe the makeup gently from her face. Help her brush her aching teeth. Rinse her mouth with a medicated wash. Put a glass of water on the nightstand for when she wakes with hot flashes, to give her something cool to reach for. Then I give her my arm so that she can lean on it to walk the few steps to the bed.

As I make a warm cocoon in the bed for her and tuck her in with a tender kiss, I think to myself again that I can do this. Never mind that I am less enthused than before. A sales job is a no brainer compared to the most recent job assigned to me. Being Jody's caregiver has completely exhausted my resources day after day, but day after day, there was no choice and nowhere that I would rather have been. I wouldn't have missed the experience of staying by her side, and all of the extra moments we've had together because of it, for the world.

CHAPTER *10*: March

The baby shower ● Radiation ● So tired ● Mom's downward spiral ● Son's fears ● Kevin's new job

March 2
KEVIN:

Around 50 people pack themselves into our designated area at the restaurant that Lori selected for the going-away luncheon arranged for me. I'm in awe of the turnout! Either they are all happy that I'm leaving or else they appreciate my accomplishments. An H.R. director can never be sure.

Earlier today, I roamed the plant and said my goodbyes. There were abundant heartfelt handshakes and warm hugs. Ever aware of the nature of my position, I've not typically made myself available for demonstrations of friendship or camaraderie, but today was different. I believed those who said I would be missed.

Of course, there's always one. My particular one disgruntled employee seizes an opportunity to announce that she is glad I am leaving. A year earlier, she says, she was not treated fairly by me.

"I think you're incompetent and ill-suited to the position," she snipes, eyes snapping. I put up no rebuttal at all. What difference does it make now? Let her have her day. Her say. She must have been thinking of this for days, worrying over how she would approach me, what she would say, how I would react. No doubt she had fired herself up for a fight, the very behavior that landed her in my office in the first place so long ago. I merely wish her well with the new H.R. director, whom I have already recruited. Perhaps it's time to get out of human resources permanently. Who needs the grief inherent to the position? I have enough grief in my life.

Lunch speeds by. Different people present me with parting gifts, make nice comments about my contributions, and wish me well in my new endeavor. I choke up when I say my goodbye to the group at large. I have the hardest time when it is time to say goodbye to Lori. I will miss her.

I go home directly from the luncheon and then get in a quick round of golf before Jody gets home. A sorely needed mini-vacation. My new job starts on Monday.

Sunday, March 4
JODY:

A script from hell: Go to a baby shower with the womenfolk of your ex-husband's family, whom you haven't seen for almost 20 years. Oh yeah, and you're bald, still have chemo-blisters on your face, and are about 30 pounds heavier than before starting treatment (which would add 50 pounds to the era when they knew you). And your fingernails and toenails are purple, rippled, and falling off.

Kevin and I spent the night with Summer and Paddy so that I could help with last-minute preparations. Now, dressing for the party, I tell myself to buck up as I look into the mirror. *Stop your whining, Brook is home on leave and this is Summer's day. Put on a little makeup and straighten the gold turban. Put a pin on it; make it look festive.* In the scheme of things, it will be no big deal. Just another day. *Be thankful you have it with the girls.*

I drive Summer and Brook to friend Moona's suburban Chicago home, the car packed full of food, gifts, and door prizes. Summer is radiant with her pretty, flowered long dress and her round belly. Brook wears a new outfit bought special for the shower; tiny Capri pants with matching powder blue sweater. Summer will have to share the spotlight with Brook today, our petite military cop on her first trip home since enlisting. We tease Boo-Bear that with her long and lush blonde hair and flawless Florida tan, she looks like a Barbie doll. They are so beautiful, my grown daughters, that it brings a lump to my throat.

Moona is radiant as well. Summer's best friend is Pakistani with mysterious brown eyes. She stands between my two blonde lasses for a picture and the contrast is startling. Soon she is a dark beauty in a sea of Irish faces. I've never seen so many Irish women in one place, as more and more guests arrive. All of Summer and Paddy's Irish friends are from a tight circle of recent immigrants and speak with the musical lilt as they share stories about being pregnant themselves with their *wee ones*. The Glynn women, second and third generation, fit right in and speak of journeys taken and planned to Ireland. Ghosts of family gatherings past are within reach as I awkwardly greet each one in turn; Aunt Erin, Kathy, Mary Lee, Annie, Denise.

We play games and I forget that I am *sick*. It is too funny, the lengths of ribbon the women cut as they try to *guess the girth* of my sweet Summer's belly. What fun! Brook helps Moona lay out the last of a huge buffet and we eat together from the feast the girls have assembled. I am exhausted, but thankful for the role of party photographer, which lets me move around a lot and masks my brief disappearances to a back bedroom to just catch my breath. As much as I am enjoying the party, I am spent and will be glad when it is over. Kevin and I are driving back to Madison and I realize that he will have to do the driving. I am nearing the end of my stamina.

"You look beautiful," Aunt Erin whispers as the Glynn family matriarch hugs me goodbye. "God bless you with your troubles."

"God has blessed me already with your kindness," I whisper in return. What a great party!

Wednesday, March 8
JODY:

I am sick of losing toenails. Sick of the eye tearing. Sick of chemo. Particularly since this part of the journey is supposed to be over!

Radiation isn't as easy as I thought it would be, either. The 90 seconds of treatment actually take 24 minutes (they count them) to shoot me four places with a huge electron machine. It doesn't hurt, but whether imagined or real, I feel the cells suddenly hypered and dancing in the area being shot, like a little buzz, or a vibration deep inside. It is very alarming.

The radiation technicians — or nurses, which are they? — stop between shots to draw a vertical line on my chest with a marker by making little dots and then connecting them to the ones tattooed on my chest. This is weird-funny because they start at the bottom of the area being radiated, where I am completely numb from the nerves being cut during the mastectomy. I feel nothing. Then suddenly they hit a "hot" or unaffected area where I can still feel something and it is startling.

Lead shields are put right inside the machine to protect my heart and most of my lungs, and they put cool, gel-filled forms on my surface skin at some locations to alter the point at which the beam hits the skin. So there is a lot of stopping and re-preparing the machine, and whirring and buzzing while I lie in the same position, my head and arms locked steady in a pre-formed plastic mold.

The beam is part of a huge arm that moves to the side and under me, and one treatment is done on my back. Later I use a liberal dose of the cream they give me to help prevent burning. Any other lotion is prohibited.

I see the radio-oncologist on Mondays after treatment, when he inspects the site for breakdown in skin (burning). This week, he was very busy and after half an hour spent waiting, I opted to see him on Tuesday instead. The quick in and out I was promised just hasn't been my experience yet.

They've doubled my dose to accommodate my schedule so we are doing this in 17 visits. The main side effect is fatigue. Kevin drove us both to work this morning, insisting that I am too tired to take a separate car. As if to prove him right, I fall asleep at my desk. One minute I'm awake and the next one, I have to lie my head on the desk. I just can't be awake any longer. When I resurface, two hours have passed. I groggily open my office door; Bill is standing just outside.

"I fell asleep," I mumble.

"I wondered. We were supposed to meet an hour ago. Are you okay?"

"Could we skip the meeting? I have more radiation in an hour."

I am so tired! But I have a job to do, too, so after radiation, I have Kevin bring me back to the office.

Mom calls me at work at 5:10 and asks if anyone is with me. I know something very upsetting must have happened. She sounds surprisingly lucid, which hasn't been the case lately. Her doctors decided today to take her off the bone marrow transplant protocol and to begin radiation for a large tumor on her spine. They told her that realistically, she has from two weeks to six months to live. Chemo is being stopped and the idea is to make her as comfortable as possible. She reports this in a rather unemotional tone. She adds that Kurt is coming home from Missouri, in part to help Bobby muddle through things like wills and insurance papers. She has a lot of paperwork that needs sorting.

I tell her that I can't be there until possibly April or May. I have the conference, then an appointment with Mike to be put on a new chemotherapy mid-April, followed by scheduled surgery to remove my port the 19th. Summer's baby is due April 24.

What is also true, a fact I don't share with her, is that I don't want to go to Denver and do a deathwatch like I did with my stepfather two years ago when he died of cancer at home. I sat at Wayne's bedside for three weeks, then flew back to Madison to honor my wedding date, and then hopped right into a car with my new husband and headed back to Denver. I don't want to move in for the long haul when it could be months away from Kevin and the kids. Still, I'd very much like to be with her now and throughout whatever time she has left. This is about the most conflicted I've ever been about anything.

After I hang up the telephone, I cry by myself before telling Kevin that now it seems Mom and I will go through radiation at the same time, too. Kevin begs me to let the journey together end there. Mom' prognosis and struggle has deeply affected him and my children for obvious two-fold reasons. But I believe I am meant to keep her memory alive for years to come. She's very afraid of dying. She has not cultivated close friends, which means she's pretty much restricted to my brothers, my children, and me. As the end gets nearer, I certainly do intend to fly out to Denver and hold her so she will have no reason to feel afraid or that she is going alone. I would like to be there to hand her to God.

I go downstairs to PJ's lair. "You and I need to talk about Grandma," I tell him. "We got some sad news today."

"Is she dead?" His words are brave, but his voice wavers.

"Not yet. But soon, I'm afraid. Would you like to talk about it?"

"She doesn't have the same kind as you, right?"

"Right."

"Your treatment is working better, right?"

"Right."

"You're not supposed to die, right?"

"That's right. My doctor still believes I will be cured."

"Okay then."

"Okay then. Do you want to talk about Grandma?"

"Not really. Not now."

"Love you."

"Love you, too."

I can't handle anymore today. I wave off supper in favor of a four-hour nap before bedtime.

Thursday, March 9
JODY:

I'm fully awake this morning, thanks largely to coffee. I have a pile of projects on my desk, so there's no lack of stimulating things to do.

But I'm not really thinking about work. I'm thinking about Katie, a 45-year old woman that Kevin and I met during my chemo sessions. She had a computer hooked up with email just so that she could correspond with me. She isn't doing well; she's emaciated and losing her hold. Her father writes to me when she can't, but when she can, there are tears in her words, and her cancer is still aggressively going after her. Her family is urging her to *be positive, be positive* when she feels like she is vomiting up the world. She needs someone who has gone through it and can hear her and validate what she is feeling. She has chosen me, and I will be with her throughout her treatment in whatever way I can.

I fire off a brief memo reminding her that we care. We're out here.

My mother is dying while I sit at a desk working. I can't do this. But I can't interrupt my own radiation treatments, either. I can't go. But how can I stay?

My vision blurs and I have to close my eyes because I am so tired… so tired. So tired of cancer. I'll just lay my head on this desk a few minutes….

Monday, March 12
KEVIN:

I arrived early this morning at the new Rockford office, dressed in suit and tie and ready to get down to business, face recently shaved. Losing the beard wasn't my idea, but I didn't want to buck Tracy's first request as my *supervisor*. Not that it was delivered that way: Last week, while in training and learning the sales tracking system, I was told by my wife that Tracy didn't think a beard was good for a salesperson. I disagree, but learned long ago to pick my battles. This is small potatoes in the scheme of things lately. I call Jody before I leave the office at 5 p.m.

"I thought we agreed that you'd put in a regular work day, including the drive time," she says — and there is no mistaking her annoyance that I'm not calling from a closer location. "I didn't expect you to leave our house at 6 a.m. and not return until 12 hours later."

Truthfully, neither did I. It was more a matter of getting wrapped up in the first day, of not wanting to leave before the other employees, of not wanting to be seen as having *special treatment* because of my relationship with our mutual boss-lady. But this is not the time to say it.

I stop on the way home to buy an Illinois map and also to break up the monotony of the drive. The *coming back* seems longer than the *going to* because I'm beat. I'm lucky I haven't fallen asleep behind the wheel. How do long-distance truckers do this every day? *Why* do they do it every day?

Jody is on the couch with both dogs, and looking at her face as I give her a quick hello kiss, I'm reminded what exhausted *really* looks like. We were warned that she was having radiation sooner than recommended after chemo because of her desire to finish in time for her upcoming conference. As a result, the side effects of both have been magnified. While she is beginning to sprout the faintest blonde fuzz on her head, she still lacks eyelashes, eyebrows, and her face is pocked with sinister-looking red blisters. She still is plagued with mouth sores and her energy is even further diminished. After 4 p.m., she's done with her day, whether she was ready to quit or not.

Still, Jody is full of questions about my first day. I share my first impressions, how it feels to work with Abby, and my concerns that her staff not think I'm going to report their days back to her. This segues into a discussion about long days, and I try to explain my hesitation to leave too early. We flirt with an argument but manage a compromise. Whenever possible, I will leave by 4 p.m.

As I'm peeling potatoes for dinner, P.J. wanders upstairs, fresh from playing his newest video game.

"What's for dinner?" he asks.

"I'm making your mother mashed potatoes. What would you like?"

"How about spaghetti? You make that pretty good."

"Spaghetti it is, if you'll bake the garlic bread."

We eat a peaceable dinner before the television, Micky and Foley posted between us, sentries watching for a dropped morsel, an offered crumb. Garlic bread is one of their favorites; we laugh at the lengths they are willing to go for bites.

Later, lying in bed while Jody finishes her bath, I review today, plan tomorrow. I've already got some good leads and I'm hopeful. Going to Rockford was the right decision.

CHAPTER 11: April

Conference in DC • Teaching PJ to drive • Port removed • Denver good-byes • Waylaid in Topeka, Kansas • The last "active treatment" clinic visit • Life, death, & remission in 24 hours

Saturday, April 7, Washington, D.C.
JODY:

As I had hoped, I finished radiation treatment in time to participate in our company's conference for college student government leaders. This trip provides more than an opportunity to travel; it is proof that I am still able to do what I've done B.C. (Before Cancer).

I still have some chemo after-effects magnified by radiation but the conference pace overshadows those and, while busy, I concentrate on the task at hand, or enjoying the simple act of walking with colleagues through historical sites during *off* periods. The effects of radiation are harder to shake off since finishing the booster treatments. The radiated site burns with a constant flame of its own, radiating from inside rather than outside my skin. There is a clear temperature difference between the area and the adjacent tissue, and there is no lack of feeling deep inside the tissue or bone.

I was told not to wear anything but loose cotton shirts, which means no bra and no prosthesis. Even so, the area under my arm is infected, green pus forming along the incision site where the lymph nodes were removed. Gross. I bite my lip as I force a cotton swab between red scalded edges to clean the wound. I wash it well with the special soap that my friend Ruth Ann made without perfumes or harsh chemicals. During every break I take from conference-related chores, I'm up in my hotel room, cleaning the site.

I put on a red cotton blouse with black jacket and brilliant red and black patterned scarf to help camouflage the missing breast. The radiated site hurts, no matter how gently I try to pull the jacket over the shirt, and

I worry that although I've bandaged the worst of the seeping area, the shirt will soon be sticking to my skin. But there's nothing I can do differently to change the outcome, so I continue to dress.

I glance in the mirror; there is a ghost of hair covering my scalp, but certainly not enough to brush. Still, my decision not to wear any scarf or hat is sound. I have been able to be myself, and much more comfortable than at the fall conference. The result is that young women attending the conference whose brief histories include mothers with cancer, or big sisters, or even themselves, have felt comfortable approaching me and sharing their stories. A very large male student said I reminded him of his mother and gave me a bear hug that lifted me off my feet. It was a very moving experience in more ways than one.

Today, Bill is returning to Madison because wife Nancy's father died unexpectedly. The news is difficult for me on many levels; my heart goes out to Nancy and the children, but we are short staffed and Bill will be missed.

Where are my shoes? Why am I always looking for shoes in a hotel room?

Thursday, April 12
KEVIN:

"Ready to take us out on the road?" I ask P.J., wondering how much longer we're going to circle the high school's parking lot before he finds the courage to enter the roadway.

"Not yet." He seems a bit mollified that operating a real car is much more daunting than driving his NASCAR computer autos.

"Okay. Once more around the lot."

He takes the Saturn in a wide loop and then pulls into yet another parking stall well away from other vehicles. He knows the drill if he opts to park: he's to get out and check the positioning of the car. He backs into another stall. Checks his position. He drives forward into yet a different parking space and right about now I'm thankful that his mother isn't with us, because as easily as she gets carsick, she'd be puking. Still, as he continues this never-ending stop-and-go park-and-ride exercise, he shows steady improvement.

"How about now?" I ask.

"You trust me on the road?" He looks at me as if I would be crazy if I did.

"If you trust yourself, then I trust you. How's that?"

"Let's go around the lot one more time," he says.

Eventually, my stepson leaves the playground behind to venture out into the real driving world of oncoming traffic, unpredictable pedestrians, and road hazards, but all he notices is that he's making his first right turn onto a public road. I settle into the passenger's seat, mindful of the bigger picture for both our sakes, and suddenly realize that I'm also watching P.J. mature before my eyes.

It's a surprisingly emotional awareness, to lay claim to a small part of the process of his metamorphosis. To be doing something with him that I know he'll never forget. Something that he'll remember when he has his own children and it's time to teach them as I taught him, as my father taught me. I missed so many of those firsts with him: his first words, first steps, first day of school. But today I am here. I direct him through the light and have him turn left. The meaning is driven home, literally, that I can now rightfully say that I am a part of the fabric that P.J. comes from.

"Nice job," I say as he pulls into our driveway. "Now go tell your mom that you got me home in one piece."

P.J. boasts to his mom of what a good driver he already is. I second his driving prowess and am rewarded with a broad grin.

"I'm gonna practice driving on Play Station 2," he says, and the boy-child is back and racing downstairs.

"Okay, how'd he really do?" Jody asks.

"Actually, he surprised me," I answer truthfully. "He showed a lot of respect and responsibility toward the act of driving. Do you want to go out with him sometime?"

Jody laughs at the mere suggestion.

I remember aloud my own driver's education experience, and being nervous as hell before taking the driver's license exam because my father had only let me drive twice and that was augmented by perhaps three driving stints with the driver education teacher. I was prematurely tested by at least six lessons. To make matters worse, I took the driving part of the exam behind the wheel of my father's 1965 Chrysler Imperial. It was an impressive luxury sedan with a huge front end and a back end to match. As a rather small youth, I could barely see over the front end, let alone properly align the car to park between two saw-horses. Parallel parking proved to be my driving Achilles' heel. This mortifying failure earned me a couple more adventures behind the wheel with my dad. Eventually, of course, I was given a license, and, just as predictably, had a car accident four weeks later with the Imperial. I wasn't hurt, but the accident made a lifelong impression. It also made a serious impression on the front end of the car, which I was never allowed to drive again.

I tell Jody that I am determined that *my* son will get enough time behind the wheel with me by his side. It probably would be good, I add, if P.J. was also able to log some drive time with his mother....

She laughs again.

Saturday, April 14
JODY:

Yesterday, on Good Friday, I had the surgery to remove the port through which I'd been given chemotherapy. My surgeon was in and out quickly, but I remember almost nothing about it because he put me out. Surgery the way it is supposed to be done!

However, I came too pretty quickly after the anesthesia wore off and the nerve endings woke up! My plan of action now is to take large quantities of painkillers and just lie around, willing time to pass so it can heal.

We have no plans for Easter Dinner. I can't imagine spending the energy to go to a restaurant (I'd have to get dressed to do that). Or to go grocery shopping. Or to cook.

Grilled cheese sounds good, with tomato soup. *If* Kevin makes it.

I'm going to bed.

Easter Sunday, April 15
JODY:

Kurt and Bobby called first thing this morning. Mom is in a coma at home and not expected to live through the day.

Two hours later, I am packed and on a plane to Denver, clearheaded. I guess I really won't be expected to cook Easter dinner....

Friday, April 20
JODY:

My nerves are on edge and I alternate between despair and panic. Watching Mother vegetate, I decided Monday evening to get off all pain medication myself, and to drop the nightly sedative and antidepressant. In my mother's house, evidence of cancer is everywhere and she is very, very heavily sedated and medicated because the cancer is throughout her skeletal system, deep in her bones. The pain is excruciating even with the most potent drugs. A pump is delivering morphine at a rate that would be fatal to anyone but an N-stage cancer victim. Plus, she is wearing two pain medication patches. Plus, we're giving her almost hourly doses of liquid Valium to control seizures. I want to separate myself as much as I can from that outcome. I will be drug-free from now on, not only for myself but also so that I can remain aware of her slightest movement or need.

She sleeps the first day I am here. Monday, with the hospice nurse's help, we gently lifted her from the coma so that she might know I've come and perhaps even communicate with me a last time. For the next three days, Mom talks nonstop, stoned, incessantly chattering. She has moments of great lucidity when she talks about her childhood and her pending funeral. Her mind wanders and I give her a stuffed animal, which she proclaims to be her pretty little baby. She holds the otter and strokes it relentlessly. Because it stops her fingers from plucking at her own skin, I make sure to keep it in her arms all the time. She looks beyond the bed, beyond me, whispering to dead relatives that I can't see, and I know that she's closer to that side than this.

My brothers and I are trying to get along but it is neither an authentic nor lasting truce. I know that Bob has been really brave and devoted in his caring for Mom; he has lived with her and also with her disease, and he was in sore need of a break. Kurt preceded me by almost a month and has watched her deteriorate. They have been here *much* longer than I, and see my presence as an opportunity to leave or catch up on sleep. Kurt's job now is to do the paperwork. Bobby's job is to keep the bills paid. My job is to look after Mom. I am exhausted from radiation and surgery, but will not let Mom be unattended. After sitting by her side for 48 hours straight without even five minutes of sleep, I am near my breaking point.

It is an especially uneasy truce when we sit down to eat lunch together, each feeling somewhat betrayed by the other, and our tempers flair at the slightest provocation. They say the most hurtful things in the most casual of tones, which makes me suspicious that they have pre-discussed their approach while outside together. *Thick as thieves is what they've become this month.* They no longer see the sense in sitting by Mom's bedside 24/7, as I am doing, Kurt observes. He adds that they've already done that for days on end. Bobby says that they no longer believe it wise to perform more than the mildest treatments, either, because they are reluctant to *bother her* by moving Mom to change her diaper very often, wash out her blood-clotted mouth, or roll her over to *really* clean her bottom. *She's dying, why disturb her? The outcome won't change.*

I have not had the luxury of practicing my part with anyone, and so I react with raw emotion. I raise my voice and soon am shouting and crying and very directly giving them both holy hell. I can't let her spend what could be her last day tasting blood clots when I have a lemon glycerin sponge that she eagerly sucks when I pry apart her clenched teeth and put it in her mouth! We are withholding food, as she can't eat and has no interest in it. We are withholding water, which gags her. *Do we have to withhold attention and love? Is she not still our mother?* Did they really

171

think I came all the way to Denver to take a walk around the block while my mother lies in a bed dying?! "What in the hell did you call me out of a sick bed for, to come all the way to Denver, if not to sit with her? SOMEBODY has to!"

Now I've really pissed them off. "She wouldn't want to be coddled like this, Sissy!" Bobby shouts. "Not if she really knew what was happening. I lived with Mom! And she told me that she didn't want to live long enough to have people sitting around watching and waiting for her to die!"

"Well gee, then isn't it just fucking inconvenient for you that she did!" I explode. "Listen, you two, I walk away and she calls out my name and reaches for me. Am I supposed to ignore her? You care for her how you want, which has amounted to sitting outside and smoking since I've been here. But you just shut up about how I handle my end of things! I'm not asking you to do one goddam thing for her, or for me either, for that matter. So butt out!"

"If you're ever like this, then I'll come and hover over you, if that's what you really want," Kurt interjects. "But this is Mom's death, not yours."

Ah, tag team.

"Fuck you both. Why don't you go back outside and have another cigarette?"

The door slams behind them. I am not a caring sister right now; I am my mother's daughter, her first born. Mom has always wanted attention and in fact, has been vocal in acknowledging that herself throughout her life. I know her as well or better than my brothers do or ever will, even if they had lived with her a million years. I don't care that they might perceive my care level as a rebuttal that they weren't doing a great job without me. I don't care if they now see me as an interloper. They don't get brownie points from me for being there longer because they had no other responsibilities. And I don't get points from them for caring enough to come to help.

The doorbell rings and soon I assist the hospice nurse in giving Mom a real cleaning. We discover horrendous pressure ulcers with chunks of missing flesh on her buttocks. The nurse has to cover the wounds with huge patches of synthetic skin and she does little to hide her disgust.

"Even though she complains, and yes, it does hurt her, she is still a person," the nurse says to me. "You need to turn her onto her side every day to relieve this pressure. I'm glad you're here – your brothers could obviously use a break. But you'll have to be more diligent in the hours she has left to her."

I am furious that this could have happened and bring Kurt to the bedside and make him look.

"Don't show this to Bob," he says. "He's had enough pain. Don't add to it so you can feel self righteous."

He has a point and I agree to that. But I tell Kurt that nobody had better say one more damned word to me while I minister to Mom in the future. Not one word. He goes back outside without another word.

Adding to the already intense family strain, my mother's wedding rings have mysteriously disappeared, which I was to inherit. I am furious beyond my capacity to express it because Mother wanted these family heirlooms to be passed to my daughters; Brook was to get the engagement ring and Summer the diamond wedding band. Neither brother has any idea where they could have gone, of course, and accusing Bobby or Kurt outright is pointless and even blasphemous because there have been many people in and out of the house as mother's co-workers have come to say goodbye. Anyone could have plucked the rings from the dish by the sink where she took them off the last time she washed dishes. Bobby remembers seeing them there just before I arrived – the day before, in fact. But I feel betrayed to the bone. After all, I am the older sister who has always looked out for both of them and helped out emotionally and financially whenever asked. How could they have let those rings slip through our collective fingers? Why didn't they put them in her jewelry box?

I have no intentions of ever returning to Mom's home after her death. Though she has already sent us copies of her will and instructed us to share her estate, I don't care about the house or her furniture. Bob and Kurt can have it all. I no longer have the patience to deal with them or the paperwork complications of inheritance taxes. This is becoming a toxic situation. If we go much further in discussions of *what's fair* in general, we will be jeopardizing any relationship we might carry into the future. I'm willing to walk away from the bulk of the inheritance... but I do want the personal items — the jewelry that belonged to my grandmother, the quilts my mother made with her own hands. The memorabilia. My mother's clothes. Items she has very specifically called for me to have in her will.

During the rarer and rarer moments that Mom actually sleeps peacefully in her hospital bed in the living room, I pack the Jeep, having made a sudden decision not to fly back, but to drive her car home to *assure* I never have a reason to return. PJ will soon need a car and Mom has always been very clear in her discussions with me that her beloved Jeep Cherokee would go to me. Apparently she did not make her wishes as known to Kurt, who walks up behind me in the garage as I'm packing and asks me what the hell I am doing.

"We just had new brake pads put on this vehicle so that I could drive it home to Missouri!" he says, indignant. "We just got it back from the shop!"

"What *we* would that be?" I yell back. "You and Mom? Did she go with you, huh? Or was it you and the little mouse in your pocket? You and the psychic that channeled Mom's change of heart to you?"

Bob comes running in response to all the yelling. I stop him just inside the doorway with a single raised hand. I wonder if he has any sense of the murderous rage I am feeling in my heart at this instant. I turn back to Kurt: "Because I can't believe you are telling me that you and Bob made that decision!" I stab Bob with a piercing stare. "You knew better," I snarl.

"I've had enough of this!" Bob screams at us both. "Stop it!" Then, unexpectedly, he backs *me* up: "Mom never said anything about you taking her car, Kurt. She said the car belongs to Jody and she can have it now. You took dad's truck when he died. Jody didn't ask for a thing but his black Stetson hat. Jody gets the Jeep. Just let's all quit fighting. Mom don't need to hear this."

I am still stung over the missing jewelry and I'll be damned if I'll back down over the car, though at this point, I honestly could care less about it. "When you sell the house, you can buy ten cars," I hurl at Kurt. I tug a piece of paper out of my jeans pocket on which I've already typed a note signing off on the house and furniture, and hand it to my youngest brother. "You can have this in return for having the jeep re-titled right here, right now. I've listed everything I intend to take when I leave, because I won't have the stamina to come back. Take the paper and we'll be done talking."

He takes it. However, Bob has power of attorney – given to him because, Mom said, she couldn't be sure I'd outlive her – and he signs over the title to the car. I honestly never thought we would come to this. I thought our family was different – closer, more intelligent than the trashy feuding families I've seen so often on Jerry Springer's television program. But here we are, the three of us fighting like children in the garage while our mother lies dying. I am ashamed.

By silent agreement, we return to our artificial truce status. I pack photos, embroidery work, and family papers, jewelry chest, the pewter trains she had set aside from Wayne's estate for PJ, sewing machine and golf clubs. Nothing is contested; both brothers concur that what I want is trivial in comparison to the actual estate. I fill suitcases with Mom's clothing, every item that carries her smell or reminds me of an event she has dressed for, or clothing we bought together or items I've sent as gifts. She has exquisite taste and fancies shoes, so I pack her personal belongings carefully but absently, moving between the living room and the bedroom in a kind of a daze.

She wakes. I sit by Mom's side, undisturbed by either man, and we talk about death and life, and life-after-death. She wants to hear again about the casket the boys selected days before I arrived, wants to be sure she'll be buried in Illinois, where I've coordinated the purchase of side-by-side plots for her and Bobby. She giggles when I tell her that she has the most gorgeous grin I've ever seen. She is my mother, but she is also childlike in her final lucid moments. I put the plush otter toy back in her arms to redirect her flitting fingers from the port and IV morphine line. She strokes, strokes, strokes the stuffed animal, pulling it to her face and cradling it like a baby.

She is heartbreakingly a mother to the end of her consciousness, cuddling her newest baby and trying to be brave when the pain is stronger than the medication. Weighing less than 80 pounds, she resembles the bald babies she has birthed, and I can only barely resist the urge to pick her up and cradle her in my arms. Instead, I hold her hand, touch her face, put my gold Irish mother's ring — the beloved claddah that my children presented to me — on her finger, an heirloom moved the other direction. I promise to have it on her finger when she is buried.

Her fever spikes and we call an emergency number to summon a nurse. The seizures aren't controllable at this medication level. She moans and cries for several minutes after each one, her mouth blood-filled from biting her tongue, her agony deep from the spasms running up her spine. It is time to re-submerge our mother into a medical coma. We hold her hands while the relief drips into her port, all of us crying. She very purposely is returned to a deep coma.

Kurt makes a last supper for us all, though he doesn't know that while puttering in the kitchen. I wonder, watching him, if he still knows how much I love him. And I love Bobby, too. These are my brothers. These are good, heartbroken men. They are doing the best they can, and probably better than I.

"I'm having Kevin fly in tomorrow morning. I'll pick him up at the airport and he'll help me drive home," I inform my brothers over dinner. "I've said goodbye to Mom and I agree with you two at this juncture; there's nothing more I can do for her now. I'll take care of things in Illinois so she can be buried there, if you two can coordinate everything here."

"I think that's best," Kurt agrees, averting his eyes.

Bob nods, tears in his eyes. There's nothing more we have to say to one another right now. It remains unspoken but very much on our minds that the next time we share a meal will likely be the day of our mother's funeral.

Saturday, April 21
JODY:

It's 9 a.m. and Kevin's plane is on time. We find a crevice between suitcases and boxes in the Jeep for his overnight bag and get on the road. We'll stop at a McDonald's in awhile, after we get some road between us and Denver.

I miss a turn to take my favorite route, which is I-90 and up into Wyoming and South Dakota. Not wanting the Nebraska-Iowa-Illinois-Wisconsin I-80 with the usual summer road construction delays, I settle on the longer route through Kansas on I-70. Still, we have no intentions of stopping for the night. I've made the trip several times over the years and know that we could be home by 2 a.m. if we pushed.

Five hundred miles later, the Jeep engine stalls in single lane traffic in the midst of a road construction zone. We lose all power and the steering and brakes are difficult at best. Kevin activates the hazard lights and manages to steer into a Texaco station at that very interchange. According to the Jeep's computer, we have a faulty fuel injector, which has shut down the entire fuel system. We're thirty miles from the next real town of Topeka, Kansas, and I'm utterly dejected by this turn of events. Kevin tries to convince me to have a soda or ice-cream at the A&W attached to the gas station, but I refuse, taking up a post outside by the Jeep. I just can't believe this is happening.

Finally, we arrange for a tow. The driver's first instruction is that a basic AAA membership only pays for the first five miles, so we better have the rest in cash. We do and so are allowed to climb aboard. The Jeep is loaded onto a flat-bed trailer headed for Topeka. We approach Sleepy-Town USA at the wrong time – 6:15 p.m. No service is available after 5:00 on a Saturday, nor will a service station re-open before Monday morning. We make the driver take us here and there (racking up extra miles, he gripes), but we refuse to let him leave the Jeep at his choice site because it is too dark and set back from the street. We realize that we can't unpack the car, and everything I will inherit, with the exception of a few boxes of clothing mailed to my office, everything else of value is in that vehicle.

"How about here?" the frazzled driver asks, pulling into a huge dealership lot.

There is sign of life inside the building, a manager closing the front office. We get his attention and he agrees to accept the car but says that he can't lock the Jeep in a secure bay. He can give us a loaner car and a promise that it will be worked into the service group's Monday morning schedule. The lot is next to a Quality Inn, where we might stay the extra two nights.

Kevin is better than I am at making the best of a bad situation. I am in tears. I am so tired! I miss PJ. I miss the dogs and cats. I want to be home! Two more days in Topeka, Kansas?

"We'll go have a nice dinner, check on the vehicle again, and get some sleep," Kevin promises. "You'll see, everything will be fine. We'll just have an unexpected vacation and a little extra time together."

"I don't know what to take out of the Jeep! I don't know what suitcase has the jewelry or the pewter trains. Or my gun that I had given to Dad. Mom took it after he died, but then Bob gave it back to me – there is a gun in a bag somewhere. I don't know where anything is and this rental car is just too damn small to move anything of consequence — to even put a dent in everything!" Now I am crying in earnest.

Kevin remains very composed: "I have a toothbrush in my overnight bag. Don't you have a small bag you could grab? Everything is going to be okay, Jody. You're exhausted. You need some rest. We're here. The worst is over. Just get a change of clothing and let's go to the hotel."

Of course, he is right.

Sunday, April 22
KEVIN:

After breakfast, Jody and I check the Jeep. It's fine at 9:30 a.m., 10 a.m. and 11 a.m. "It's fine," I keep repeating, though Jody continues to harbor an unfounded premonition of continuing disaster. Finally I convince her to set aside her angst long enough to accompany me to a neighborhood mall, where we might see a movie. It's raining and I don't know what else to offer, but I need do something because we have changed our paradigm to pretend we are *on vacation*. We should be having fun about now, but we are not because she can't let go of her disappointment over the breakdown. Nor can she set aside this uncharacteristic pending-doom mentality. She has called Bill twice to keep him informed of our situation, and she's phoned P.J. at least three times. The movie selection isn't great, but anything would be a most welcomed diversion.

Just after 3 p.m., I discover that the car has been burglarized. Actually, we both do, but I see the Grand Cherokee first, though Jody is driving the rental car. I drop my head into my hands as she pulls into the lot, hoping against hope to will away the vision. I look up again. "Oh, my god," I moan. "This can't be happening." But it is.

The driver's window and a back passenger window are shattered; there is glass everywhere and crazy as it looks, plastic garbage bags taped to where the windows should be. I can see that a few of Jody's possessions litter the lot. It appears that bags were checked, deemed worthless, and tossed aside. But then, oddly enough, it also appears that the burglars taped plastic on the car to protect what they left from the rain!

There is no sheltering my wife from this. "Oh god, oh god, oh god," Jody whispers. But before she can bring the vehicle to a complete stop, a man and a woman pull up next to us in a pickup truck and the man jumps out. "Is this *your* vehicle?" he demands.

I'm wondering if they are the thieves. If so, are they now going to rob us? "Maybe," I challenge with quite a bit more boldness than I really feel. "Who are you?"

He identifies himself as the dealership manager. He says he was called from home by his cleaning crew, who discovered the break-in and taped the plastic to the car. He suspects that his employees may have even scared off the thieves because there are still possessions in the car, including an embroidery sewing machine in clear sight which would be valued at about $5,000.

Jody is absolutely hysterical. She leaps out of the car and takes a frantic inventory, pawing though the contents still in the Jeep with total disregard for glass pellets. She quickly concludes that at least seven suitcases are missing. I have no idea what was in any of them, or what else was taken. But I can see that Tupperware containers and paper bags and cloth bags seem to have been left behind. Everything, however, is in shambles, contents strewn everywhere.

I use our cell phone to call the police and I'm told by the dispatcher to call another number. I'm then connected to a taped message with an invitation to leave a message on voicemail.

"Call the department back and *make* them send an officer out here right now!" Jody shrieks. "Tell them that we have been robbed!" She begins crying great heaving, wracking sobs and then gags. She bends over but quickly straightens. I take a step toward her but she holds up a hand as if to push me back. "Hurry up!" she yells, "before the rain compromises the scene any more than it already has!"

I want to comfort her, but at the same time, I can't really accomplish anything with her screaming orders at me; I walk away and dial 9-1-1 again. This time I'm far more forceful and the dispatcher promises to send someone as soon as possible.

My wife completely dissolves. She alternately cries like a baby and swears like a sailor. There is no consoling her so I allow her some space, hoping she'll soon spend herself. She actually kicks the Jeep and then drops onto an overgrown grassy area alongside the curb. It's still raining, but I can still see the snot on her face, though she is oblivious or uncaring. I have never seen Jody act this way in all of our time together. She's always been a rock in times of crisis... it's who she is and how she's been formally trained. But apparently my bride is not intending to suffer this final indignity quietly. Instead, she is in full acting-out mode.

Likewise, I am furious with whoever had the audacity to steal from a grieving daughter, whether they knew it or not. Jody implicates the tow-truck driver, whom she now suspects led somebody to the booty. I agree it is a possibility, though I am just as angry with the dealership manager who would not lock the Jeep in a bay in spite of the goods he was told were in the vehicle. Jody is mad at Kurt, who told the mechanic not to replace the challenged fuel injector when it showed up on a computer analysis as needing replaced. Instead, Kurt had instructed the mechanic to just spray "some stupid anti-stick crap" on it, apparently planning to fix it later himself.

"Won't *he* find this funny?" Jody fumes.

I assure her that Kurt will not. No one could. Certainly her brother did not wish this on her.

She is also angry with her other brother, who, she says, was upset at her for moving out her mother's things before the woman was dead. "Bobby just can't understand that I can't come back later. He doesn't know how I feel or how hard all of this is for me. My god, doesn't he realize that I could be exactly how my mother is, two months from now? Doesn't he know that I'm not well? Why did he have to make me feel like a thief?"

"Nobody can make you feel like anything, honey," I tell her. I find a blouse in the litter left in the car and wipe off her face. I hold her close to me. I don't know how I know it, but I do: she isn't mad at Kurt or Bobby. She's mad at herself.

She pushes away and turns her back to me, drops again to her knees. "Oh, God, what have I done?" she moans, confirming my suspicion. She babbles on and on.... "I've lost my children's inheritance and any tangible connection to Mom and Nana because I just had to take the car. I couldn't wait there and ship the goods later, like I should have.... I just had to pack up everything and try to drive across the nation. Then, when the damn thing broke down, I didn't even have the sense to listen to my instincts and to sleep in the car! I said we should, I knew *I* should.... I should have protected this stuff with my life. Oh God, what have I done? What have I done, God, to deserve all this? *What in the world have I done?*"

A police officer arrives, thankfully interrupting my wife's pitiful spectacle. She gets to her feet and tries to answer his questions, but his only interest seems to lie with the stolen gun. He makes the mistake of asking Jody a third or fourth question about it.

Jody just absolutely erupts, obscenities spewing out of her mouth. "Don't you get it? I don't give a fuck about the gun!" she yells at the cop. "I hope one of the goddamn thieves accidentally shoots another one with it! What do you think about THAT? Stop asking me about the fucking gun! Who gives a *shit* about the gun?! I lost my grandmother's priceless 1940s ball gown! Why don't you take fingerprints or do *something* to help me get the important things back instead of grilling me about a legally registered gun?!!"

Moments later, the dealership manager makes an offhand comment that there have been lots of these kinds of burglaries all over town. My wife reacts to that insult as well; she strides over to the Jeep and opens a car door and slams it. Open it again and slams it. Opens it again and slams it even harder.

"Your wife isn't taking this very well," the cop observes.

Honest to God, I am about to give up myself. Between Jody, the cop, and now knowledge of the night manager's lack of concern about our vehicle when we brought it to his property fully loaded with robber-bait, I'm about to start slamming some car doors myself! NOW the dealership is willing to push it into a locked area for safekeeping? As Jody would say, big fucking deal. My wife stops slamming the vehicle's door only to again sink in the depressed spot by the curb and cry.

All I see, when I look around me, is another shining example of the chaos that continues to ambush our lives.

"My mother is probably dying this very second," Jody wails, "and I have lost everything she held dear. My god, Kevin, what have I done to deserve all of this?"

Monday, April 23
JODY:

"What an interesting little shit-hole Topeka, Kansas is turning out to be," I remark to Kevin. "I didn't think places like this really existed anymore."

"We'll be out of here pretty soon," he promises. "Just be patient a little longer. *Please?*"

There is nothing else to do, since we've already checked out of the hotel and turned in the rental car. Where are we to go? What are we to do after being told that only a Kansas City dealership, some 30 or 50 miles away, has the right glass for the car? That's why the car is not ready as promised. The dealership apparently sent for it and received smoked privacy glass, which we do not have on the car. So a runner was sent back to Kansas City.

He returns with the right glass and it is put in. Oops. There is no fuel injector for a Jeep to be found inside the city limits of Topeka. They thought they had one in stock that would fit, but it will not. Back to Kansas City. An hour-plus later, someone yells out that the new filter is the wrong size. Back again to Kansas City, but the courier just called in to say that the parts person there is taking a 3:00 lunch, so it'll be awhile.

We sit in the dealership waiting area from 7 a.m. until 5:45 p.m. Parts and labor top $680 because the dealership's insurance will not even cover the broken glass. When we finally get on the road, I refuse to stop anywhere and only to pull over for gas and a drive-through restaurant. I will drive. I will drink coffee. I will get us home. We will drive all night if we have to, to get from this godforsaken place where tornadoes leveled a neighboring town just last night.

There's no place like home. There's no place like home. There's no place like home. We will drive all fucking night if we have to.

And so we do.

Tuesday, April 24
JODY:

We slept until noon; not very long, considering we never got to bed until 5:00 this morning.

Now I am unpacking the Jeep with little heart or purpose. I stack the Tupperware boxes in one pile, cloth bags in another. There are dozens of pairs of socks. Goody, goody, glad those weren't stolen.

I open a small Tupperware box and see a glint of gold. Could it really be my mother's metallic evening bag, into which I believe I remember putting her jewelry? I am amazed and absolutely delighted to find roughly half of the pieces I believed forever out of the family's hands! And then to find PJ's pewter trains, all except two. And the family papers and albums and quilts!

I am so grateful that I get down on my knees and thank God on the spot. Then I thank my grandmother, whom I consider to be my guardian angel; how could I have doubted her powers? And Daniel, my special angel. And I call out to Kevin and sing the news and I am laughing and laughing and touching these things because they are more than things.

181

More than property. They are memories. My mother's legacy. My children's umbilical cord to their past.

True, the thieves did get my mother's ball gowns and best suits and my new camera (a replacement for the one stolen during our last trip to Florida) and new noise cancellation earphones that I'd worn on the plane. I don't know what else. Oh yeah, the pistol. But my grandmother's cameo and her wallet, with her driver's license and a picture of me as a child, was left behind. I still don't understand why I would have packed such treasures in boxes instead of suitcases, except that I had packed in a daze.

Had we traveled north, as I'd wanted, who knows where our car would have died? There were 16" snowstorms in Wyoming; we might have frozen to death before being found. And on 80, you don't want to have a breakdown in the middle of construction. The Texaco station was a Godsend, and the rental car a blessing.

It's all in how you look at it, I guess… though I will never willingly set foot in Topeka, Kansas again.

Thursday, April 26
JODY:

"So, has your life settled down since radiation?" Mike asks.

"Our little wee one was born late yesterday!" I tell him. "Can you believe it? I've lived long enough to become a grandmother! And I have you to thank!"

We tell him about the last couple weeks. About the conference and the call from Denver. About being at mother's bedside, and the trouble on the road coming home.

Mike takes a deep breath. He asks, "Am I to understand that your mother died?"

Kevin takes my hand. This is why he is with me; because I knew Mike would ask and I would be unable to answer.

"Jody was called at work earlier today. Yes, her mother is dead."

"I'm so sorry, Jody." Mike takes my other hand in his. True to my innate prediction, I can't talk at this moment. It hurts too much yet to say the words myself. I simply nod.

When Bobby called, he kindly told me that he and Kurt were able to tell Mom about the birth of her great grandson early this morning because she amazed them by rallying one last time and opening her eyes. Tears ran down her cheeks, Bobby said, and they knew she understood — and they understood that her crying was for joy. Then she closed her eyes as the hospice nurse raised the dose of drugs to the highest dose yet, and Mama dreamed her final dreams.

Mike is obviously affected by Mother's death, but I am his primary concern. "You've had every stressor on the books in the last couple weeks," he says gravely. "It's time to give your immune system a rest and heal now."

We leave with what we came to Mike to get – my official release from active treatment. Today Mike put me on a maintenance chemo program (pill form daily), and instructed me to report back for a checkup in three months on the anniversary of my diagnosis. Otherwise, I am advised to enjoy and to live my life as best I can for the coming year and to go forward without fear – to forget that this is the period when reoccurrence would be most expected. Most women with my type of cancer live, on average, 18 months; no single day can be taken for granted by me ever again. Each will be a gift.

It has been nine months *to the very day* since both Mom and I were diagnosed with cancer. Of the two types we had, mine was considered the most deadly, hers the more difficult to manage. After my surgery, we would both walk parallel paths in terms of chemotherapy and radiation, and even share my oncologist for a month. I wonder now whether on some level she chose to share this journey with me, and I can't help but believe that she would have volunteered to do it if she thought it would make the experience easier for me. I don't know what I think, really. There's just too much to process.

Nine months … time to create a life. In the same week nine months ago that two lives — the lives my mother and I knew as ours "before" cancer — would end, another was created.

Yesterday Summer gave birth to Patrick Daniel Cassidy, my grandson. Today, my mother, Marilyn Joyce Webster, died.

Today, I was given back my life. Different, certainly, than it was *before* and even *during*. Today is the first day of *after.*

Mother, God rest your tortured body and tormented soul. I will keep your memory alive with me all of the days that I am given on earth. All I ask of you in return is to please give Daniel and Nana a kiss for me. And Wayne a swift kick.

Hello, Mother – never Goodbye. Always hello from me to you.

KEVIN:

Please, God, let it *really* be over. Amen.

CHAPTER 12: *After* word
by Kevin Patrick
Fight for second mastectomy • Drive-by surgery • Lymphodema swelling • Family news • Living in the moment

As the door closed on active cancer treatment, another door opened on a seemingly more empowered life for both Jody and me. The passing of our neighbor Bill was a sad reminder of how lucky we were that we had missed Door Number Three, and my wife took his death (and her "second chance") to heart.

Jody's passion to complete the projects she felt were unfinished, both at home and at work, has turned even the most casual of her previous interests into all-consuming undertakings. In a matter of months, she created a family legacy that already fills 15 scrapbook albums. She then set aside scissors and photos long enough to paint every room in our home in brilliant color. Within the same month of her painting spree, she replaced the flooring in the kitchen and bathroom ("I've never done tiling, but..."), installed wood moldings and hung wallpaper trims. She topped it all off with sewn curtains. As usual, I was the support person laying drop cloths and cleaning paint brushes, balancing family matters and managing the routine chores of our lives, but I went to bed every night amazed at her focus and her dedication toward seeing each project to its completion.

Around the time of this hectic home renovation activity, we had a serious scare that the cancer had returned. Fortunately, further medical testing indicated it had not: Jody had (and continues to have) prolonged complications due to lung scarring from the radiation. Even as I began to breathe more naturally again, however, the psychological toll of the false alarm and the real fact of having one breast continued to torment my wife.

Jody asked for a second mastectomy and it was explained to her why it was *not medically necessary*. She went back and asked again, and again. This willfulness indicated that having one breast was a much deeper-level trauma for my wife than even I had realized. Initially I thought she wanted another surgery because she was so fearful of a new occurrence in the other breast – and she had reason to fear that. But then I came to understand that it was also very much about body image.

Primarily, her struggle manifested itself in a withdrawal from normal activities. She elected not to go swimming with a gel breast form, or to work out at the gym. (She was probably right not to exercise with it, because the form had fallen out of her bra on more than one occasion already.) After she came home from work and removed the bra and form, she wouldn't answer the door for even a pizza delivery person. Jody even cradled a pillow in front of her chest while watching TV in the privacy of our home, in the event that unexpected company dropped by. It was becoming more and more uncomfortable to watch her quiet suffering, yet nothing I said made her feel better.

Still, her oncologist continued to resist another request for a second mastectomy. "Your insurance won't cover it for at least two years," Dr. Frontiera explained.

It wasn't the answer Jody wanted. "Why? Because that's the window in which I'm supposed to die?" she challenged. "Are they worried that doing it sooner might later prove to be a needless payout?"

He looked away without answer.

"It isn't ending here, today," Jody stated matter-of-factly. "That isn't acceptable. I've checked: the cheapest cost is $5,000, if I don't spend the night in the hospital, and I'll spring for it if there is no other way. But as a matter of principle, I've just this minute decided that the insurance company will pay."

Shortly thereafter, Jody's surgeon agreed to the procedure – provided she got the proper authorizations. Jody then put into writing an impassioned plea to her oncologist, reminding him of the constant strain of waiting for the next lump to form. In addition, she confessed to Dr. Frontiera that she felt like a freak because she couldn't have reconstructive surgery to augment the missing breast:

My 16-year old son comes home unexpectedly in the company of his friends, and he is noticeably embarrassed if I've already removed the uncomfortable form (and so it is obvious that I have one breast). His face reddens. This is humiliating to us both.

Why is it mandated that insurance companies must pay for plastic surgery augmentation to add a breast — if that's what a woman decides might make her feel *normal* after a single or double mastectomy — but they need not approve my similar request to remove a remaining breast? Having a single breast is even more noticeable than being flat chested! Please help me end this nightmare, Mike. I'd rather be permanently disfigured on both sides of my chest under my clothing than to have to hide from my own son to spare his feelings... and mine.

Jody added verification from a psychiatrist that she was making a rational decision with full appreciation of what she was doing. Dr. Frontiera told her that her description of her emotional life actually changed his understanding of what some patients went through, and he then added his petition to the psychiatrist's note, the surgeon's letter, and another entreaty written by Jody's new family practitioner. My wife had covered all the bases. THEN the insurance company reluctantly agreed.

When booking the surgery at the hospital, Jody showed her appreciation by arranging for a drive-by mastectomy so that she would not spend even one night in a hospital, keeping the insurance payout to a minimum. She choreographed her release, asking the surgeon to let her go "just before the sedatives wear off, so that I can be home before I really need a pain pill. Don't worry if I'm out of it... Kevin will get me home safe and put me to bed." She was right, of course.

Three days later, Jody accompanied me to a movie and then, upon on our return home, asked P.J. if he wanted to see the scars. He surprised us both by saying yes. Summer and Brook have also been shown the ragged lines that travel from breastbone to arm pit either direction. "What they fear is worse than the actuality," Jody insists, though I doubt that is true.

It isn't all over for her, however. We bought a companion to her original breast form so that if she feels that a business obligation demands it, she has access to a more feminine form. I've noticed that's her decision when she's asked to be a keynote speaker or lecturer, and I suspect she is more publicly confident on stage with breasts. However, most of the time she is content with her angularity. I frankly don't even notice at first glance anymore and couldn't tell you, right now, if she had breasts today or not. She's equally beautiful to me either way.

More of an acute nuisance is the lymphedema in Jody's left arm that causes her to need to wear a compression sleeve to keep the swelling in check. Initially the distension was unbelievable; now we hope to maintain the left arm at about twice the size of her right arm. We believe the ballooning was caused by Jody's having flown in an airplane twice in the span of one month — the change of air pressure often causes sudden and permanent swelling problems for people lacking lymph nodes. But regardless of the cause, she can no longer wear her business suits and has necessarily changed her fashion style again; this time to camouflage an unnaturally large arm. She's nicknamed the fat limb

Elfrieda after a favorite oversized aunt. She also jokes that because of her decision to keep her red hair in a buzz cut, and because of her having a flat chest and no wedding ring on her left hand, she gets offers from some pretty attractive ladies. Very attractive ladies, she teases. Still, she assures, she'd never leave her pool boy for anyone.

Perhaps Jody's sense of humor was more affected by chemotherapy than she'd admit. She often laughs at her own jokes... which makes one of us. But seriously, I don't begrudge my darling any laugh she might find or manufacture because the lymphedema has cost her months of physical therapy and necessitated sessions where she has had to endure scar massages. Jody hates to be intimately touched by strangers, but she goes and she returns without comment. This is her life now. It's a part I no longer really share, since she's substituted a compression sleeve for the five layers of elaborate bandaging I used to wrap around her arm nightly. We're learning what options we have therapist by therapist, claim by claim.

She's a warrior, my wife, but believe me, even she has limits. For example, Jody was deeply affected by her inability to directly influence daughter Brook's safety. Our military police officer was stationed in the Middle East on 9/11, and again just before the war in Iraq began. Brook remained deployed near the Iraq border long after the war was declared over, during which time her mother became a CNN addict and returned to sleeping pills. Then Jody had an *aha*: if she couldn't get Brook out of the Middle East, at least she might bring sorely needed supplies to her daughter. Toward that effort, she spearheaded a drive with the Dane County Salvation Army to send critically needed items (including medicine, food, clothing, books, and personal grooming items) to any troops she could reach.

For three months, Jody spent a great many hours alongside other volunteers packing boxes of supplies, phone cards and letters of support from school children. I did my own share of box packing and taping, but no one put in more hours than Jody. The program consumed her weekends and workday evenings. She used Brook's connections to provide a pickup point for the soldiers and airmen in even the most remotely-situated outposts. Brook's face appeared larger than life in the newspaper and on the web, and Jody was on every area radio station and television station. Before it was declared mission over, the troop support action resulted in more than 3,000 pounds of goods being shipped under the Salvation Army's label. Since then, we've received appreciation letters and flags from soldiers in Afghanistan, Iraq and Kuwait who benefited from the project.

My lady is equally zealous in her demonstrations of love for the rest of the family. (Some might say overboard, but I pick my battles and this won't be one of them.) Little Patrick likely has been the most obvious recipient of his grandmother's affection. Jody makes frequent trips, both with me and without me now, to Chicago to see her wee one. Once there, she throws open her arms... arms Patrick immediately and gleefully runs into to collect yet another installment on the million kisses due from his beloved Nana.

"This little boy is why I lived!" Jody exclaims. "He is my reward for making it through chemo!"

He is <u>our</u> reward, I think, knowing that helping keep Jody alive has also afforded me the opportunity to be Patrick's grandfather. He calls me his *Ding Dong* (long story, don't ask) and Jody isn't the only one who carries his picture in a wallet.

As long as I've got out the brag book, I'd like to add that our kids (I do claim a chunk of their hearts these days) are all now young adults and having many successes of their own. They show the same drive and determination as their mother, though to varying degrees, thank God. Summer is happily married to Paddy (a masterful plasterer), and she recently completed her college studies and won a scholarship to attend a prestigious nursing school in Chicago. Brook will be returning to the Windy City as well when her enlistment period is up, to become a Chicago cop alongside her detective father. As of this writing, she is stationed in Florida and recently was given an early promotion to the role of desk sergeant.

P.J., now 18, is still our young pup ... though thankfully he's no longer the sullen teenager. He's had his share of adventures but none of them left the car wrecked, landed him in jail, or really put him in harm's way, and he's more of a man every day. I wear a father's ring given to me by my son and I can lay claim to being more and more of an influence on P.J. as time passes. At least I hope so. He'll never join the Navy (he's made that clear), but he is job hunting! He smiles with ease, and there is less and less time between his seemingly random acts of kindness to both his mother and me.

Unexpectedly, extended family has also become very important to me. Jody reconnected with an aunt and uncle and her cousins on the day of her mother's funeral, and the uncle has since assumed a fatherly position in her life and also has become a wonderful surrogate parent for Bobby, who moved from Denver to within blocks of his Uncle Gene and Aunt Sherrill. We make the five-hour trip to Bushnell, Illinois to celebrate holidays and I have come to cherish the experience of again having a large *family*. I warn my wife that this small-town clan loves me so much that if this here pool boy was ever to find himself tossed out, his new *cuzins* would surely create a puddle in their collective back yard so he'd have a place to land.

"They love you more than they love me," Jody grouses, but I see the smile on her face. She smiles a lot now. Mostly, her wacky relatives like my impersonations and strange voices, which they beg to hear (and talk sassy back to) at every family dinner ... and so I oblige them because hey, they're kin in my book (and this IS half my book!).

Jody and her brothers quickly mended fences, particularly with a couple serious cancer scares to prod them in the right direction, so all talk of jeeps and rings and Topeka, Kansas has been forgotten. When they meet now, they often stand together before their mother's grave holding hands, each remembering their respective childhoods, I imagine. I don't know firsthand... my own parents lack grave markers to visit. What do people think, looking down? I hope not to know for a very long time....

Completing the family story, Jody and I found a local United Methodist church whose congregation warmly embraced us the first time we visited. This is another new experience for me, but forging a relationship with this religious community has brought a balance to our lives and even more strength to our marriage. While it has challenged my belief system, it has also made me aware of the importance of having a belief system. Now I think, I know and I believe — and understand the true significance of each.

On a less positive note, *In Business: Rockford* magazine closed as a result of the manufacturing town's economic tailspin in the war's aftermath. However, the Madison-based magazine is still doing great under Jody's leadership, and she and Bill are continuously evaluating new ventures.

As for me, I've changed jobs a couple times, but that is my nature. I haven't yet found a job that is the best fit for me but I'm getting closer to it. I can feel it.

In the meantime, I tend to remain overprotective, always watchful and, it seems, forever wary. I don't think I'll ever get used to the continuing cancer scares or ever come to expect them. I guess, truth be told, I still feel pretty helpless against this disease. Jody is my girl. If I have to be the hypochondriac in this relationship to watch over her, so be it.

But between scares, there is life! I bought my wife piano lessons for Christmas so that she might further her playing skills... another project she had identified as being incomplete. Now, many nights I lie on the couch to listen to her at the keyboard playing several variations of her beloved Canon in D, Foley draped near her feet as she works the pedals. Micky nestles next to me but keeps his eyes on his mistress just the same. She is the heart of our family -- we all know it just as we all know our own roles. Charlie Cat perches on the bench beside her and Little Cat sleeps in a curled ball atop the piano.

"This is *my* reward!" I think during such exquisite moments. "This is why she *has* to live!"

The love story continues...

About the Authors

Jody Glynn Patrick is publisher of *In Business* magazine, which, she jokes, makes good use of both her writing talent and her crisis counseling training.

Before moving to Madison, Wis., Jody won the highest achievement award given by the American Newspaper Association for a column published in more than 20 newspapers in the Milwaukee-Chicago marketplace. She has earned numerous awards for in-depth news and special features, and she has also written the guidebooks, "Crisis Training for Hotline Intervention" and "Coping: A Death in the Family." Her other works have been published in *Guideposts* magazine and *Elements Literary Magazine*.

A crisis counselor as well as author, Jody has served as Director of Western Illinois University's Hotline Crisis Center, and as Manager of the Chicago Ronald McDonald House. While a crisis interventionist for the Cudahy, Wis., Police Department, Jody's work was highlighted on a "Positively Milwaukee" television broadcast. She was nominated for the Jefferson Award and the national JC Penney community service award for her work with community crisis situations.

Other jobs include Director of the Cudahy/St. Francis Interfaith Program for the Elderly, and Supervisor of the Jefferson County (Colorado) Human Services Child Protection Intake Unit. After moving to Madison, she has continued to be a spokesperson for many community organizations.

Co-author **Kevin Patrick** left his hometown of Louisville, Kentucky to join the United States Navy. He had various assignments — ranging from surgical technician to career counselor — during 23 years of active service. Kevin lived in cities across America, as well as in Japan, Turkey, and Guam. He also served a stint at the National Security Agency as a Russian crypto-linguist before retiring at the rank Senior Chief Petty Officer.

After leaving the Navy, Kevin was a human resources manager for two international companies. Now he is a sales training coach for Apex Performance Systems in Madison, Wis.

Kevin's volunteer experience has been as varied as his work history. He has been Santa Paws for the Humane Society, a statistician for the Ronald McDonald House, and a bell-ringer for the Salvation Army. He enjoys his many church activities and entertaining others with voice impersonations and character roles.

Order more copies for friends and associates!

ORDER FORM

DURING.. A Couple's Intimate Experience With Breast Cancer Treatment
by *Jody Glynn Patrick & Kevin Patrick*

Order Information:

Number of Books   _____

Amount ($19.95 ea.)   _____

Shipping &Handling (\$5.00 ea.)   _____

Sales Tax (Calif. residents add $1.57 ea.)   _____

(Int'l. residents, please call for shipping rates.)

Total Amount   _____

Shipping Information:

Name _____

Company _____

Address _____

City _____

State _____ Zip _____ Country _____

Phone _____

Email _____

Payment Information:

❑ Visa ❑ MC ❑ Amex ❑ Disc   ❑ Check

Expiration Date _____

Account #: _____

Signature _____

Send to the publisher:
Veda Communications Co.
4709 N. El Capitan, Suite 103, Fresno, CA 93722

ONLINE ORDERS

Visit our website to: 1) Place orders online;
2) find out about distribution of the book;
or 3) arrange presentations for the authors
www.DuringBreastCancer.com
